THE DEMANDS OF RECOGNITION

WITHDRAWN
UTSA Libraries

SOUTH ASIA IN MOTION

TOWNSEND MIDDLETON

THE DEMANDS
OF RECOGNITION

State Anthropology and Ethnopolitics in Darjeeling

STANFORD UNIVERSITY PRESS

STANFORD, CALIFORNIA

Stanford University Press
Stanford, California

Printed in the United States of America on acid-free, archival-quality paper

Library of Congress Cataloging-in-Publication Data

Middleton, Townsend, author.
 The demands of recognition : state anthropology and ethnopolitics in Darjeeling /
Townsend Middleton.
     pages cm—(South Asia in motion)
 Includes bibliographical references and index.
 ISBN 978-0-8047-9542-5 (cloth : alk. paper)—
 ISBN 978-0-8047-9626-2 (pbk. : alk. paper)
1. Gorkha (South Asian people)—India—Darjeeling (District)—Politics and
government. 2. Gorkha (South Asian people)—India—Darjeeling (District)—
Government relations. 3. Gorkha (South Asian people)—India—Darjeeling (District)—
Ethnic identity. 4. Ethnology—Political aspects—India—Darjeeling (District)
5. Ethnicity—Political aspects—India—Darjeeling (District) 6. Identity politics—
India—Darjeeling (District)
7. Darjeeling (India : District)—Scheduled tribes—Government policy. I. Title.
II. Series: South Asia in motion.
 DS432.G87M58 2015
 301.0954'14—dc23
                                        2015007352
ISBN 978-0-8047-9630-9 (electronic)

Designed by Bruce Lundquist
Typeset at Stanford University Press in 10.75/15 Adobe Caslon

CONTENTS

LIST OF ILLUSTRATIONS

ACKNOWLEDGMENTS

This book has been a journey through many years and places. Along the way, I have gathered a rucksack full of thanks to the communities, individuals, and institutions that have made it possible. With gratitude, I necessarily begin this story by acknowledging their contributions. There is no other starting point.

First and foremost, I would like to thank the people of Darjeeling who allowed me into their lives and political struggles. Over the years, I have had the good fortune to work with a number of different communities within the Nepali-speaking Gorkha conglomerate. But I owe a special thanks to the Gurungs and Tamangs with whom I lived and worked throughout fieldwork. The ethnic associations of these communities—for the Gurungs, the Tamu Choj Din and the All India Gurung Buddhist Association; for the Tamangs, the All India Tamang Buddhist Association and the Tamang Buddhist Gedung—opened their doors to me and made me feel welcome. My friends and neighbors in the village of Bidhuwā Busti (a pseudonym) gave me a much-needed sense of home. I remain as grateful for their everyday company as I am for the window they opened for me onto everyday life in the hills. One cannot navigate Darjeeling's steep terrain without also navigating its contentious party politics. Given the powers that be, I would be remiss not to pay my respects to the Gorkhaland National Liberation Front, which ruled Darjeeling until 2008, and the Gorkha Janmukti Morcha, which has controlled the region ever since.

In my engagements with the postcolonial state, I have had the unique privilege to learn the ropes of government anthropology with the members of West Bengal's Cultural Research Institute. The team allowed me to shadow them during their fieldwork and be a frequent visitor to their Kolkata offices. Doing so, these civil servants showed me how tribal recognition works inside the state. This book owes a great deal to their willingness to embrace the similarities and differences of our respective anthropologies. I also benefited from various meetings with members of the Registrar General of India—Social Sciences Wing and the Ministry of Tribal Affairs, both in New Delhi. For historical perspective, I consulted several archives, and at each one of them certain individuals made a significant difference. Bidisha Chakrabarty was of great help at the State Archives of West Bengal (Kolkata). Jaya Ravindran got me situated in the National Archives of India (New Delhi). At the British Library (London), Ramesh Dhungel oriented me to the Hodgson Collection, which at the time was in considerable flux.

Countless individuals facilitated my work in India. I would like to especially thank I. C. Agrawal, Sanjay Basu, Jiwan Bhandari, Dr. Bharati, the late M. S. Bomjun, Dr. S. M. Chakrabarty, Kakoli Chowdhuri, Captain Debnath, Ranen Dutta, N. K. Ghatak, Anand Gurung; Brigadier Gurung, D. B. Gurung, Karma Gurung, K. K. Gurung, the late Madan Gurung, M. B. Gurung, Saritha Gurung, Tilaak Gurung, the late Tika Khati, Amar Lama, Nima Lama, Niraj Lama, Ishamani Pakrin, Shyam Pakrin, Vikash Pradhan, Anmol Prasad, the late K. S. Ramudamu, Sonam Sherpa, Pradeep Tamang, Sujata Tamang, Nirmal Thapa, and Nima Ting. I am similarly indebted to the following organizations: the Akhil Bharatiya Newar Sangathan; the Akhil Bharatiya Magar Sangh; the All India Gorkha League (Darjeeling); the All India Kirat Yakkha (Dewan) Chhumma; the Anthropological Survey of India; the Darjeeling Bharatiya Khas Hitkari Sammelan; the Darjeeling Gorkha Hill Council's Department of Information and Cultural Affairs; the Gorkha Janjati Manyata Samity; and the West Bengal Backward Class Welfare Department (Darjeeling).

In the academy, I am grateful to those who have helped me find my anthropological way. George Mentore got me started down this path during my undergraduate days at the University of Virginia. He remains my friend, and aptly named. Matthew Kapstein at the University of Chicago provided guidance at a pivotal time of my intellectual development. At Cornell, I found a special connection with Viranjini Munasinghe, a personal and intellectual bond that I continue to cherish. Similarly, David

Holmberg became a friend, guide, and proof positive that good people make great ethnographers. Dominic Boyer honed my interests in the anthropology of knowledge and has provided sage counsel ever since. Additionally, Kathryn March, Andrew Wilford, and Terence Turner were integral to my training, as were the students and the department as a whole. A warm thanks also to my Nepali teacher, Shambhu Oja, and Cornell's South Asia Program. From 2010 through 2012, I was a postdoctoral fellow at Duke. My colleagues in the Thompson Writing Program helped me discover a vital balance between teaching and research, which has served this book well. Colleagues and friends in Duke's anthropology department provided disciplinary connection during my short stay at Duke. Sumathi Ramaswamy, Philip Stern, and others kindly introduced me to the local South Asian Studies community—in particular, the North Carolina Consortium for South Asian Studies, of which I remain a part.

Since 2012, I have been glad to call the University of North Carolina at Chapel Hill my professional home. My colleagues in the Department of Anthropology have been nothing short of outstanding. I am deeply grateful for their continued support. Chris Nelson has been a terrific mentor, as has Rudi Colleredo-Mansfield. While drafting this book, I benefited from a junior faculty writing group led by Silvia Tomášková. My colleagues in this group—Amanda Thompson, Anna Agbe-Davies, Jocelyn Chua, and Jean Dennison—provided timely feedback on some of this book's trickier sections. Beyond anthropology, I am thankful to be a part of UNC's Curriculum on Global Studies and a growing South Asian Studies collective, where I have found great colleagues across the campus. I completed this book as a Faculty Fellow at UNC's Institute for the Arts and Humanities. My thanks to the IAH and its fellows for such a productive and enjoyable experience.

A number of other scholars have helped me along the way. Saurabh Dube and Ishita Bannerjee-Dube have been tremendous friends and colleagues over the years. Akhil Gupta, William Mazzarella, Alpa Shah, Sara Shneiderman, and Ajantha Subramanian have done much to shape my work. I remain grateful for their friendships and collaboration. I convey a similar note of appreciation to Douglas Holmes, Pinky Hota, Aftab Jassal,

Mara Kaufman, Christian Lentz, Megan Moodie, Chérie Rivers Ndaliko, Peter Redfield, Emma Shaw-Crane, Adriane Smith-Lentz, Gabriela Valdivia, Saiba Varma, and others who read and commented on different aspects of the manuscript. I presented various components of this project at conferences and talks in the United States, Europe, and South Asia. The venues, organizers, and participants are too many to list, but the conversations remain positively part of this book's genealogy. The last decade has been an especially dynamic time to be an ethnographer in the Darjeeling region. During this time, I have crossed paths with a number of fellow researchers, including Rune Bennike, Jenny Bentley, Sarah Besky, Miriam Bishokarma, Chelsea Booth, Mona Chettri, Nilamber Chhetri, Barbara Gerke, Bengt G. Karlsson, Swatasiddha Sarkar, Thomas Schor, Debarati Sen, Sara Shneiderman, Tanka Subba, and Mark Turin. I have learned a great deal through these scholars' work, and I look forward to more to come.

This project has benefited from various sources of institutional support. Foreign Language and Area Studies Fellowships supported much of my graduate training. Research travel grants from Cornell's Maurio Einaudi Center for International Studies, Cornell's South Asia Program, and Duke's Thompson Writing Program allowed me to make several trips to India for short-term fieldwork. I received a Fulbright-IIE Fellowship to conduct research on the history and contemporary life of anthropological knowledge in India. Following my dissertational fieldwork, a Sage Fellowship from Cornell and a Dissertation Completion Fellowship from the American Council of Learned Societies provided precious time and security to write. I am thankful also to UNC and the Department of Anthropology for the funds and time for additional trips to India. In the fall of 2014, I became the Pardue Faculty Fellow at UNC's Institute for the Arts and Humanities, which excused me from teaching in order to finish this book.

Parts of this book have been adapted from some of my earlier publications. The following journals and press have graciously allowed me to reprint those sections: *American Anthropologist*; *American Ethnologist*; *Focaal: The Journal of Global and Historical Anthropology*; *Political Geography*; and Oxford University Press.

My experiences working with Stanford University Press have been excellent. Michelle Lipinski acquired this book and shepherded it through the review process. My editors with the South Asia in Motion series, Jenny Gavacs and Thomas Blom Hansen, have lent a steady hand and sharp editorial eye in shaping the manuscript into its current form. I am grateful for their contributions and honored to be a part of this promising new series. My reviewers with Stanford engaged deeply with my work. I take this opportunity to publicly thank them for their time, care, and intellectual generosity.

I save a final round of thanks for three of my closest interlocutors and friends. Jaideep Chatterjee has remained part of my thinking and life since this project began. I owe many long nights and breakthroughs to him. My writing partner, Jason Cons, has read every word of this book more times than I care to admit. As one of my closest allies and sharpest critics, he remains a friend and intellectual partner *hors catégorie*. In the field, this project would have been something wholly different were it not for my exceptional research assistant, Eklavya Pradhan. Eklavya's connections, social agility, and critical eye were indispensable. We have written about our dynamics elsewhere, but suffice to say I cannot imagine my research or this book without him. Eklavya transformed my understandings of what ethnography could and should be. I think he would say the same of me, though you would have to ask him. So it is with gratitude (and a wink) that I acknowledge Eklavya—my friend, colleague, and conavigator of the ethno-contemporary.

Finally, to the friends and family who have supported me every step of the way: thank you for providing me with a sense of belonging amid what I know must seem like a nomadic life. I will refrain from mentioning you by name—only to say that your love and support grace these pages in ways that cannot be written.

TECHNICAL NOTES

TRANSLATION AND ORTHOGRAPHY

I have tried to make the language of this book as accessible as possible. I conducted fieldwork in Nepali and English. In Darjeeling, these languages intermingled to varying degrees depending on with whom I was speaking—not just for mutual intelligibility but also because English anthropological terms were in widespread circulation. People frequently interchanged words like "culture" and "identity" with Nepali equivalents like *sanskriti* and *astitwa* or *chinhāri*. "Tribe" increasingly became synonymous with *adivāsi* (a term used throughout India and Nepal, meaning "autochthonous or original inhabitant") and/or *janājāti* (which loosely translates as "indigenous community" or perhaps "ethnicity"). These linguistic interplays were important, but made for difficult transcription. Darjeeling Nepali also differs significantly from that spoken in Nepal. Hindi, Bengali, and English words are common throughout the lexicon. To make the text more reader-friendly, I have accordingly opted to translate fully into English (adding Nepali terminology where relevant). My research assistant often worked with me in translating and transcribing the many hours of recordings I collected during fieldwork. However, all translations and shortcomings remain my own.

Where I include Nepali terms, I have used Turner's *Comparative and Etymological Dictionary of the Nepali Language* (1931/2001) as a general guide, with certain spelling modifications for phonetic clarity for those unfamiliar with South Asian languages. For proper nouns such as the names of organizations, I have used the most common emic renderings. I have rendered popularly transcribed words like "Dasain" without diacritics. Where necessary, I have pluralized Nepali terms by adding an "s," as is done in English.

PRIMARY SOURCE REFERENCES

All primary sources (archival files, periodicals, etc.) are referenced fully in the notes. Throughout the book, I draw upon findings from a number of different archives. For simplicity's sake, I have used the file's call number to reference these archival materials. For example, a file referenced as India, Foreign, July 1864, 132–133, Political A comes from the Government of India, Foreign Department, dated July 1864, Proceeding Number 132–133, of File Type A.

PSEUDONYMITY

My research protocol has been to render all individuals and sensitive places pseudonymous—the one exception being well-known public figures, for whom it would be pointless due to their notoriety. Ethnic organizations and government departments, where appropriate, are presented by their most commonly used names.

THE DEMANDS OF RECOGNITION

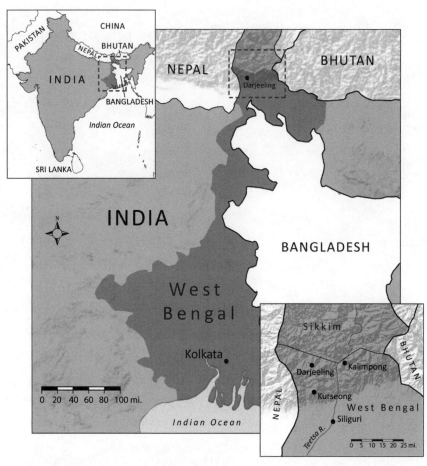

MAP F.1 *Map of West Bengal, with insets of South Asia and the Darjeeling Hills*

TABLE F.1 *From Gorkha to Tribal and Back*

A Chronology of Recent Movements	
1986–1988	**Gorkhaland Movement**: The Gorkhaland National Liberation Front (GNLF) agitates for a separate state of Gorkhaland within India. After three years of violence, the movement fails.
1989	The Darjeeling Gorkha Hill Council (DGHC) is established, providing limited autonomy within the state of West Bengal.
1990s/2000s	**Movements for Scheduled Tribe Status**: Ethnic groups within the Gorkha conglomerate mobilize for recognition and affirmative action as Scheduled Tribes of India.
2005–2007	**Movement for Sixth Schedule Tribal Autonomy**. The GNLF attempts to make the Darjeeling Hills an autonomous "tribal area", as per the Sixth Schedule of the Indian Constitution.
Sep 2007	Prashant Tamang wins *Indian Idol*, triggering riots, and a violent political upheaval.
2007–2015	**Gorkhaland Movement II**. A new Liberation Front, the Gorkha Janmukti Morcha, launches a second Gorkhaland Agitation, effectively ending the bid for tribal autonomy.
2011/2012	The Gorkhaland Territorial Administration (GTA) is established, again providing limited autonomy within West Bengal.

BECOMING TRIBAL IN DARJEELING

An Introduction to the Ethno-Contemporary

MONSOON FOG sweeps across the Darjeeling Hills. The ghostly seren-ity of the morning is cut only by the drone of diesel engines, as two gov-ernment jeeps ply their way along a road dripping with the season's rains. From the back of one of these jeeps, I watch the heads of the three passen-gers in front of me loll back and forth to the rhythms of the winding road. A head careens off a headrest; a chin digs into a slouching chest; an ear finds the unwelcoming shoulder of a colleague. Asleep, but without com-fort, they are anthropologists of the Cultural Research Institute (CRI) of the Government of West Bengal. They have been sent from Kolkata to determine the tribal identities of ten communities seeking recognition as Scheduled Tribes of India, a designation that affords coveted affirmative action benefits—what in India are commonly referred to as "reservations."

For more than a week now, these civil servants have been bombarded with astonishing displays of tribal identity. Overnight, communities have transformed their villages into elaborate ethnological spectacles. Shamans have shaken in trance, their eyes rolled back in their heads, to the sound of thunderous drums. Women bedecked in tribal attire have danced and sung their most traditional folk songs. Men have shown their primitive wares and performed signature rites of passage. There have been sacri-fices and exorcism, bows and arrows, blood drinking, and packs of youth howling into the monsoon skies—all in the name of the "primitiveness,"

1

"animism," and "backwardness" necessary to attain tribal status. All the while, elite ethnic leaders dressed in suits and armed with cell phones have roamed the perimeter, orchestrating the encounters. These elites have ensured that the anthropologists were looking in the right direction at the right time and speaking with only the right people. They have coached the locals on what to say and how to act. And they have peered over the anthropologists' shoulders to make sure the facts were properly recorded—all for the good of their community.

The anthropologists have set about their work in a manner befitting their bureaucratic duty. They have conducted the required number of interviews, filled out their surveys, and dutifully documented the details of culture, custom, and ritual. But amid the chaos, fulfilling their classificatory responsibilities has proven virtually impossible. "Nothing is raw. Everything has been cooked," they have quipped. And yet day in and day out, these civil servant anthropologists have taken to the field, notebooks in hand, to meet the demands of recognition.

In the middle of this tussle for ethnographic truth have been the everyday residents of these villages. Hand-selected by the "big men" (*thulo mānches*) of the ethnic associations, they have been asked to sing, dance, and all the rest. But seldom have they been allowed to speak. Thrust under the ethnographic lens, they have been made to appear to be the consummate objects of tribal recognition, living embodiments of the tribe. Nevertheless, many have remained largely unaware of the stakes of the encounter. "We are tiny little bugs," they would tell me later. "We wouldn't know." And yet they have been central to this classificatory moment.

For a week now, the anthropologists have been searching for proof of these communities' tribal identity. Today is the final day of the Ethnographic Survey, and they are tired. And so, as their jeeps carry them to another remote corner of the Darjeeling Hills, these civil servants sneak some precious sleep.

But there is little rest for the weary. Within an hour, the diesel engines rattle to a stop, and the anthropologists awake from their slumber to find another community ready to convince them that they are a proper tribe. The anthropologists climb down from their jeeps with an air of authority. They are treated accordingly. Here, civil servants, ethnic leaders, and everyday citizens—all with their own agendas, understandings, and capacities—meet one another in an encounter shot through with power, promise, and paradox.

For the communities under investigation, the stakes are high. A successful demonstration of tribal identity will bring these groups much-needed affirmative action benefits. Their recognition as Scheduled Tribes will, in turn, give Darjeeling the tribal majority needed to bring the region autonomy as a constitutionally recognized tribal area. Eyeing these prospects, many have heralded the anthropologists' arrival as the dawn of a new tribal era—not just for the groups under investigation but for Darjeeling writ large. And so, with rights, autonomy, and a new form of belonging hanging in the balance, a people long relegated to the margins steps into the ethnographic spotlight.

AN ANTHROPOLOGIST
AMONG THE ANTHROPOLOGISTS

The Ethnographic Survey of 2006 was to be a defining moment. For generations, the people of Darjeeling have searched for, yet been perennially denied, their place in India. Historically, the majority of these Nepali-speaking (Gorkha) groups moved eastward across the Nepal Himalayas into the Darjeeling area—especially in the nineteenth century to sell their labor in the budding industries and tea plantations of the British. They have suffered anxieties over being-in and being-of India ever since. Despite being the region's demographic majority and citizens of India, they continue to be called "outsiders" and "foreigners." They remain subject to enduring forms of precarity and exclusion. Throughout the twentieth century, these Nepali-speaking groups came to collectively identify as "Gorkha," eventually launching a violent agitation for a separate state of Gorkhaland in the 1980s. Encompassing the Darjeeling Hills, a region that includes the subdivisions of Darjeeling, Kurseong, and Kalimpong (Map F.1), and reaching into the plains below,[1] Gorkhaland was to provide a homeland *within* India and redress for generations of marginalization. But the Gorkhaland Movement failed. In its wake, politics took a decidedly ethnological turn.

Throughout the 1990s and 2000s, movements for tribal recognition and autonomy swept through the hills, as communities sought new routes to rights and inclusion in the nation-state. By definition, these newfound tribal movements would work to rewrite the terms of ethnopolitics, sociality, and subjectivity. The promise of becoming tribal was twofold: first, Scheduled Tribe status would bring these groups increasingly competitive affirmative action advantages. Second, attaining a tribal majority would facilitate the Darjeeling Hills' becoming an autonomous tribal area, the provisions of which are laid out by the Sixth Schedule of the Indian Constitution. Where Gorkha politics failed to deliver recognition and autonomy, tribal politics would succeed. The Ethnographic Survey of 2006 was to be a pivotal moment in this calculus of tribal becoming.

For me, riding alongside the government anthropologists was an awkward but important experience. I did not come to Darjeeling to work with these agents of the state, but instead to live and work among the people of Darjeeling as they strove to attain tribal recognition and autonomy. By the summer of 2006, I was well into fieldwork with these communities. I spent those early months of research engaging the ethnic associations and political parties leading these tribal movements, attending protests, and trying to get a sense of what becoming tribal meant at the community level. Toward that end, I was living in a local tea estate village (which I call Bidhuwā Busti)—a steep hour-long walk from Darjeeling Town—where I was beginning to understand how these movements were affecting everyday life. Coincidentally, Bidhuwā Busti was situated just above one of the villages investigated by the government anthropologists during the Ethnographic Survey. So, between my work with Darjeeling's ethnopolitical leaders and my village neighbors, I was familiar with many of the people who found themselves the objects of state ethnography during those pivotal days of 2006. It was with these communities—and in their vehicles—that I first arrived to this encounter with the Indian state.

The event quickly opened up new research opportunities. Since I am white, there was no hiding amidst the spectacle that ensued. The Indian government anthropologists quickly pegged me as one of their own. Over the cacophony of the encounter, I did my best to introduce myself.

Soon the team was showing me the ropes of state ethnography. Recognizing the opportunity at hand, I did my best to keep pace with these civil servants as they went about their work. On the final day of the weeklong study, it was with them—and in *their* vehicles—that I made my way to the day's field site. Crammed into the back of that government jeep winding through the hills, I found myself an "anthropologist among the anthropologists," seeing tribal recognition from an entirely new angle.

My relationship with the government anthropologists deepened in the months that followed. Shadowing these civil servants in the field and in their offices in Kolkata, I gained new appreciations of the challenges the Indian government—and its anthropologists—face in managing the demands of its people. These engagements with the postcolonial state allowed me to explore recognition from the inside out—a complement to the outside in perspective I was gaining with Darjeeling's aspiring tribes. Among my friends and neighbors in Darjeeling, the movements' effects were puzzling. The prospect of becoming tribal was breeding hope, but also unexpected tensions. As I began moving across the interface of recognition, it became clear that what was happening in Darjeeling was inexorably tied to what was going on within the state. This involved as much the written policies of affirmative action as it did the unwritten prejudices and practices of the postcolonial state itself. Accordingly, studying these bureaucratic inner workings became vital to understanding the politics—and impacts—of tribal recognition in Darjeeling.

I subsequently began developing the multi-sited, multi-sided ethnographic approach that is this book's backbone. Throughout fieldwork, I carried on with my work among the people of Darjeeling. But I added to these engagements a concurrent study of the civil servants deciding their fate. My jeep ride with the dozing anthropologists, in this regard, marked the start of a sustained effort to marry the critical attentions of the anthropology of indigeneity and recent ethnographic studies of the postcolonial state.[2] This multi-sided, interface-based approach posed ethical and logistical challenges, which I address in the chapters that follow. It also generated unique insight into how recognition works and how its ethnologics transform communities in new and un/intended ways.

Examining these interfaces of communities and the state, this book seeks to raise a broader set of questions about how sociocultural difference is recognized, managed, or otherwise denied at our current conjuncture. This question of difference and its rightful recognition has emerged as a crux of what Elizabeth Povinelli aptly terms "late liberalism."[3] With her, I am specifically concerned with how postcolonial states manage those claims of collective difference that have emerged and gained steam since decolonization. While the trajectories of postcolonial democracy vary considerably from country to country, the quandaries of late liberalism are particularly pronounced in India. Like other anticolonial struggles, India's independence movement forged new political possibilities for minorities. The struggle put into play new categories and new state-based mechanisms of social justice. Since 1947, however, the terms and forms of minority politics have mounted and morphed, putting immense pressure on a government that is at once bereft of resources and wedded to outdated systems of recognition. This book explores these quandaries of late liberalism through those people who arguably know them best—aspiring minorities and government workers. Government anthropologists necessarily figure in this analysis. My main concerns, however, remain with the people of Darjeeling. Through *their* struggles for rights, autonomy, and belonging (tribal and otherwise), I seek a deeper questioning of what forms of life and politics are possible amid these regimes of late liberal recognition.

This is a book about a people and the state that governs them. But it is also the story of a discipline and its gradual seep into the world it studies. Since the British colonial period, anthropology and its subfield ethnology have been central to the governance of diversity on the subcontinent. Today, the paradigms and practices of these human sciences extend from the policies of multicultural governance to the bleeding edge of minority politics. The scholarship of Bernard Cohn and others has demonstrated how these budding disciplines became modalities of colonial rule, informing a litany of devices (censuses, ethnological surveys, etc.) to "scientifically" know and rule India's diverse masses.[4] The story played out to varying degrees throughout the Euro-colonial world, as these sciences of Man were deployed to address the "native question" in contexts ranging from South Asia to Africa and the Americas.[5] The imperial implications of anthropology, ethnology, and other academic disciplines are, consequently, undeniable. Postcolonial critique has accordingly set about the difficult work of bringing these skeletons in the disciplinary closet into the open—a project that continues to this day. Yet, as we confront these problematic pasts, we must not be lulled into thinking that these operations of ethnological knowledge-power are only a thing of the past. They are present, and not always in ways we are accustomed to recognizing.

Ethnology continues to be pressed into familiar services. The Ethnographic Survey of 2006 is a case in point. Here we see the sustained operation of ethnological categories (tribe) and practices (state ethnography) as a means to govern diversity. The survey extends a long history of ethnological governmentality in India. Yet this may be only half the story. Communities throughout the world are now turning liberalism's ethno-logics back upon the state—and themselves—to redefine their community, their politics, and their worlds. For many, the ability to represent culture, identity, and custom in certain ways (and not others) has become a prerequisite to the achievement of rights and social justice. Indigenous peoples from Australia to Nicaragua and the United States are taking their struggles to court, and increasingly putting anthropological experts (native and academic) on the stand to testify on their behalf.[6] Majorities and minorities in Indonesia have refashioned native tradition (*adat*) into a resurgent political force.[7] First Nations in Canada and indigenous communities worldwide continue to invest in archeology and heritage (museums, etc.) to re-present themselves locally and to broader publics.[8] And, as we saw earlier, minorities in India continue to confound the logics of state multiculturalism by performing categories like "tribal" to a T.

Ethnological self-concern has become integral to a new politics of difference—indigenous, tribal, and otherwise—at the global level. There is more at stake in these endeavors than an opportunistic appropriation of static categories. Communities are reworking ethnological paradigms in newly generative ways, posing fresh challenges to governments, the human sciences, and community members themselves. For the academic, it may seem strange (even uncanny, in a Freudian sense[9]) that populations—many of them ethnology's erstwhile objects—are taking up and taking on disciplinary paradigms. But for the marginalized, repurposing disciplinary norms may be vital to the achievement of rights, prosperity, and survival itself.

These dynamics are part and parcel of a world deeply affected by ethnological thought—what I call the *ethno-contemporary*. We are hard-pressed to go anywhere without encountering claims of the *ethnos*. On the one hand, notions of tribes, natives, and indigeneity, each bearing their attendant forms of culture, identity, and difference, have become seemingly ubiquitous fixtures of public policy and the popular imagination. On the other hand, these concepts are under fresh—and urgent—renegotiation. Now in non-academic hands, ethnological knowledge has become central to efforts to redefine the ethnos for the twenty-first century. Deployed by governments, co-opted by the market, and put to increasingly inventive uses by communities themselves, ethnology, as such, continues to shape and reshape the contemporary in unforeseen ways.

This book sets out to explore these untold "lives" of ethnology. Through the people and processes of tribal recognition in India, it examines what happens when disciplinary knowledge travels from the domains of scholarship and governance to the lives and politics of everyday people seeking their rightful place in the modern world. I ask several questions: How are states and communities using ethnology to redefine themselves and their futures? What are the stakes of these ethnological (re)turns? And what might this all mean for difference and recognition in the future?

Ethnology, as the visionary poet William Butler Yeats might say, is now "loosed upon the world." My project is to shed some light on this *second coming*.[10] As I hope to make clear, classificatory moments like the Ethnographic Survey figure as defining moments for much more than just a people seeking rights and belonging. They are defining moments for a state struggling to meet the needs of its people. And perhaps, too, of the ethnologically marked times in which we live.

ESCALATING DEMANDS

There are, at present, more than 700 Scheduled Tribes of India—a population that amounts to more than 8 percent of the country's population, or roughly 100 million individuals (a figure exceeding the combined populations of Great Britain and Canada).[11] ST status affords these groups a range of affirmative action advantages, including employment quotas in government posts, lower standards of admission to educational institutions, and eligibility for special tribal development packages. As India has embraced liberalization since the 1990s, the demands and need for this kind of affirmative action have escalated. Officials I interviewed estimated upwards of a thousand minority groups aspiring to tribal status. The demands are all the more telling considering the Indian government's formal criteria for Scheduled Tribe recognition: (a) indication of primitive traits, (b) distinctive culture, (c) geographical isolation, (d) shyness of contact with the community at large, and (e) backwardness.[12] Pejorative connotations and echoes of colonial anthropology aside, becoming tribal has nevertheless emerged as a twenty-first-century desire for millions—and a veritable problem for the postcolonial state.

The timing of all this matters. The increased demand for tribal status has coincided with a global proliferation of indigenous movements, the 1990s uprisings of Latin America being the most notable. These struggles have thrust indigeneity and its signature claims of culture, identity, and difference into the forefront of international concern. In response to this movement of movements, the United Nations declared 1995 to 2004 to be "A Decade for Indigenous People," instituting its Permanent Forum of Indigenous Peoples in 2000 and adopting its Declaration on the Rights of Indigenous Peoples in 2007. These events punctuated the development of a global discourse of indigeneity that has become a vital resource for marginalized groups throughout the world.[13] The Indian government, for its part, refuses to legally recognize indigeneity—preferring instead categories like "tribal" and *adivasi*.[14] But this has not stopped India's tribal movements from indexing and participating directly in this global arena of indigenous struggle.[15] The last two decades have consequently seen indigeneity become a key trope of minority politics across South Asia.[16]

At the national level, the growing demands for affirmative action have coincided with the liberalization and privatization of India's economy. Amid the turbulence and rising inequalities of neoliberal reform, more and more communities have turned to the state for aid. The Indian government consequently finds itself in a signature paradox of late liberalism.

On the one hand, it cannot abandon the commitments to state welfare that have defined its legacy since independence in 1947. Any retreat from the entitlements upon which people have come to depend is sure to be met by significant public protests. On the other hand, the Indian government continues to do all it can to usher India into the neoliberal world economy, where—in theory at least—the state would gradually retreat from daily life at the behest of the market. Given the expectations and politics of the people, this has proven impossible. The postcolonial state thus finds itself in an acute bind, as it struggles to reconcile its socialist past, the needs of its people, and its designs for a neoliberal future.[17]

Affirmative action has emerged as a flash point for these contradictions. In the 1990s, shortly after India began to privatize its economy, the government announced a significant increase in the quotas for Scheduled Castes (SC), Scheduled Tribes (ST), and Other Backward Classes (OBC) in government posts and public universities from 22.5 percent to 49.5 percent. This initiative had been on the books since 1980, when a special governmental commission known as the Mandal Commission recommended the redoubling of affirmative action to combat India's rising inequality. A decade later, when it was suggested that these recommendations would become a reality, violent protests ensued. Claiming reverse discrimination, upper-caste Brahmins took to the streets, lighting themselves on fire in protest. The scene repeated itself in 2006, when it was announced that a 27 percent quota would be established for OBCs in institutions of higher learning. Concerns of caste have typically dominated these controversies, and for good reason. Caste has been at the fore of India's inequality debates since before independence. As Anupama Rao elegantly argues, the caste question has done much to shape liberal democracy's particular trajectory on the subcontinent.[18] That said, something else was brewing in the closing decades of the twentieth century—a different kind of category with a fresh set of claims upon the present: the tribe.

Since the 1990s, the politics of tribal recognition have escalated significantly in volume and volatility. Throughout the country, and particularly in India's Northeast, the uneven allocation of ST status has become a source of considerable ethnic tension.[19] In Assam in 2007, for instance, the Guwahati public turned on *adivasi* communities protesting their un-requited bids for ST recognition. The ensuing massacre left two dead and hundreds wounded in the streets. That same year, similar violence ripped through the northwestern state of Rajasthan, as tensions flared over the Gujjar community's struggle for tribal status.[20] The clashes were between both the Gujjars and the police and Gujjars and their Meena neighbors, a community that had enjoyed ST status for generations and now was willing to go to violent extremes to prevent others from eating into its advantage. Since 2007, the strife has spilled over into neighboring states, leaving more than sixty dead in the name of tribal recognition. These episodes thrust the tribal question to the fore of India's affirmative action debates, underscoring, at once, the volatility of these demands and the extraordinary salience of this category to the politics of modern India.

THE TRIBAL TURN IN DARJEELING

The prospects of becoming tribal appeared especially promising—and timely—in Darjeeling. In the early 1990s, the Nepali-speaking Gorkha communities were just emerging from the throes of subnationalist agi-tation. From 1986 to 1988, the Gorkhaland National Liberation Front (GNLF), a political outfit spearheaded by its charismatic leader, Subash Ghisingh, waged a violent struggle for a separate state. The movement's ultimate failure left the Gorkhas' longings for autonomy and belonging in India unrequited. Further, it signaled the unviability of the conglom-erate Gorkha identity itself. The individual communities that made up the Gorkha conglomerate subsequently began searching for alternative routes to rights and recognition. These they found in India's massive af-firmative action system—particularly its provisions for Scheduled Tribes. Four local communities—the Bhutia, Lepcha, Sherpa, and Yolmo—had enjoyed ST status since 1950. Now others felt they were due.

Darjeeling's aspiring tribes framed their cause in overtly comparative terms. They argued they were equally deserving of recognition as their ST neighbors. Taking the government to task for its unequal distribution of positive discrimination, they claimed that their current disadvantage was not just unfair. It was unjust. They also made more-regional comparisons, pegging their cause to a variety of well-known ST cases in West Bengal and India's Northeast. There and elsewhere, the government's conferring of ST status upon other groups provided inspiration—and above all, leverage—as the people of Darjeeling brought their demands to the state.

Darjeeling's tribal turn coincided with related developments unfolding in neighboring Nepal, where ethnic (*janājāti*) identity had recently become a galvanizing force of political change in the Himalayan kingdom. Nepal's People's Movement of the 1990s saw marginalized hill communities like the Tamangs, Gurungs, and others unite under the banner of *janājāti* rights to reinstitute representative democracy in the once-Hindu monarchical state. The assertion of *janājāti* political identities went hand in hand with a sharpening attention to ethnic difference and cultural revitalization.[21] Forging a new kind of Himalayan ethnoscape,[22] leaders in Darjeeling networked directly with their counterparts in Nepal, exchanging vital knowledge and tactics. Through these exchanges, Nepal's *janājāti* movements provided invaluable guidance as communities in Darjeeling ventured their own politics of difference in India. Indeed, *janājāti* and tribal became synonymous banners for the movements afoot—indexing, at once, pan-Himalayan dynamics and a newly global discourse of indigeneity.

The Tamangs and the Limbus pioneered these new forays into Indian political society.[23] Others, like the Gurungs and the Rais, followed close on their heels. By the mid-2000s, becoming tribal was a pan-ethnic phenomenon, as every major non-ST community of the hills had filed for ST status.[24] The race to become tribal was on.

This marked an abrupt shift in identificational practices and politics. Whereas notions of a hybrid, conglomerate Gorkha community dominated identity politics throughout the twentieth century, in the 1990s and 2000s, the terms quickly shifted from "Gorkha" to "tribal." Becoming tribal necessitated the undoing of the Gorkha identity on a number of registers. Politically, the go-it-alone tactics of aspiring STs like the Tamangs and the Gurungs atomized the Gorkha conglomerate, effectively refiguring the unit of ethnopolitical mobilization. Socially, the exigencies of ST recognition amplified inter-ethnic competition and distinction. Analytically, there were also tensions. For while the Gorkha identity was predicated on hybridity and the amalgamation of multiple ethnicities into one, ST recognition—with its mandates of cultural isolation, distinctiveness, and purity—called for hybridity's undoing. If groups like the Tamangs and the Gurungs were to attain ST status, they would need to extract their discrete cultures from an already stirred melting pot. While it is true that many continued to self-identify as both Gorkha and, for example, Tamang, it was also clear that the Indian government had little provision for such segmentary configurations. And so, an identity one hundred years in the making began to come undone.

The calculus became more complicated in 2005, when Subash Ghisingh and his ruling GNLF Party began mobilizing to make Darjeeling an autonomous tribal area as per the Sixth Schedule of the Indian Constitution. Originally designed for India's Northeast, the Sixth Schedule incorporates existing tribal political institutions into autonomous District Councils with powers to regulate forest and property rights, social customs, and local administrative structures (for instance, the appointment of headmen and chiefs).[25] Again, Darjeeling's leaders looked to India's Northeast, where the Sixth Schedule had become instrumental in the creation of various "ethnic homelands" for hill communities not unlike their own.[26] Certainly, the Sixth Schedule was no Gorkhaland, but it promised increased autonomy nonetheless. How exactly it would take form in Darjeeling was unclear, however. To date, the region was only 32 percent ST, far short of the tribal majority thought necessary. Due to the Gorkhas' history of migration and ethnic intermixing, there were no discrete tribal political institutions to build upon. And despite the various movements afoot for ST recognition, tribal identification remained, for many, an alien concept. Making matters even stranger was the fact that just twenty years earlier, Subash Ghisingh, the then-political face of Gorkhaland, had rejected the idea, claiming definitively, "We are not tribals. Such a status is bestowed upon people who are uncivilized, very backward, whose men go around naked and whose women go bare breasted. But we are advanced people. We are civilized."[27] Now, a less-militant Ghisingh was reconsidering.

The tribal turn therefore unfolded on two fronts: (1) individual ethnicities' quests for affirmative action as Scheduled Tribes; and (2) a region-wide movement for autonomy as a constitutionally designated tribal area. Crucially, these movements were connected. The Ethnographic Survey of 2006 was the link. If Darjeeling was to attain autonomy, more of its communities needed to be recognized as Scheduled Tribes. This meant convincing the government anthropologists that they were indeed tribal. A proper performance of tribal identity would bring recognition to the individual communities in question and thereby tip Darjeeling's ST population into the majority, bringing autonomy to the region as a whole.

Importantly, the tribal turn entailed more than just a categorical politics—more, that is, than an opportunistic appeal to state-sanctioned categories of difference. These movements were intimately bound up in programs of cultural revitalization and tribal awakening. As the movements unfolded, the prospect of recognition galvanized new forms of ethnic consciousness. Ethnic associations offered language courses, cultural programs, and an array of ethnic media to help their constituents rediscover the linguistic and cultural practices they had "lost" (*harāyo*) since migrating to Darjeeling generations ago. Thus, while the tribal movements looked outward toward the tangible incentives of affirmative action and autonomy, they also moved inward to reform what it meant and how it felt to be a tribal subject. The logics of recognition and subject reformation were often impossible to separate.

Ethnology figured into these reformations in intriguing ways. Communities turned to academic, governmental, and native ethnology to represent—and remake—themselves as proper tribes. Study teams combed through the literatures in search of the tribal subject. Ethnographic delegations traveled to the interiors of Nepal to find their original and "true" culture (*maulik sanskriti*). Native intellectuals generated memorandums, books, and documentaries by the score. These endeavors were taken up not merely in the Geertzian spirit of thick description, but also sociocultural prescription. Leading political parties and ethnic associations implemented dress codes, codified ritual practice, mandated attendance at public ceremonies, and leveled pressures spoken and unspoken to fall into ethnological line. Evoking the troubling tropes of ethnic cleanliness, they launched programs to purify socioreligious practice of the corrupting traces of hybridity. Recognition demanded cultural purification. Revitalized tribal culture, in turn, demanded recognition. As they advanced this agenda, politicians, ethnic associations, and born-again ethnics reaped considerable credence from the ethno-logics of the Indian state. With multicultural governance dangling the carrot, and political cadres wielding the stick, becoming tribal became the order of the day.

The logics of becoming tribal were compelling—animated, as they were, with promises of affirmative action, autonomy, and self-rediscovery. Yet my research tells a more complicated story. Precisely at the moment when the prospects of tribal recognition were giving birth to new kinds of political subjects and possibilities, they were also dividing communities in unexpected ways. Among my neighbors and across the hills, there was a general consensus that people needed whatever advantage they could get. Virtually everyone wanted the benefits of tribal status. It was with the ethnological mandates of becoming tribal that the disagreements began. Determining what constituted tribal culture proved a contentious affair. Factions within communities championed one rendering of culture, custom, tradition, etc., while deriding others as inauthentic, corrupt, and

FIGURE I.1 *Enacting the Tribal Turn*

politically unviable. These politics of authenticity reached into the most intimate spaces of life, as ethnic leaders and local experts proffered their particular versions of culture. There was little hiding from the ethno-logics at hand. Cultural practices that had once been taken for granted now had real social and political repercussions. Those who refused to reform ran the risk of estrangement and, in certain cases, even fines. Worse yet, they would undermine their community's chances of attaining affirmative action and long-denied autonomy. Lines were being drawn. Choices had to be made.

In villages like Bidhuwā Busti, Tamangs and Gurungs, who for generations had intermingled with relative ease, were now actively distancing themselves from each other. Inter-ethnic tensions intensified in 2003 when the Tamangs received Scheduled Tribe status, thereby establishing their advantage over their Gurung neighbors. The Gurungs felt this was unjust. But the Tamangs, wanting to be "the last in the gate," had little interest in helping the Gurungs' struggle for ST status. The Tamangs, meanwhile, had their own divisions to manage, as two rival factions had emerged with competing renditions of Tamang culture and its appropriate political trajectory. Each faction laid claim upon the village, putting everyday citizens in the crosshairs of a veritably cultural politics. These were not isolated events. The scene was repeating across the hills. Such were the conditions in 2006 when the news broke that the anthropologists were coming.

Even at that early point in my fieldwork, these dynamics weighed on me. As an ethnographer, what stories could I tell that my neighbors—who, with so many ethnological expectations already thrust upon them—could not? What forms of critique—of a system and its real-life impacts—could I develop by following *their* politics and *their* lives? How might this ethnographic perspective help to rethink recognition in India and beyond? Now, many years later, I offer answers to these questions. As I hope will be clear, my critiques are of a process, not a people. By following the communities of Darjeeling in their struggles for the rights, recognition, and belonging they need—and I believe, deserve—my aim is to throw some critical light on a *system* within which they (and many others) have little choice but to operate.

This requires thinking beyond classificatory moments like the Ethnographic Survey of 2006 to consider how the ethno-logics of a particular liberal order are reconfiguring life and community beyond the circumscribed arenas of political recognition. In these more intimate realms of sociality, subjectivity, and embodied affect, the exigencies of tribal recognition have transformed communities' lifeways in unforeseen, perhaps irrevocable ways. Some of these impacts have been desirable. Others have proven more troubling.

THE ETHNO-CONTEMPORARY

These dynamics mark but the latest chapter of ethnology's ever-evolving legacy in India. But while ethnology's salience on the subcontinent is pronounced, it is hardly unique. Consider some associated snapshots from around the world:

I. *Geneva, 1996.* The Boers of South Africa, descendants of Dutch colonialists, crash the United Nations' inaugural Forum of Indigenous Peoples demanding that they too be recognized as "indigenous." Claiming to be under threat by Nelson Mandela's African National Congress, the Boers evoke tropes of victimhood, distinctive culture, and territory to constitute their claims for UN recognition. They are denied, but not without underscoring the currency of "indigeneity" on the world scale. Citing the Boers' gate-crashing as emblematic of this global proliferation of "indigeneity," Andrew Kuper designates this movement of movements as "The Return of the Native."[28]

II. *Alaska, late 1990s/early 2000s.* Pushing the envelope of Native heritage, the Alutiiq of southwestern Alaska bring native and scholarly testimony together in a collaborative museum and book project, *Looking Both Ways.* Combating the essentialist tendencies of other Native heritage representations, the project works to provide "a multivocal, nonessentialist account of a fundamentally interactive tradition." James Clifford roots the initiative in the intensifying Native and First Nations claims in Alaska and Canada, propelled by new land-rights policies and the global discourse on indigeneity. Clifford goes on to conclude, evoking Marx, that while "not always in conditions of their choosing, people do make history.

The unexpected resurgence of Native, First Nations, Aboriginal, etc., societies in recent decades confirms the point."[29]

III. *Honduras, 2002.* Garifuna activists campaign against a proposed tourist project funded by the World Bank. To bolster their claims, they contract the services of the Caribbean Central American Research Council (CCARC), a collective of academics and activists, to provide the anthropological and legal bases for securing the land titles necessary to prevent these neoliberal encroachments. Anthropologist Charles Hale, himself a founder of CCARC, explains, "Oppressed peoples, in the vast majority of cases, have no alternative but to wage struggles for rights and redress using the language, the legal and political tools, and even the funding of their oppressors."[30] Or as Garifuna leader Gregoria Flores puts it, "We are using the system to fight the system."

IV. *South Africa, 1990s/2000s.* Indigenous communities of South Africa launch a variety of capitalist enterprises to effectively brand their ethnic identity. Selling ethnic goods, creating "authentic" encounters with indigenous peoples, and exploring venture capital as ethnic corporations, these tactics turn on the possibilities of transforming cultural capital into financial capital and back again. The leaders of this self-commodification claim it will not lead to alienation, as a good Marxist might expect, but rather to a renewed sense of identity and purpose. Tracking these developments through the expanding domains of ethno-tourism, ethno-commodities, and ethno-futures, John and Jean Comaroff label this phenomenon "Ethnicity, Inc." They go on to raise the fair question of whether the future of ethnicity may well lie precisely "in taking it into the marketplace? In hitching it, overtly, to the world of franchising and finance capital? In vesting it in an 'identity economy'?"[31]

These are snapshots of the ethnologically affected present I call the *ethno-contemporary*. Read alongside earlier scenes from Darjeeling, they bring into view a world in which ethnological knowledge is being used in old and new ways to redefine the ethnos. Marking this global moment, the ethno-contemporary has emerged as a field of vital negotiation over the terms and very possibilities of human difference. Encompassing a web of institutions, forces, and social movements—indigenous, tribal, and otherwise—it is an arena of political operation and contested intelligibility. Beyond all else, the ethno-contemporary is a time-space of struggle over what it means to belong to a range of often-competing framings of community. Culture, identity, and difference are its key tropes. Recognition is one of its key battlefields.

Figured at the global level, the ethno-contemporary represents a particular kind of conjuncture. It has emerged from traceable histories, yet its contours remain patently unstable and contingent. What then are the forces that have come together to shape this current moment of ethnological concern? To begin, neoliberal economic reforms, by lowering barriers to transnational capital, have rendered minorities and native peoples ever more vulnerable to advancing regimes of resource extraction. With their land and lifeways under threat, communities have responded with demands that their rights and cultural identities be recognized and protected. As the above snapshots illustrate, ethnology (broadly conceived) has become integral to their new engagements with the state, the market, and international bodies like the UN and the World Bank.

Communities' appropriation of scholarly paradigms is, in itself, nothing new. Anticolonial struggles frequently turned to history to define the nation and its right to independence.[32] Subsequent ethno-nationalist movements made occasional use of anthropology for similar purposes.[33] What sets our current moment apart, however, is the *degree* and *innovation* of these ethnological turns. As communities, academics, NGOs, and activists forge new alliances, recombination and experimentation have emerged as the modus operandi of these suddenly urgent efforts to define and defend cultural difference. Whereas earlier movements evoked history to establish their modern (or "civilizational") equivalence, indigenous peoples have now turned to anthropology and ethnology to assert their fundamental difference. Marginalized groups have made use of communicative technologies like the Internet to take their message to broader publics and to network with other movements. Working together, these communities have accordingly constituted the ethno-contemporary from the ground up. With the pace and moral force of indigenous politics growing,[34] governments, transnational corporations, and organizations like the UN and the World Bank have had little choice but to respond with appositely ethnological gestures to "multiculturalism," "native culture," "heritage," and so on.[35] The result is an arena co-constituted and shot through with competing claims upon the ethnos. These are the conditions that define the ethno-contemporary today.

If the ethno-contemporary is a time-space of global scale, its forms and consequences remain intensely local. Because it emerges through particular convergences of local, national, and global histories, the ethno-contemporary looks different in South Asia than in Latin America— and different in Darjeeling than in other Indian contexts like Manipur, Tripura, etc. Which is not to say that trajectories of indigeneity (and its synonyms) in widely dispersed geographies have not informed one another. They have. Neither is it to deny that there are structural similarities and connections between these contexts. There are. The challenge is to develop an analytic that is capable of accommodating the particularities of life and politics in places like Darjeeling, while also capturing the global conditions (and indeed, conditionality) of the ethnos today. Navigating this problem-space, the ethnographer must take stock of the local, regional, and global forces that define the ethnos *at present*—and thereby shed some light on the actual human experiences of these convergences. This is my project in the chapters that follow.

The intellectual histories of anthropology and ethnology are important parts of this story—particularly in India, where these disciplines have directly informed the management of diversity since the nineteenth century. But it is not academic knowledge alone that I focus on here. My concerns lie with ethnological paradigms that circulate through the offices of ethnic associations and the corridors of the state, through struggles for autonomy and recognition, and through the village tea stall and everyday life. In these realms, particular paradigms of ethnological distinction have gained extraordinary traction. Categories like "tribal" have become normative, at once loaded with history, possibility, and seemingly unarguable sociopolitical sanction. This is not to say that they are static. Quite the contrary—people are reworking ethnological paradigms in newly instrumental ways, just as paradigms like "tribe" are reworking them. Pressed into new kinds of service, the ethnology of the self has accordingly become a realm of intense and uneven negotiations.

Governmentalized systems of recognition have done much to structure these circumstances. There is no denying the normativity of the categories they put into play. But to write off dynamics like the tribal turn in Darjeeling as merely derivative of late liberal governmentality would be to miss the generative tensions, effects, and affects that shape the ethno-contemporary. It would likewise be to overlook the transformative—potentially productive—potentials at hand. Given the grids of ethno-intelligibility, a more fair place to begin would be to question how ethnology, however conceived, can be both an instrument of modern governance *and* a resource for emerging sociopolitical forms. From there, we may find ourselves in a better position to discern what is old, what is new, what calls for celebration, and what beckons critique amid these contending claims upon the ethnos.

To enter this fray is, in the spirit of Paul Rabinow, "to find oneself among anthropology's problems."[36] There, we may begin a critical pondering of the discipline's past, present, and future implications in the world that it studies. Embraced accordingly, implication serves as the starting point—not the end—of this book's inquiry. For though anthropology may always have been a part of the problem, that is not to say it cannot be a part of the solution. The aspiring tribes of Darjeeling would be the first to confirm this point. The question these communities put to us is whether—and how—anthropological knowledge can help to create a different kind of future.

Rendered in these terms, this book is about more than life and politics in a distant corner of India. It is about the transformative possibilities of disciplinary knowledge itself. What is to be made of ethnology's second coming remains an open-ended question, especially for the people of Darjeeling, who continue to experiment with ethnological strategies to reshape their futures and themselves. With them, this book sets out to explore how an ostensibly "academic" way of knowing the world may shape our very being in it. For all of us, this is among the more pressing philosophical questions of the ethno-contemporary—one that asks academics, non-academics, and civil servants alike to think critically and collaboratively about who we are, what we do, and how our knowledge(s) might make for a more just and desirable future. My hope is that this book provides some grist for these conversations to come.

DESIGN OF STUDY

This book draws on a decade of involvement with the tribes and politics of the Indian ethno-contemporary. I first began tracking Darjeeling's tribal movements during preliminary research visits in 2004 and 2005. Over 2006 and 2007, I conducted fifteen months of fieldwork, living and working among the people of Darjeeling. My days typically began with a steep hour-long walk from Bidhuwā Busti to Darjeeling Town, where I made my rounds to political and ethnic association offices, attended rallies, and conducted interviews with the various subjects of these movements. In the evenings, I returned to Bidhuwā Busti, usually exhausted from my work up in town, to spend time with my village neighbors and friends. My work in Darjeeling Town was primarily with the men. My village life offered a more gender-balanced outlook. Traveling up and down Darjeeling's steep topography allowed me to gauge how these movements were affecting life and politics at a variety of socioeconomic strata.

My encounters with the government's anthropologists started a second, complementary line of study. Observing the team's day-to-day operations in Kolkata and conducting interviews at various ministries in New Delhi, I delved into the bureaucratic lives of government anthropologists and their knowledge. During 2006 and 2007, this multi-sited, multi-sided approach became my key methodology. I continued with this interface-based approach throughout additional fieldwork in 2010, 2011, and 2013 to constitute a decade of coverage. Over this time, I augmented my ethnographic work with research in the archives of Kolkata, New Delhi, and London in order to understand not only the current contours of the ethno-contemporary in Darjeeling, but also the pasts from whence this ethnologically affected present spawns.[37]

The chapters that follow are accordingly ethnographic and historical by design. They track a series of interfaces that are constitutive of life and politics in postcolonial India. The first interface is that of a *people* and the *state*—specifically, Darjeeling's aspiring tribes and their government anthropologists. The second is that of the *present* and the *past*. Here I ask how paradigms of old (like "tribe") return to shape the present anew. The third is that of *concepts* and the *ways we world our worlds*. The question here concerns how ethnology structures what it means (and how it feels) to be a recognized community. Of the various interfaces that constitute the ethno-contemporary, this is perhaps the most difficult to apprehend, but also the most meaningful and in need of careful consideration.

The first half of the book (Chapters 1–3) charts the origins and formations of the ethno-contemporary in Darjeeling and India more generally. In the second half of the book (Chapters 4–7), I move into more purely ethnographic engagements with the peoples and processes of tribal recognition today. These chapters travel into the inner sanctums of government anthropology and aspiring minorities to investigate the real-time dynamics by which difference is reckoned—and in certain ways, made—at the contemporary conjuncture. The book's seven chapters come together to trace an analytic arc that extends beyond the formal parameters of late liberal recognition to ask how particular ways of knowing and governing the ethnos have come to rework even the most intimate spaces of present-day life.

By definition, such an inquiry must be open-ended, yet grounded in local realities. Chapter 1 accordingly begins by taking a closer look at the fluctuating forms and energies of ethnopolitics in Darjeeling. Here I lay out the tribal turn as a working example of the ethno-contemporary. Chronicling the shift from *Gorkha* to *tribal* politics, I ask what drives communities into such intermittently violent and ethnological relations with the state and themselves. This involves a look at the hard realities of history at the margins of India—as well as a consideration of how these histories are embodied. Venturing an affective history of the present, Chapter 1 foregrounds these communities' anxieties over belonging in India—what I term *anxious belonging*—to explore the mercuriality of ethnopolitics in this particular corner of the country.

Chapter 2 shifts registers to consider the origins of ethnological governmentality in India. It focuses, in particular, on the colonial history of tribal recognition. On the surface, "tribe" would seem to be the most colonial of categories. But a simple genealogy of "colonialism and its forms of knowledge"—to borrow terms from Bernard Cohn[38]—proves insufficient for understanding the problem of tribal recognition today. It was not epistemic hubris that animated the know-and-rule rationalities of the British Raj, but rather uncertainty.[39] So severe was the colonial discontent with the category of "tribe" that by the time the British were pulling out of India, they had all but given up on its utility. At independence, what was left were the scattered remains of classificatory systems torn asunder by the shifting persuasions of ethological thought and imperial rule. How then did tribal recognition become a centerpiece of state multiculturalism in postcolonial India?

Taking on this question, Chapter 3 shows tribal recognition to be a postcolonial problem demanding postcolonial answers. Here I view the escalating politics—and violence—of the category as a mandate to consider these more-recent intercalations of knowledge, power, and policy. The postcolonial part of this story begins with the Constituent Assembly debates of the 1940s, a crucible of postcolonial nation-making, where Dr. B. R. Ambedkar and his fellow "architects" of India gathered the remains of the tribal category to make it a hallmark of postcolonial affirmative action. Traveling through the various commissions and policies that brought the category to its current form, Chapter 3 exposes the emergence of a conspicuously Hindu-centric form of liberalism, the prejudices of which continue to shape the recognition of minorities across the country. As I show, the impacts in places like Darjeeling have proven particularly deleterious. Chapter 3 thus works to unpack the paradoxes and persuasions of a particular late liberal order.

Chapter 4 turns to the pivotal events of the Ethnographic Survey of 2006. Taking this encounter of anthropologists and tribes as an object of analysis, I begin with the frenetic days leading up to the survey, going inside the "emergency meetings" and eleventh-hour preparations of the groups under investigation. I then shift to the spectacular events of the survey itself in order to explore the contending tactics of government anthropologists and aspiring minorities to determine the ethnographic truth. This was more than a one-off performance of the "tribal slot," however.[40] This classificatory moment epitomized the conditions, possibilities, and impossibilities of becoming tribal in Darjeeling. It was, as I noted at the start, a defining moment.

Chapter 5 follows the anthropologists and files of Darjeeling's tribes back to Kolkata to chart the inner workings of today's ethnographic state.[41] In this analysis of postcolonial bureaucracy, I shadow government anthropologists as they produce and defend their soft science in the hard places of late liberal governance. Investigating affirmative action from the inside out, I reveal a system that, by all accounts, is overburdened, under-resourced, and severely out of date. Government anthropologists, in this regard, face impossible demands. On the one hand are the growing demands of the people; on the other, a crippling knowledge politics within the Indian government itself. Crucially, these technocratic discrepancies within the state directly affect the success and failures of applicant ST communities (not to mention the lives and careers of civil servants themselves). Chapter 5 accordingly goes inside the postcolonial state to provide a humanized understanding of the operations and operatives of ethnological governmentality today.

Chapter 6 returns to Darjeeling to assess the effects and affects of tribal recognition. The analysis focuses on the work of ethnic associations, political parties, and my village neighbors to remake the tribal subject. Buoyed by the prospects of affirmative action and autonomy, these programs induced sweeping sensations of ethnic rebirth. Following Foucault,[42] one might here trace a trajectory of biopower from the liberal state, through the organs of political and civil society, and into the body of the born-again ethnic. But, as I argue, this would overlook the formative tensions of becoming a twenty-first-century tribe. The Foucauldian optic of governmentality here proves ill-equipped to understand how people are negotiating and reworking late liberalism's ethno-logics. Populations are things. People are not. People feel. People categorize back.[43] For some, tribal reform engendered newfound senses of self. For others, it bred controversy, confusion, and division. Sorting through these intended and unintended outcomes, Chapter 6 examines how ethno-logics do and do not make their way into the body and body politic. It is necessarily a phenomenological inquiry.

Just when the people of Darjeeling seemed on the cusp of attaining tribal recognition and autonomy, the terms of ethnopolitical mobilization suddenly shifted. In the fall of 2007, a Gorkha of Darjeeling won *Indian Idol*, India's version of the television sensation *American Idol*. Reactivating long-standing desires for belonging in India, the victory brought euphoria to the hills. But pop culture can be cruel. Just days after victory, a radio DJ in Delhi made discriminatory remarks about the Gorkhas' newly crowned idol, triggering communal riots and a political upheaval beyond anyone's imagination. Chapter 7 takes a closer look at this shocking sequence by which a television show sparked a violent subnational agitation for Gorkhaland—this, the second in as many generations. At first glance, the tribal turn appeared to be at an end. But as time would tell, the champions of Gorkhaland 2.0 only redoubled the ethnological tactics of the earlier regime: mandating political/cultural conversion, engineering public rituals, implementing dress codes, and forcing the populace to fall into ethnological line. Chapter 7 draws on fieldwork in 2010, 2011, and 2013 to demonstrate the perpetuation of precisely the same ethnological paradigms discussed over the course of the book. It goes on to chart the repeated failures of these movements to deliver to these communities the rights, autonomy, and belonging they need and deserve.

Crucially, these failures fall not to the people of Darjeeling but rather to the systems of recognition they must negotiate. As I discuss in the Epilogue, these circumstances implicate us all. To conclude, I accordingly step back to ask what all of this means for communities, difference, and the human sciences broadly conceived. Framing the ethno-contemporary as an intellectual problem and opportunity, I offer some thoughts on how the twenty-first-century ethnographer might navigate its protean contours and work with its various "tribes" (anthropologists included) to develop new modes of recognition—and new ways of being—that can better serve us all. Amid this ethnologically affected present, thinking beyond our current systems of recognition figures to be vital for forging an alternative future.

First, though, we need to critically consider the contemporary at hand. This requires taking a hard look at our current grids of ethno-intelligibility—and, beyond all else, the relative im/possibilities of their habitation. Toward that end, I turn now to the struggles of a people whose ways of being—whose kind of difference—have never quite fit the norms of the day.

CHAPTER 1

A SEARCHING POLITICS

Anxiety, Belonging, Recognition

HOURS AFTER DARK, I find the village council president squatting over a small fire, seething with anger at the anthropologist in his midst. He casts me a sideways glance, then turns away with sudden revulsion. In his hands is a dead chicken. Feathers stick to his calloused fingers; others float seemingly suspended on the tense air between us. I squat down beside him as the flames ribbon over the lines in his face before they leap into the night. He appears to be trembling.

"Sir," I say, "I heard you came to my house this afternoon looking for me."

He shoots a look of disgust into the fire, responding gruffly, "No."

He works the bird with redoubled vehemence. I try again. "But, sir, my landlord told me you came."

"No, I didn't come!" he snaps back, now visibly shaking.

I don't know what I have done to upset him, so I wait. As he plumes the last feathers, I engage him again. "I heard there was some problem with my survey."

"What is this survey? You come here and ask these questions: 'When did your family migrate from Nepal? Why did they come? How long have they lived in this village?'" Suddenly, his upwelling anger cuts off his speech.

"No, no . . . let's talk about this. I didn't mean to upset anybody. Why are you so upset?"

"I am the president of the village council. If you want to ask questions about the village this is fine, but these questions of 'When did you come? Why did you come?' I am the president! You can't ask these questions!"

Suddenly it starts to make sense. Earlier that day, I met with a new assistant to help me conduct a simple survey of the village.[1] Having lived there for seven months, I assumed it would be a straightforward project. I left the survey forms with my assistant and told him to await further instruction. Apparently, he had not. And now something had gone terribly awry.

"Please forgive me," I tell the president. "Now I understand that I should have cleared this survey with you."

"Oh, yes, you should have . . . but this business of 'When did you come to Darjeeling? From where in Nepal?' You can't ask these questions." His temper resurging, his tone again becomes aggressive.

"Wait!" I say assertively. "What's the problem? Listen, you and I both know, we all know: the people here, their ancestors came from Nepal."

His antagonism checked, he is taken aback. He begins shaking his head back and forth, before begrudgingly admitting: "Okay, Okay. We know, we know that! But you can't ask these questions . . . That would be proof. If we put our signature here [inscribing his signature on his hand like it was paper] . . . That would be proof!"

This admission of the obvious now out in the open, the tension dissipates and I breathe a tempered sigh of relief. Clearly, this is not the time to hash out these matters, so we agree to a meeting (for me, more like a tribunal) with the village leadership the following morning. As I get up to leave, I place my hand on the president's shoulder in hopes of conveying my sincerest apology. He shakes his head, staring only into the fire.

. . .

The village night can be especially dark when one is in trouble.[2] On the clock and with the imperatives of apology pressing upon me, I thus began a frenetic search for understanding. As I moved through the village long after gates had been shut and front doors locked, it was easy for me to reconstruct the immediate backstory of an overzealous research assistant, a wary village leader, and a gag order that spread like wildfire. The deeper history of anxiety was more opaque, yet frighteningly present.

Since arriving in Darjeeling, the Nepali-speaking Gorkhas have been beset with uncertainties over their place in India. Generations of discrimination, precarity, and exclusion have imparted to these groups deep-seated anxieties over being-in and being-of India. These anxieties about belonging—what I call anxious belonging—are deeply rooted in body and time.[3] Through the years, they have fueled an array of identity-based movements. These movements have, in turn, constituted a categorically searching politics, in which the terms of mobilization may suddenly shift—say, from *Gorkha* to *tribal*—but the affective undercurrents remain alarmingly the same. Surging one moment, receding the next, taking this form, then that, anxious belonging has consequently made for a particularly volatile—or charged—ethnopolitics in Darjeeling. My goal here is to understand the nature of that charge.

I begin with my harrowing encounter with the village president not to relive the regrettable disturbance I caused my neighbors, but rather to foreground the histories, anxieties, and desires that animate the ethno-contemporary in Darjeeling. Doing so, I offer an alternative reading of these struggles for rights, recognition, and autonomy. I frame these movements as, beyond all else, *a politics to belong* in India. This requires tracing a history of anxiety from the precarious conditions of colonial life in Darjeeling, through the violent Gorkhaland Agitation of the 1980s, and into the designs of the twenty-first-century tribe. Involving, as it did, a shift from a violent ethno-nationalist movement to a more indigenous-based politics,[4] the tribal turn provides a compelling case study of the ethno-contemporary—one that signals the broader contours of this global conjuncture while underscoring the specific histories (and energies) that shape the ethno-contemporary in particular places at particular times. Examining this shift from Gorkha to tribal politics, this chapter aims to raise a deeper set of questions about the conditions that drive communities into intermittently violent and ethnological relations with the state and themselves. Toward that end, let me return to the crisis with which we began.

. . .

Minutes before my meeting the next morning, I am pacing nervously near the village temple when I run into my friend and neighbor Deepak. "Deepak, what happened?" I ask.

"It's fine, there is just that one question that is a problem," he tells me.

"Which one?" I ask, pulling the form from my bag.

Scrolling down the questions with his finger, "This one," he says. "'How many generations ago did your family migrate from Nepal?' The people around here are scared of what will happen to this information. If we put our signature on this, then people are scared it will be proof, and if the government gets it, they will send us back to Nepal."

"No! That's impossible!"

"You see, this is a political thing. We had the Gorkhaland Agitation where we tried for our own state. The people of India think we are foreigners. We have tried for the Sixth Schedule [tribal autonomy]. There is discrimination from the people of the plains. So there is history there."

"But, Deepak, everyone's ancestors came from Nepal, right?"

"Yes, but we can't say that. People think we are foreigners. Like, you know, the situation with the Bhutanese refugees that got sent back to Nepal. If the Ministry of External Affairs somehow gets hold of this form and it has all of our information: where we came from, when we came . . . people think they could send us back."

He breaks off to check his watch. We're late.

ANXIETY, BELONGING, RECOGNITION

Deepak's explanation came not a moment too soon for an ethnographer in trouble. As we made our way to the meeting, I was glad to have him at my side and glad to have a bit more understanding of the crisis I had caused. Thankfully, this meeting commenced with less intensity than that of the night before. Clearly, I was guilty on two counts: first, for failing to clear the survey with the village leaders; and second, for violating a people's sensitivities. The latter was the more serious offense. I therefore began the meeting with an earnest apology. Having heard my side of the story, the council members reciprocated with apologies for their overreaction to my honest, but insensitive, mistake. With an awkward shame lingering among us, conversation shifted to friendlier matters, suggesting that the case was closed. But there was clearly more to this encounter.

As Deepak pointed out, his people's place in India remains a "political thing" with a real and problematic history. Since the nineteenth century, he and his people have been severely marginalized. Despite being the region's majority and bona fide citizens of India, they have been shunned as "outsiders" and "foreigners," and geo-racially typed as "hill peoples" and "chinkies." Economically, the Gorkhas remained pegged to the lowest rungs of a plantation economy dominated by tea. Morally, they have been constantly questioned about their national and nationalist loyalties. Politically, they remain under the thumb of West Bengal and thus lack the representation, autonomy, and homeland they desire. The Gorkhas consequently find themselves relegated to a literal and figurative corner of the nation.

National dynamics have compounded their anxieties over belonging. Throughout India, Nepali-speaking groups have suffered prejudice and periodic bouts of ethnic cleansing—particularly in India's Northeast, where targeted expulsions in the 1960s, 1970s, and 1980s established alarming precedents.[5] The Bhutanese refugee crisis of the 1990s only exacerbated the unease, as roughly 100,000 Nepali-speaking refugees, unwelcome in India, passed through Darjeeling, en route to the interminable refugee camps of eastern Nepal.[6] These events hit close to home in Darjeeling. As Deepak's testimony shows, they powerfully inform the Gorkhas' collective sense of vulnerability.

The anxieties came to a head in the 1980s when the Gorkhaland National Liberation Front (GNLF) launched its violent agitation for a separate state of Gorkhaland. When asked why the name Gorkhaland, the GNLF's charismatic founder, Subash Ghisingh, explained, "[Because] only the ethnic name of any place or land . . . can germinate the real sense of belonging in the conscience of the concerned people."[7] Three years (1986–88) of violence failed to deliver to the Gorkhas the homeland they desired, leaving the people unrequited and in search of political alternatives.

The quests for tribal recognition and autonomy followed soon thereafter. These movements reset the terms of ethnopolitical mobilization—effectively replacing the failed banner of the Gorkha with the more ethnologically savory figure of the tribe. This reset was not coincidental either at the local level or at the national level. Becoming tribal presented a way *out* of the violent failures of the 1980s and *into* a mainstream quickening with India's 1990s embrace of economic liberalization. At this conjunction of local and national history, the tribal turn was equally logical and timely. For a people consistently denied recognition and autonomy, it marked an innovative engagement with the ethno-logics of late liberal governance. Following Partha Chatterjee, we might productively see the tribal turn as a "politics of the governed"—in this case, a strategic renegotiation of governmental categories in the name of social justice and economic gain.[8]

But there was more to these tribal politics than the pursuit of rights and entitlements. Their political instrumentality notwithstanding,[9] these newfound tribal movements also operated on a more affective register. They were geared as much toward the attainment of affirmative action and autonomy as they were toward that sacred stuff of recognition to affirm these communities' being-in and being-of the nation—and themselves. They were, in other words, always also *a politics to belong*. It was Hegel, of course, who first emphasized the self's need for recognition.[10] Recognition, he argued, was vital to self-fulfillment. I mean to suggest something similar—namely, that the promise of these movements lay not only in the tangible advantages of affirmative action and autonomy but also in the more existential realms of affect, belonging, and self-realization.

These dialectics of recognition and belonging became especially clear in the tribal rhetoric of the times. As but one example: on the occasion of Bhadra Purnimā in 2006, Subash Ghisingh's Department of Information and Cultural Affairs (DICA) commandeered the town plaza (Chow Rasta) to put on a massive celebration of tribal identity. DICA officials decorated the plaza in classic "animistic" fashion and set up a PA system with enough power to rattle windows across town. Thousands observed the spectacle, as shamans recited their chants, pounded their drums, and shook violently with the gods that possessed them. As tourists, journalists, and the greater public took in the sights and sounds, DICA officials watched over the event with a careful eye. Proper orchestration was imperative. To conclude the festivities, a high-ranking GNLF official took the stage to offer a few closing remarks. As he explained,

> the rituals and practices that you have witnessed here today give us our iden-
> tity as tribals. We have drifted away from our identity. We have to know
> ourselves . . . We have not been able to recognize ourselves. We have not been
> able to recognize ourselves as tribals . . . That is why the Sixth Schedule is
> a great opportunity for us to understand our identity and our customs and
> traditions . . . There are great mysteries hidden within, and these mysteries
> are to be revealed.

Note how the speaker hails the Sixth Schedule as an "opportunity" for re-discovering the tribal self. "We have not been able to recognize ourselves," he exclaimed. "We have not been able to recognize ourselves *as tribals*." With these last words, the speaker struck upon *the* crux of the tribal turn: how were the people of Darjeeling to find themselves in this category of the state? How were they to recognize themselves *as tribal*?

Enter ethnology. Throughout his remarks, the speaker repeatedly called upon intellectuals to facilitate the discovery of the tribal self. "What is important," he insisted, "is to get research done on our traditional heal-ers, sorcerers, and shamans. We would like to tell the intellectuals to take up this research . . . We need to help each other. We need to get deeply into this." As the speaker implored native intellectuals to take up this work of tribal revitalization, the message was clear: auto-ethnology was to be, at once, politically expedient and socially and subjectively transfor-mative—a way of revealing, as it were, the "great mysteries within."

These were designs for a tribal future and, as such, an idealized vision of these dialectics of recognition and belonging. The past tells a more un-settling story—not so much of belonging, but rather of its perennial lack and therefore anxiety. Embodied by a people over time, anxious belong-ing has become a historical fact and a political force in Darjeeling.[11] Pre-cisely in its ability to galvanize bodies and the body politic, this collective anxiety over belonging has proven an action potential for ethnopolitical mobilization. Yet its mercurial nature has also made for a highly unstable field of political operation, wherein regimes, demagogues, and the very terms of identification rise and fall with sometimes stunning caprice.

Shifting so suddenly from "Gorkha" to "tribe," the categorical instability has only amplified these communities' anxieties over who they are, who they should be, and what kinds of belonging they might accordingly find within the nation-state and themselves. Herein lies the paradox of these categorically searching politics.

Crucially, if we are to understand how anxious belonging frequents the present, we must ground it in the hard realities of Darjeeling's past.[12] Let me then turn to the Gorkhas' earliest days in Darjeeling to search out the origins of these anxieties about being-in and being-of India.

COLONIAL UNEASE

Since their arrival to colonial Darjeeling, the Gorkhas have endured considerable insecurity. By the 1850s and 1860s, outbreaks of anxiety were flashing across the hills. Captured by the archive in the affective language of alarm, flight, and unease, the panics foretell a broader pattern to come. Indeed, they bear directly on the crisis I caused in 2007:

Archival Excerpts

I. *October 1854:* The Deputy Commissioner of Darjeeling, A. Campbell, alerts government of "universal" rumors of an invasion by Nepal, inducing "much alarm among the population."[13]

II. *November 1854:* Campbell continues, "The alarm amongst the Nipalese subjects employed here . . . rose to such a pitch . . . that about 500 men employed on the government works were not to be found."[14]

III. *September 1858:* Campbell describes rampant rumors of a proclamation by Nepal's prime minister that "all the Nipalese who do not return to their country before the end of the Durga poojhā [a major Hindu holiday] shall be shut out from ever going back to Nepal and shall be considered in the light of British subjects, or as enemies in the approaching invasion of Darjeeling from Nipal." This time 1,000 laborers fled in two days.[15]

IV. *October 1858:* Under what he terms the "pressure of failing labor," Campbell reports hearing that the prime minister "had issued a proclamation to all Nipalese wherever located that now or never was the time to return to their allegiance . . . The whole native population became uneasy at these rumors, the sappers got alarmed, and the European community did so also." Between October 9th and 19th, 700 more men on government hire: gone.[16]

V. *October 1864:* The superintendent reports that "considerable excitement exists among the Nepalese laborers and Emigrants in this settlement in consequence of Jung Bahadoor's [Nepal's prime minister] approaching visit to our Terai . . . The coolies and others are reported to be selling their property at a loss and leaving in large numbers . . . Many of the Nepalese Laborers and settlers are refugees, and I have no doubt that they fear that Jung Bahadoor's visit is made with a view to obtaining the extradition of such persons."[17]

The last case is particularly intriguing. In 1864, Nepal's notorious prime minister Jung Bahadoor Rana reportedly had his sights set on a fabled white elephant rumored to be foraging in the Darjeeling foothills (Terai).[18] Jung Bahadoor made almost yearly forays into Indian territory in quest of game, and he seldom traveled light.[19] On this particular trip, his entourage was reported to include six hundred cavalry, seven regiments of infantry, seven hundred elephants, two guns, and just for good measure, two Europeans.[20] That the coolie populations of Darjeeling would notice such a force is no surprise. What is intriguing is the anxious response it triggered. What were the origins of these anxieties about being in India?

Ever since the 1830s, when the British began developing Darjeeling as a hill station sanatorium, colonial administrators encouraged the immigration of labor from Nepal and surrounding areas.[21] Clearing the rugged landscape, building roads, and peopling the region's budding tea industry required far more labor than the local populations (primarily Bhutia and Lepcha) could provide. Nepal's hill tribes, moreover, were seen as uniquely suited to this type of mountainous labor.[22] The British therefore turned to neighboring Nepal to pursue the "most vigorous and enterprising of the Nepali races."[23]

Circumstances in Nepal facilitated the endeavor. Nepal at the time was undergoing tumultuous land reform and excessive taxation policies, which put considerable strain on its ethnic hill populations. Forced-labor regimes, bonded labor, and slavery were commonplace.[24] British India, meanwhile, offered wage labor and an escape from Nepal's oppressive hierarchies and feudal circumstances. With these push-pull factors, thousands of "sturdy hillmen" were soon pouring across the border.[25] Given the proximity and the types of people that flowed in, Nepal was, for the British, an ideal and decidedly ethno-logical labor pool. But there was a problem: the Nepali government did not approve.[26]

The colonial planters accordingly turned to informal labor recruiters known as *sardārs* to do the dirty work of moving bodies across borders. These native *sardārs* used ethnic kinship networks and the promise of a new life in India to bring labor to market.[27] Working closely with the planters, the *sardārs* became linchpins of a migration that would quickly see Nepali laborers become the region's majority. The numbers are unreliable (more on this in a moment), but by the 1870s there were well over a hundred tea gardens in the area, and the Nepali population had grown to almost 40,000. By the turn of the twentieth century, the number of Nepalis in the Darjeeling district had swelled to 152,000.[28]

For these laboring populations, liminality was a way of life. Since they were no longer Nepali and not yet Indian, status of any sort was tenuous at best.[29] Colonial officials and planters encouraged the influx of labor, promising food, clothes, shelter, employment, and freedom.[30] What they did not provide, however, was legal protection and recognition as British subjects. With the responsibility of labor outsourced to the *sardārs*, the entire system operated in a realm of quasi-legality that obviated the possibility of formal papers, acknowledgment, or bona fides of any sort. From the outset, this was a history of migration that could not officially exist.[31] By juridical rule, any traces of this history, any residues of quasi-legality, would have to be rendered on a different register.

Extradition was a real, albeit rare, possibility. Along with formal extradition cases, the archive tells harrowing stories of Nepali raiders crossing into Darjeeling in the dark of night to recapture escaped slaves.[32] In the reports of these cases, the colonials' ambivalence toward the Gorkhas is clear. Administrators wished to claim these people as British subjects, but recognized they had little recourse to do so. The ambivalence largely mirrored the empire's relations with Nepal. At some times, the British treated the Himalayan kingdom as a sovereign nation; at others, they treated it as merely a princely state, with nominal sovereignty from the British Empire.[33] Reflecting the equivocations of the empire of which they were a part, British administrators and planters in Darjeeling relied on—and encouraged—Nepali immigration, but nevertheless refused to claim these groups as British-Indian subjects. Such were the conundrums of quasi-legality.

These juridical ambiguities were to play a critical role in shaping the Gorkhas' questionable status in the future nation-state. To this day, many Gorkhas, including those in the village where I lived, feel they lack "proper papers." This is why my neighbors reacted so strongly to my survey questions about household ownership, immigration, and so on. The aftereffects (and affects) of this colonial history, in this sense, remain hauntingly present. The fear of being sent back to Nepal, the lack of papers, the hair-trigger sense of panic—the resonances with the crisis I caused in 2007 are uncanny.

RECKONINGS OF DIFFERENCE

In policy and the post/colonial imagination, Darjeeling has always been a special place. It is well known that India's human and ecological diversity presented major problems to British imperialism. In the interest of "good governance," the British periodically instituted special arrangements—exceptions to the standard rules of law—for aboriginal, frontier, and/or "backward" peoples and places. The Scheduled Districts created in 1874, Backward Tracts created in 1919, and Excluded and Partially Excluded Areas created in 1935 are examples of these special forms of governance. Border regions and hill tracts like Darjeeling often fell under this ambit of exceptionalism. Beginning with the carte blanche authority vested to Superintendent A. Campbell to develop a proper sanatorium in the 1840s and extending through the most recent administrative arrangements, Darjeeling has always been a place apart—a "zone of anomaly," as K. Sivaramakrishnan might have it.[34] In theory, these exceptional forms of governance were implemented in response to local ethnopolitical and ecological configurations. In practice, they also produced them.

In 1874, Darjeeling was declared a Scheduled District, exempting it from standard governmental procedures. With tea flourishing in the hills, ample labor to bring it to market, and Darjeeling coming into its own as a hill station, local British interests favored this largely unregulated status. It seemed only right that the "queen of the hills" was kept above the fray of the "real" India in the plains below. In 1917, the Scheduled Districts Act of 1874 came under review as part of the Montagu-Chelmsford Reforms. In question were the extant laws of the districts, as well as the character of the natives. Not coincidentally, it was at this time that the first articulations of a collective Nepali-Indian identity appeared in the historical record.[35]

In 1917, the Hillmen's Association (comprising ethnic elites from Darjeeling's Nepali, Bhutia, and Lepcha communities) sent a memorandum to the British Indian government arguing that Darjeeling should remain excluded from standard governance. Evoking geographic, racial, historical, religious, and linguistic difference, the Hillmen argued, "No real affinity exists between the peoples of this Himalayan and sub-Himalayan region and those of the plains of Bengal. The evolution of our political life should be towards a distinct local government of our own."[36] The Planters Association and the European Association of Darjeeling lobbied along with the Hillmen to sustain the status quo of exceptionalism, though they stopped short of advocating for native self-rule, as had been proposed by the Hillmen.

These claims of difference were not unanimous, however. Other groups lamented being set apart from the rest of India. The Gurkha Memorialists called the proposed "Backward Tract" designation an "insult to injury." "The Gurkha race is not inferior to any other community in India, and has a brilliant tradition of military and civil services," they argued. "There is no difference between the people of Bengal and Gurkhas, geographically, historically, religious and linguistically, except racially and they do not therefore want Darjeeling to be separated from Bengal."[37] The Darjeeling People's Association concurred. Even factions of the Hillmen's Association—namely, the Kalimpong Samiti—expressed dissent over exclusion from the all-India reforms scheme. Tellingly, the British Planters quickly brought this rogue faction back into line. And so, with the planters' capital backing Darjeeling's unregulated, anomalous status, the region was declared a Backward Tract in 1919.

Similar debates arose in the late 1920s when Darjeeling's status again came under review—this time by the Simon Commission. In question again was the ethnopolitical character of the native population, in particular their "backwardness," their capacities of democratic citizenship, and their alterity vis-à-vis the Indians of the plains.[38] The reckoning touched off considerable debate, including *within* the native populations. The outcome, however, was similar to those of years past. Darjeeling was made a Partially Excluded Area, extending its exceptional status.

One will not find these native voices of dissent in the popular histories of the Gorkha, but they deserve mention for several reasons. First, they illustrate the political interests undergirding the early articulations of a Nepali-Indian identity. State formation and ethnic difference were here entangled from the start. It is not coincidental that this Nepali-Indian identity emerged at a time when the governance of Darjeeling was thrown into question. Second, the internal dissension suggests that this conglomerate identity did not yet have the cohesion it accrued in later generations. This situation changed in time, but in the early twentieth century, the Nepali-Indian identity remained largely a political construction. It was what Bakhtin would call an intentional hybrid, a conscious cobbling together of communities into a political interest group.[39]

More-organic processes of hybridity were under way, however. Across the hills, once-discrete ethnic groups like the Tamangs, Gurungs, Newars, and Lepchas were mixing to unprecedented degrees. Plantation life proved to be a crucible of inter-ethnic hybridity, where linguistic, cultural, and religious distinctions blended in generative ways. Nepali soon emerged as the lingua franca among these groups. Old languages and practices were "lost." New practices and solidarities were born. These developments lent the Nepali-Indian identity increasing sociocultural and affective substance.[40] Gradually, this ethnic conglomerate came to look and feel more like a culture-bearing community. And so, as organizations like the Hill People's Social Union (established in 1934) and the All India Gorkha League (established, in Darjeeling, in 1943)[41] advanced the cause of Nepali-Indian rights and autonomy in the decades to come, their identificational claims increasingly reflected the evolving realities of everyday life. Gorkha identity politics gained steam accordingly.

IMPERIAL BAGGAGE

Being Gorkha in India comes with baggage. When Nepali speakers in Darjeeling and across India began making claims under this appellation, they confirmed a dangerous slippage in terms. Already imbricated in the colonial imaginary were the famed Nepali "Gurkha" regiments of the British Indian army. Since the mutinous Rebellion of 1857 when they stood by the British in their desperate defense of Delhi, the Gurkhas had been a trusted ally in combating sedition.[42] But as the tables of empire began to turn, so too did the legacy of this "brave and chivalrous" "martial race."

With India accelerating toward independence in the 1930s and 1940s, the Gorkhas' national(ist) loyalties were increasingly called into question. The issue concerned not so much their ties to Nepal as those to the British. Anticolonial nationalist propaganda took the Gorkhas to task for their service to empire. Pamphlets intercepted in Darjeeling's post office in 1931, for instance, implored the Gorkhas to forsake the British and join the nationalist anticolonial struggle. "What have you gained by giving your lives for the English?" the pamphlets proclaimed. "The Gurkhas should rectify their mistake and help India."[43] Importantly, the propaganda laid the burden of history not only on Gurkha soldiers. "Civilian Brethren!" it hailed. "It is your religious duty to make amends for the work supplied by military brethren. It is your religious duty to bandage the injuries inflicted on account of their mistakes." The message was agonizingly clear: the once-heralded identification of this "martial race" would now be problematic for a minority seeking moral inclusion in the nation-to-come.

The Gorkhas' colonial past was an inconvenient truth for a people already uneasy about their place in India. That their belonging came to be weighed on moral grounds reminds us of the more affective dimensions of national inclusion. Theorizing related dynamics of *affective citizenship*, Lauren Berlant and others have argued that national inclusion involves not just the formalities of papers, rights, and recognition, but also shared structures of feeling.[44] Per these attentions, the Gorkhas' quasi-legal history of migration, the precariousness of their colonial labor, their ethnological difference, and their service to empire rendered them lacking in both formal and informal credentials of national belonging. Accruing on multiple registers, these conditions of non-belonging compounded through time, giving rise to increasingly anxious forms of life and politics in the process.

POSTCOLONIAL FRUSTRATIONS

India's independence brought new hope, but little respite for the Gorkhas. Decades before 1947, the Gorkhas were already maneuvering for a favorable place in a free India. Correspondence between Gorkhas across India and the Indian National Congress in the 1930s stressed the urgency of an "authoritative declaration on behalf of the Congress that the Gurkhas were their own brethren forming an integral part of the Indian community."[45] With the blessing of nationalist leaders like Nehru, Patel, and Bose, the Congress Party assured the Gorkhas equitable minority status in the independent nation-to-come. Subash Chandra Bose personally proclaimed the Gorkhas' grievances "just and legitimate." He further promised to remedy these grievances "as speedily as possible" once Congress was in a position to do so (i.e., after independence).[46]

But the Gorkhas hedged their bets. Gorkha League leaders in the hills appealed to both the British and the Congress throughout the 1940s. In 1943, they wrote to the British governor general highlighting the Gorkhas' "steadfast loyalty" to the British during the Rebellion of 1857 and in more recent events like the Jallianwala Bagh massacre of 1919. Yet "in spite of their long and loyal services," the memorandum explained, "they have been consistently ignored . . . and not recognized as a community of India."[47] When lobbying the Congress, however, the Gorkha League strategically removed reference to the Gorkhas' service to the British, yet sustained the demands for rights and inclusion. Playing it both ways, the Gorkhas navigated the inconvenient truths of history, with an eye toward securing their place in the future nation-state. If these dynamics illustrate the baggage of being Gorkha in India, they likewise demonstrate the complicated politics of minority belonging that attended decolonization.

Whatever stroke-of-midnight hopes the Gorkhas in Darjeeling harbored for national integration were quickly dashed by the realities of postcolonial life. Discrimination, political marginalization, and a pronounced neo-colonization of the hills by West Bengal and the "people

of the plains" only redoubled earlier exclusions. The call for ethnic autonomy, by this point, had been through numerous iterations. Yet with the
newly empowered Congress resisting the idea,[48] there was no substantive
progress. As India transitioned from colony to modern nation-state, Darjeeling remained a place apart: exceptional in every way, but not worthy
of native self-rule.

Material conditions further frustrated the Gorkhas. In the 1950s,
West Bengal instituted sweeping land reforms designed to break up the
massive landholdings of the *zamindars* and aristocratic elites. Acreage
ceilings were implemented to do away with this feudal land tenancy system. Notably, Darjeeling's massive tea estates remained largely exempt
from these reforms.[49] In the interest of tea and capital, the exemption
allowed the industry to function much as it always had.

Which is not to say that important changes were not afoot. As British
planters sold off their interests, they left a vacuum at the highest echelons
of the local political economy. Bengalis and increasingly Marwaris capi-
talized on the opportunities at hand, replacing the British planters. Once
again, the Gorkhas found the land and resources that otherwise might
have been theirs in the hands of outsiders.[50] With the land came labor.
When Bengalis, Marwaris, and others bought up Darjeeling's tea plantations, they also "bought" the livelihoods of those who lived and worked
in the estates. The geo-racial overtones of this internal colonization were
obvious. Suffice it to say: while independence may have altered the upper
tiers of the local economy, for the average Gorkha, little had changed but
the faces of domination.

Exclusion at the national level punctuated local grievances. The Nepali Language Movement offers a case in point. In 1972, the All India
Nepali Language Committee began a protracted struggle to make Nepali
a national language as per the Eighth Schedule of the Indian Constitution.[51] The movement had strong activist roots in Darjeeling, but it
struggled to gain ground at the national level for the millions of Nepali
speakers across India. The initiative suffered a most telling rebuke in
1979, when Indian prime minister Morarji Desai publicly declared Nepali to be "a foreign language" spoken by foreigners in India.[52] Desai's
words struck a particular nerve in Darjeeling—that of anxious belong-

ing. They have since lived in infamy, becoming fodder for subnationalist politics. The Nepali Language Movement, for its part, eventually succeeded in making Nepali a national language of India in 1992. As for Desai's rebuke, the damage was done.

Nepali speakers meanwhile found themselves the targets of escalating prejudice and violence throughout the country, particularly in the Northeast. Ethnic cleansing in Mizoram in 1967, in Assam and Meghalaya in 1979, and in Manipur in 1980 underscored the tenuousness of the Nepali-Indian identity. For the Gorkhas of Darjeeling, these instances tapped into their own insecurities over being-in and being-of India, inflecting them with the corporeal threats of displacement and violence.

As local rhetoric increasingly had it, the Gorkhas did not have an identity; they had an identity crisis. Relegated to the geographic margins of the nation, lacking political voice, economic opportunity, and a secure sense of being-in and being-of India, anxious belonging would soon engender new political forms—these of a more radical kind.

AGITATION

In the 1980s, anxious belonging reached a breaking point. Gorkhaland National Liberation Front (GNLF) leader Subash Ghisingh explained, "The growing fears of the Gorkhas had spread like a cancer. No ordinary medicine would cure this malady—it was a very, very old disease. There was just one capsule which could clean the system of this affliction—Gorkhaland."[53]

Ghisingh, like the people he represented, had been called many things: "anti-nationalist," "foreigner," and "traitor," but the classic anthropological character of the shaman is more apt. Given his propensities for the mystical (he frequently claimed magical abilities), it is unlikely that Ghisingh himself would have shed that label like he did xenophobic pejoratives: "Me! An anti-national!" he once exclaimed, aping an epithet he described as "far removed from reason. For, weren't we just *longing to be* called Indians?"[54] (emphasis added)

Ghisingh's words bring to mind Elspeth Probyn's writings on the longings that inhere in belonging itself. Recognizing belonging to be a "profoundly affective manner of being," Probyn sees these longings as a source of "immense political possibility."[55] Ghisingh would concur. Gorkhaland was a "longing to be," an embodiment that cannot be understood sans the framings of nation and the political genius of Subash Ghisingh. For there, in the ambiguous netherworlds of national belonging, we find this political sorcerer and his magic. Like the healer of Levi-Strauss's fascination, Ghisingh was a master of abreaction, a conjurer of malady who could affect the traces of a "very, very old disease" so as to prescribe its notional cure—Gorkhaland.[56]

Under the auspices of Ghisingh, the GNLF waged a deadly three-year (1986–88) agitation for a separate state. The Gorkhaland Movement was one of many ethno-nationalist agitations in India. In the Punjab, the Sikhs' movement for Khalistan had been ongoing since the 1970s. Meanwhile, insurgencies in India's Northeast had proven that ethno-nationalist agitations could indeed lead to the creation of new states.[57] Across the country, these struggles (some secessionist, others not) differed in important ways, but they also bore common features, among them vitriolic demands for territory and self-rule; violent engagements with the state; and the willingness to radically disrupt life among their constituents in the name of achieving their goals. These movements affected one another in indirect and direct ways, through both precedence and the networking of leaders. Their trajectories informed the political imagination in Darjeeling. As Ghisingh and the GNLF launched the Gorkhaland Movement, they studied and frequently invoked other struggles to justify their cause.[58] During the 1970s and early 1980s, political outfits like the All India Gorkha League and the Pranta Parishad made similar demands for a homeland. Ghisingh's innovation was to inject a viral politics of anxiety into this milieu. The seeds were already sown. Under Ghisingh's spell, anxious belonging metastasized into what the man himself called a full-blown "cancer."

With a curious blend of poetics, paternalism, and paranoia, Ghisingh cultivated anxiety as the fuel of political conflict. He and the GNLF fixated on the Indo-Nepal Treaty of 1950, which granted "reciprocal" rights (of property ownership, business, movement, etc.) to Nepalis domiciled in India and vice versa. The treaty said nothing of dual or "reciprocal" citizenship. Moreover, the Indian Constitution states unequivocally that all those residing in India at the time of independence were legal citizens.[59] This included the majority of Darjeeling's population. Yet Ghisingh preached otherwise. Speaking to the Gorkha masses on June 2, 1985, he warned:

> This word "reciprocal" has become a blemish for we (Nepalese in India). This word indicates that we have come to India after the 1950 Treaty as immigrants. Accordingly, we are not bona fide citizens of India. Life and future is not secure for us in India.[60]

Note how quickly Ghisingh's rhetoric of doubt slips from a juridical to an affective register—from a legal "word" to a "life and future not secure." Only through political conflict and the achievement of a separate state of Gorkhaland would the Gorkhas find the security they longed for. On July 27, 1986, the GNLF ceremoniously burned the Indo-Nepal Treaty of 1950 at rallies throughout the hills.[61] But the question of citizenship remained a centerpiece issue throughout the agitation, making "reciprocal" a household term.

Leading the Gorkhaland Movement, the charismatic Ghisingh became an icon of the hills and an operator on the national stage. As his fame grew, he took the Gorkhas' plight to the Indian public:

> [Prime Minister] Morarji Desai described us as foreigners and said we were welcome to go back to Nepal … We Indian Nepalis who have nothing to do with Nepal are constantly confused with "Nepalis," that is, citizens of Nepal, a foreign country. But if there is Gorkhaland, then our identity as Indians belonging to an Indian state (…) will be clear.[62]

This was classic Ghisingh. Reintroducing the threat of extradition (first evidenced in the 1850s), he and his party reminded the people of their sensitivities precisely by aggravating the anxieties in question. With each iteration, those nerves became simultaneously more raw and more real—fueling, in turn, an escalating guerrilla insurgency. Ghisingh and the GNLF were not just summoning a history of anxious belonging. They were producing it.

The agitation generated new anxieties. Throughout 1986 and 1987, GNLF guerrillas targeted state police and the Central Reserve Police Force (CRPF) using bombs, snipers, arson, and more-organized assaults on CRPF camps. By definition, these tactics were unpredictable and unsettling. More distressing were the state's retaliations. Where GNLF guerrillas worked through pinpoint strikes, the CRPF responded with village raids and sweeping attacks through market towns like Manebhanjang. These counterinsurgency measures left hundreds of homes burned, thousands homeless, and hundreds more injured, tortured, and/or killed.

Adding to the day-to-day uncertainties were the GNLF's increasingly lengthy *bandhs* (strikes), which shut down all travel and commerce. What began as two- and three-day strikes, by June of 1987 had grown to six- and thirteen-day affairs.[63] If these tactics demonstrated the GNLF's power, they also radically unsettled life in the hills. Agitation thus became, simultaneously, a political project and a socially embodied state—something akin to the internal-external dialectics exposed by Michael Taussig in *The Nervous System*, his study of conflict-torn Colombia.[64]

Making matters worse, the movement entailed volatile cycles of progress, setback, and intensity. In the fall of 1987, for instance, tensions eased as negotiations between the GNLF, the Government of West Bengal, and the national government in New Delhi progressed toward an imminent peace accord. The optimism and relative peace were short-lived, however. Negotiations faltered in December amid a sudden uptick in violence. The situation worsened in early 1988, as GNLF cadres (increasingly operating beyond Ghisingh's control) became more brazen in their attacks, and the CRPF more severe in its responses. With the situation spiraling out of control, Ghisingh announced a forty-day strike to begin on February 10, 1988. This period would come to be remembered as the most traumatic chapter of the movement.

The embodiments of the Gorkhaland Agitation—and its failures—must not be underestimated. The three-year agitation left an estimated 297 dead and some 1,164 private homes destroyed.[65] Today, vivid memories remain: of decapitated heads appearing in the bazaar, of atrocities committed by military and paramilitary forces of the Central Government and the Government of West Bengal; of razed villages, disappeared loved ones, and countless other atrocities. Crucially, the movement failed. On July 25, 1988, Ghisingh signed a Memorandum of Settlement, ending the agitation. As part of the deal, a *Gazette* notification was issued by the Indian government to clarify the question of Gorkha citizenship.[66] Further, the Darjeeling Gorkha Hill Council (DGHC) was established— a makeshift government with limited autonomy that the GNLF and Ghisingh would control for the next twenty years (1988–2008). These conciliatory measures did little to assuage the people. Nevertheless, with Ghisingh at the helm (and answering directly to West Bengal), the energies of agitation were kept at bay—largely by their onetime instigator. In the end, then, the Gorkhaland Agitation did not "cure" the people's anxieties over belonging. It exacerbated them, rendering them ripe for alternative forms of mobilization.

THE TRIBAL OPTION

With the failures of the Gorkhaland Movement fresh at hand, the people of Darjeeling sought new political possibilities. The violence of the 1980s had left the public on edge and unrequited. India meanwhile was embracing unprecedented socioeconomic transformation. The liberalization of the national economy in the 1990s was attended by increasingly violent controversies over affirmative action, as the government moved to implement the Mandal Commission's suggestions to increase the quotas for Scheduled Tribes, Scheduled Castes, and Other Backward Classes. Of these official designations, it was the tribal distinction that captured the public imagination in Darjeeling. Individual ethnicities reset the terms of ethnopolitical mobilization from "Gorkha" to "tribe" to venture a different kind of engagement with the late liberal state. Movements for Scheduled Tribe status quickly spread through the hills, bearing promises of recognition, rights, cultural rebirth, and new forms of social belonging. Indeed, by 2005 every major ethnic group that was not yet ST had applications pending.

These newfound tribal politics spawned from a particular conjuncture of local, national, and global histories, but they introduced new questions about who these communities were and should be. The tribal movements largely worked against the grain of the previously hallowed Gorkha identity. Where inter-ethnic mixing had been constitutive of a shared Gorkha culture, the exigencies of tribal recognition made hybridity something to be combated and/or suppressed. The imperatives of ethnic singularity divided the Gorkha conglomerate. The prerequisites of ST recognition likewise triggered acrimonious debates within aspiring tribes over what constituted distinctive culture, custom, tradition, etc. Once-taken-for-granted practices now became both objects of political scrutiny and sources of inter- and intra-ethnic tension. The social and subjective divisions were undeniable. But so too was the hope—and real socio-material gain—that tribal recognition promised.

For decades, Darjeeling's unrecognized communities had watched their ST neighbors reap the advantages of positive discrimination. These included economic opportunities (quotas for government jobs, preferential promotion, access to special development packages); political rights (reserved seats in legislative assemblies, legal protections against discrimination, etc.), and a variety of educational benefits (relaxed qualifying minimums, matriculation quotas, tuition stipends, scholarships, and special support cells to support SC/ST minorities in universities). My friends and neighbors saw these educational provisions as especially vital to the success of their children and future generations. With few job prospects in the hills, Darjeeling's youth have increasingly sought schooling and work in cities like Kolkata, Delhi, and Bangalore. These are places where, as "hill people," they experience palpable discrimination.[67] Affirmative action accordingly promised a more level playing field as these minorities ventured beyond the hills to participate in India's increasingly competitive economy.

What ST status promised in terms of recognition and affirmative action, the Sixth Schedule promised in terms of autonomy and place. Like the bid for positive discrimination, the movement to make Darjeeling an autonomous tribal area emerged at a similar conjuncture of local history and late liberal governance. It too augured a shift away from the ethno-nationalist struggles that preceded it. Representing a more pragmatic approach, the quest for tribal autonomy exchanged the violence of an earlier era for a more legal engagement with the state—one couched in the globally salient language of cultural difference, recognition, and rights. These new idioms of engagement marked what B. G. Karlsson, Tanka Subba, and others have elsewhere argued to be the "indigenization" of ethnopolitics in India.[68]

The bid for tribal autonomy made this paradigm shift clear. When Ghisingh, West Bengal, and the Centre signed the agreement declaring their intention to bring Sixth Schedule autonomy to Darjeeling, they did so with a particular mind to redress the people's histories of violence and nonbelonging.[69] The written agreement (formally, a Memorandum of Settlement) spoke directly of the Gorkhaland Movement and promised to "fulfill the aspirations of the Hill people of Darjeeling District (West Bengal) relating to their cultural identity, language, education, and economic development." Perhaps most importantly, it declared the Sixth Schedule the "full and final settlement" to the question of ethnic-based autonomy in the hills. Tribal autonomy thereby was framed as the endgame of anxious belonging and subnationalist desire. No further demands would be necessary. Neither would they be entertained.[70]

To bolster the cause, Ghisingh used his administration's Department of Information and Cultural Affairs (DICA) to organize massive spectacles of tribal identity. Attendance was requested. Dress codes were

FIGURE 1.1 *Demonstrating Tribal Identity*

enforced. Aspiring STs like the Gurungs proved willing participants, since they believed that the Sixth Schedule and Ghisingh could provide the push they needed to secure ST status. With the GNLF cadres out in force to ensure compliance, the mobilizations were massive. Parades of tribes snaked through town, demonstrating the Gorkhas' newfound tribal identity. Jeeps with loudspeakers blaring and GNLF banners flying overhead led the way, as shamans, cultural troops, ethnic delegations, and thousands of citizens bedecked in tribal attire moved to the syncopated rhythms of the shaman's drum—an ancient beat carrying fresh promises of recognition, autonomy, and belonging.

As the details of the deal were being worked out behind closed doors in Kolkata and New Delhi, Ghisingh himself took to the stump. On October 11, 2006, his identical bulletproof limousines rolled into the town of Lebong, where he was to inaugurate a new community hall. This being a rare appearance for the increasingly reclusive (and paranoid) Ghisingh, I took my seat among the thousand or so GNLF cadres in attendance. After the requisite performances of tribal identity, Ghisingh stepped to the podium to begin a rambling diatribe on culture and politics. "We are hill tribes!" he proclaimed. "Our civilization, our culture, our tradition, all that we have here in Darjeeling are of ancient times. . . . The Indian Government may have knowingly or unknowingly tried to break us. But this could not be broken."

Ghisingh went on to accuse not only the "Britishers," but also "international spy agencies" such as Pakistan's ISI, Russia's KGB, and the United States' CIA, of trying to destroy their tribal culture. For years, Ghisingh had warned that foreign spies were operating in the hills, though he never gave any reason *why* such operatives would care to meddle in either the politics or the "ancient culture" of this particular corner of India. That wasn't the point. Ghisingh stared down these imagined foes with great bravado. He explained the passions of his tribal politics as follows:

> Though my blood is still hot, I have kept it under control. Locking horns with the Government of Bengal and Delhi is not going to work. The way forward is the kind of politics I am doing these days. In today's context of the

Sixth Schedule, it is the policy of protecting the tribals. Not a separate state
of Gorkhaland, but security for the tribals!

Ghisingh's appeal to the "security of the tribals" reprised a politics of anxiety that he himself had pioneered during the Gorkhaland Movement. But whereas in the 1980s he harped on the vulnerability of the Gorkhas, now it was the tribes who needed security. The "hot-blooded" passions coursing through these identifications, Ghisingh professed, were one and the same.

Philosopher Charles Taylor reminds us that the politics of recognition may do their most insidious work through processes of misrecognition. Says Taylor, "People can suffer real damage, real distortion, if the people or society around them mirror back to them a demeaning or contemptible picture of themselves."[71] Certainly this is true in Darjeeling. Terms like "foreigners," "outsiders," and "martial races" mark the misrecognition that has attended and defined the Gorkhas' questionable place in India. Yet in light of the tribal spectacles devised by Ghisingh and his administration, I think we might take Taylor's insight a step further. The question here becomes how the politics of recognition may engender not merely misrecognition, but also misidentification. That is, to what extent do classificatory systems push people to self-identify as something they are not? Or, as Fanon and the young Marx might have framed it, to what degree did these objectifications of tribal identity engender alienation for the people of Darjeeling?[72] Amid the crosscutting categories that shape the ethnocontemporary, this issue of alienation—or finding oneself amid contending claims upon the ethnos—remains a less explored, but timely question.

In fact, opponents of the Sixth Schedule seized on this very point. Tribal identity, they argued, was an absurdity that flew in the face of current sociocultural practice. Equally, it was an affront to the Gorkhas and the cause of Gorkhaland, for which so many had lived and died. The opposition further suggested that the Sixth Schedule posed a direct threat to inter-ethnic solidarity. For example: the Sixth Schedule promised exclusive land rights to existing STs. With unequal inheritance rights, non-STs would find themselves at a sudden disadvantage with their ST neighbors. There was also serious concern about the proportional makeup of the legislative council. Seats would be reserved for STs and non-STs, but how many? When the people of Darjeeling looked to places like Assam and Meghalaya, where the Sixth Schedule had been in place for years, they saw disturbing precedents. In those areas, tribal autonomy privileged some and severely excluded others. Political scientist Sanjib Baruah has argued that the Sixth Schedule creates a system of "two-tiered citizenship" by conferring upon tribal majorities exclusive rights to land, employment, and political representation, while relegating non-tribal minorities to positions of extreme disadvantage. Rather than ameliorate ethnic strife, Baruah goes on to note, the Sixth Schedule has fomented inequality and tension in India's Northeast, leading to frequent episodes of inter-group violence and, in the worst cases, ethnic cleansing.

Mapping these precedents onto Darjeeling, one had to ask, Was the Sixth Schedule an attempt to divide and rule the Gorkhas? Prophesying future unrest, Darjeeling's non-STs sent a collective memorandum to the government invoking precisely these concerns. It read:

> The state and Central governments' decision of dividing the single entity of Gorkha community into Schedule Tribes and not yet Schedule Tribes and keeping them as such even in the coming or proposed Schedule VI of the Constitution of India is actually unjust . . . Then why should the State government and our government at the Centre adopt this partial and unjust pick-and-choose system, which will definitely give rise to discontent and chaos in this region?[73]

With arguments like these, the people began to wonder whether the Sixth Schedule was a conduit to autonomy and belonging or a hollow promise riddled with the seeds of communal disharmony. What this "full and final solution" would really mean remained an open question. Nevertheless, throughout 2006, the public turned out en masse to support these newfound tribal movements. For a community long relegated to the margins, the promises of becoming tribal were sufficiently compelling.

A HAUNTING PRESENCE

The tribal turn intensified throughout 2006, as Ghisingh and company took their message to the streets. My involvement also deepened. The ethnic association leaders I was working with were becoming increasingly comfortable having me around. My research assistant Eklavya, meanwhile, had introduced me to the head of Darjeeling's Department of Information and Cultural Affairs (DICA)—Ram Bahadur Koli.[74] Our budding friendship gave me access to DICA and with it an inside look at the political engineering of tribal culture. There was considerable overlap between DICA and the ethnic associations I was working with. The quests for Sixth Schedule autonomy and Scheduled Tribe status, after all, were linked. Transcending any line between political and civil society, these were sites where late liberalism's ethno-logics were being negotiated and redeployed in meaningful ways. My experiences in the village testified to their transformative effects, both positive and negative. The consequences were a growing public concern, but there was nevertheless an optimism in the air. The future looked bright—and decidedly tribal.

My sources inside the Indian government confirmed this point. The government anthropologists had completed their Ethnographic Survey. The reports were being written. Everything was on track. The left-out communities would have ST status conferred, and the Sixth Schedule would follow suit soon thereafter. By all accounts, Darjeeling was on the cusp of becoming tribal.

Or so people thought—a point to which I return later in the book. For now, there is much to be learned from this deeper, more longitudinal reading of life and politics in Darjeeling. We see here a history where the terms of mobilization may shift, but the underlying anxieties and desires remain largely the same. The tribal turn, in this regard, offers a case study of the ethno-contemporary not only in its forms and contexts, but also in its energies. Concerning form, the tribal turn marked a pragmatic shift away from the violent subnationalist agitations of the 1980s and toward a more indigenous-based politics of cultural difference, legal recognition, and rights. That this shift followed the failed Gorkhaland Movement and coincided with both India's economic liberalization *and* the proliferation of indigenous struggles throughout the world is not coincidental. Add to this conjuncture the ethnological dispensations of late liberalism in India, and the stage was set for the tribal turn of the 1990s and 2000s.

As the coming chapters will show, ethnology's post/colonial entanglements have played a pivotal role in constituting this field of ethnopolitical possibility. There remain, however, other histories at work—deeper, more local, more affective histories that animate the ethno-contemporary in their own ways and by their own terms. Anxious belonging is one such history. Embodied through more than a century of discrimination, insecurity, and exclusion, anxious belonging remains the lifeblood—and charge—of a categorically searching politics in Darjeeling. Alive in the body and the body politic, it continues to spawn palpably anxious forms of life and politics. This haunting presence was what I failed to see before that dark night with the village president in 2007. His trembling body, my neighbors' panic, and all the rest made it painfully clear: the tribal turn was about much more than rights and entitlements. It was about belonging, and the enduring struggle of a people for their place in the nation-state.

It will be worth keeping this haunting presence in mind as we move through the subsequent twists and turns of the chapters to come. For now, I turn to a different historical register to chart the birth of ethnological governmentality and the uncanny return of the category "tribe" to the politics of modern India.

CHAPTER 2

DURGA AND THE ROCK

A Colonial Category and Its Discontent

IN WEST BENGAL and throughout much of South Asia, Durga Pujā is a holiday of dazzling celebration. Despite its Hindu origins, Durga Pujā (also known in Nepali as Dasain) has traditionally been celebrated by communities across the religious spectrum in Darjeeling. It is a time for visiting family and an apt alibi for libations and celebratory spirits of all kinds. Presiding over the merrymaking from her sumptuous *pandal* has always been the fierce, compassionate, and, at this time of year, particularly bloodthirsty Hindu goddess Durga.

In 2006, though, instead of unveiling the ornate idol of Durga that usually sits at the center of the spectacle, the Darjeeling Gorkha Hill Council (DGHC) rolled out an enormous rock (*shilā*), plucked from the bed of a nearby river by a local shaman (*jhankri*). Chosen for its spiritual prowess, the stone was then ensconced onstage at Chow Rasta, the town plaza, in its own *pandal* of opulence. For days, shamans hovered around the rock, shaking in trance, bedecked in ritual attire. Suited bureaucrats monitored the proceedings from deluxe chairs situated around the stage. Musical troops commissioned by the DGHC were brought in to sing devotional songs to the *shilā*. These were then broadcast across town at mind-numbing pitches. Processions came and went, as did politicians, party loyalists, tourists, and everyday townspeople. Through it all, the *shilā* sat dumbly onstage, enwreathed in incense, flower garlands, and vermil-

FIGURE 2.1 *Paying Homage to the Rock*

lion, just as Durga would have in previous years. This year, however, it was the Rock—the centerpiece of a bizarre, animistic, tribal mise-en-scène.

The ritual was one of many put on by the local administration from 2005 to 2007. It was no secret that these tribal displays were part of Subash Ghisingh's ongoing efforts to bring Sixth Schedule autonomy to the hills. The Sixth Schedule agreement was signed, but there was still considerable work to be done to make Darjeeling a tribal area. As Ghisingh negotiated the details of the bill, his administration took the initiative to the public. Supplanting Durga with the Rock was one of the many tactics deployed toward this end. Yet who was to be convinced of Darjeeling's tribal identity remained an open question. The government needed to be convinced, but apparently so too did the people of Darjeeling.

Few denied the political motivations of these spectacles. The veneer of authenticity was thin at best. As a resident anthropologist, I was often summoned to such performances and treated as a VIP. My presence, it seemed, functioned as a tacit endorsement of the tribal identities being performed. And so I found myself sitting with the vice president of the municipality, stage left of the *shilā*, watching as the Rock steadily accumulated offerings from the party loyalists who had come to pay their respects. With hundreds of spectators looking on, even the vice president conceded the cultural engineering at hand. Leaning toward me, as though to share a secret, he explained, "We started bringing the rock last year. We have to prove that we are not Hindu. We worship an ancient religion of *bon*. It came before, and Hinduism only came later. Hinduism was imposed on us. Our ancestral religion, you know. This *kul* ritual is animistic. *Bon* means animism. The *shilā* is animism, nature worship."

I nodded along. By this point in my research, I was well versed in these logics of tribal becoming. The vice president, in this regard, was only reiterating an oft-repeated maxim: *To be tribal, one mustn't be Hindu.* The absolute dichotomy between tribes and Hindu castes was an ethnological fact in the public imagination. The vice president made it plain: "We have to prove that we are not Hindu." This frank admission from a high-level politician was surprising only insofar as it came straight from the horse's mouth. Otherwise, it merely restated the obvious.

Everyone knew these fashionings of tribal identity to be stilted affairs. Yet it was nevertheless the case that even as the vice president confessed to me the underlying motives of the ethnological pomp and its political circumstance, a steady stream of devotees—men and women, rich and poor—ascended to the stage to bow before the Rock and receive its blessings. From where I sat stage left, I was in no position to judge the sincerity of their moment with the *shilā*, only to note the political import of the ethnological forms of which they were partaking.

RETHINKING TRIBAL RECOGNITION

Why the Rock and not Durga? To broach this question is to ask how particular ethno-logics—in this case, the binary of tribes versus castes—come to structure the ethno-contemporary in particular places at particular times. More specifically, the question begs reconsideration of the history through which tribal recognition has become a platform for rights, entitlements, and social justice in modern India. Given its official and popular connotations of primitiveness, isolation, and backwardness, "tribe" would appear the most colonial of categories. Scratch the surface, though, and the category's history suddenly appears to be a morass of nebulous conceptions and broken epistemologies, born out of the patently unstable collusions of anthropological thought and liberal governance. Throughout the colonial era, "tribe" was seldom the self-assured category one might assume. It was instead dogged by persistent doubts over its integrity and administrative utility. Even as tribal classification became integral to British rule, this epistemic discontent—what Ann Laura Stoler elsewhere calls "epistemic anxiety"[1]—led to a pernicious cycle of the category's demise and subsequent resurrection in "better" forms. These categorical instabilities make for a particularly troubled genealogy. Yet it is precisely these discontinuities, contradictions, and uncanny returns that have made tribal recognition the calling card for rights, autonomy, and social justice that it is today. This chapter examines how this has come to be the case.

Understanding tribal recognition today requires a new reading of "colonialism and its forms of knowledge." Since Bernard Cohn's seminal work on the subject, we are well aware of anthropology and ethnology's involvement in the colonial project in India.[2] The know-and-rule strategies of the British birthed a palpably ethnological form of governmentality. That ethnology became a technology of liberal rule in nineteenth-century India comes as little surprise. This was a time when governments (imperial and otherwise) were increasingly concerned with understanding and managing populations. Populations became targets of rule and entities to be manipulated, governed, and, in the liberal parlance of the times, "improved." Along with economics, sociology, and psychiatry, ethnology was but one of the human sciences that emerged to meet these designs of liberal governance.[3]

The long-term effects are immeasurable. From Africa to South Asia, scholars have worked to unveil the colonial underpinnings of identity politics today.[4] Sudipta Kaviraj and others have shown how mechanisms like the census ossified communal distinctions, becoming, in effect, not just models *of*, but also models *for*, communities and their politics.[5] Nicholas Dirks has gone so far as to argue that today's caste system is itself a colonial construction.[6] More-tempered readings of the impacts of colonialism on ethnicity, race, and gender are now common features of colonial historiography.[7]

Despite its conspicuous coloniality, the figure of the tribe has largely eluded this line of critique in India. Genealogical concerns have focused primarily on the British's nineteenth-century designation of "criminal tribes" and their subsequent twentieth-century "denotification."[8] But there are deeper issues to consider when historicizing tribal recognition. As a category of distinction, "tribe" has had a particular—and peculiar—history in India. Since the earliest days of British ethnology, the category has been counterposed to "caste." As we saw with Durga and the Rock, this contradistinction continues to inform tribal politics. And not just within the politics of minorities. The radical alterity between tribes and Hindu castes issues from within the Indian state itself. As I will illustrate, it articulates a subtle, but powerful, Hindu-centricity of late liberal governance in India. As such, tribal recognition provides a way of prying open the persuasions of a particular late liberal order and its epistemologies of difference. In contrast to "caste," "tribe" offers a different vehicle for exploring the history of Indian democracy.[9] Along the way, it throws fresh light on the contingent origins of biopolitics and governmentality more generally.

As an instrument of imperial knowledge and power, colonial ethnology in India did not develop in isolation. Its operatives worked in dialogue with anthropological and proto-anthropological thinkers throughout the European world. As the discipline of anthropology began to find its institutional feet in the late nineteenth and early twentieth centuries, it exerted considerable influence on conceptions of India's tribal peoples. Which is not to say academic anthropology lent tribal recognition any surety. Quite the contrary. Paradigmatic shifts within the discipline periodically undermined existing taxonomies, thereby driving a cycle of epistemic turnover wherein the criteria and practices of tribal recognition were constantly revised, torn asunder, and revised again. Uncertain, protean, and fraught from the start, tribal recognition thus epitomized the colonial state of which it was a part. The colonial knowledge regime, per these terms, appears in fact to be something other than the monolith it is often made out to be.

By the 1930s and 1940s, when Indian lawmakers began to assume the reins of governance, the category's reputation lay in shambles. British administrators had deemed the category "worthless" and the whole enterprise of tribal recognition "dubious." By the time of independence, they had all but given up on its analytic and administrative utility. Yet precisely when it seemed the death knell of this problematic category would finally be sounded, the bits and pieces that remained were gathered and liberally reworked by the founders of independent India. Their discursive-qua-juridical re-assemblage of the tribal would condition the possibilities for millions in the post-1947 era—including the people of Darjeeling.

Re-engaging this history is indispensable to understanding the politics of tribal recognition today. To return to the vice president's maxim "We have to prove we are not Hindu," it bears asking, Why the cultural engineering to eradicate the influence of Hinduism, a religious tradition that until very recently was held in high esteem by these groups? Why the turn to ethnology to represent—and where necessary, remake—the people of Darjeeling as proper tribes? Why the performative evocation of animism, primitiveness, backwardness, and the like? In short: Why the Rock and not Durga?

To begin answering this riddle of the ethno-contemporary, I turn now to a particularly influential figure for colonial ethnology and the people of Darjeeling.

FOUNDATIONS: "BROKEN" AND "UNBROKEN"

In 1819, a budding colonial official received his first appointment in the East India Company (EIC). His name was Brian Hodgson. Of impeccable pedigree (he studied at the East India Company College at Haileybury before doing a year of training at Fort William in Calcutta), Hodgson was sent to serve as assistant commissioner of the mountainous region of Kumaun in northwestern India. There he worked under George William Traill, who like Hodgson was a young man, adventurous in both mind and body. Largely left to their own devices on the northwest frontier, throughout 1919 and 1920 Traill and Hodgson explored their jurisdiction by foot, interacting with the locals in their native tongue, garnering firsthand information with an ethnographic rigor that would stay with Hodgson throughout his career. Their findings would be published and republished for decades to come in forms ranging from official settlement reports (1842–48) and scholarly articles (1822, 1828) to the *Statistical Survey of India* (1877) and *Imperial Gazetteers* (1886).[10] When Hodgson conducted this work, he was just nineteen years old.

In 1820, Hodgson was appointed assistant resident in Nepal, later becoming the British's official resident to Nepal from 1833 to 1843. There, Hodgson worked as the lone agent of empire in a technically noncolonized land. He managed the testy relationship between the EIC and Nepal with remarkable acumen. During this time, he became a committed scholar of the Himalayas and its people. When he finally resigned from his post in 1843, the raja of Nepal reportedly burst into tears when bidding him farewell.[11] His ties to Nepal—and the peoples of the Himalayas—were nevertheless established. Illness befell Hodgson, but after a brief hiatus in England, he returned to India. He found his new home in Darjeeling, where he lived from 1845 to 1858. Now free from the burden of administration, but not from his tireless dedication to the empire, Hodgson continued the scholarly work he had begun in Kathmandu. He was a naturalist, a religious scholar, and a collector extraordinaire, but it was his obsession with the tribes of the Himalayas that is of importance here.

Hodgson used the term "tribe" with little precision. In this regard, he was not unlike other colonials of his era. In the parlance of the time, "tribe" meant anything that we might today call race, nationality, community, or group. Hodgson's writings on the "martial tribes" and "hill tribes" of Nepal took a more pointed form, however. As early as 1832, he began studying the martial tribes of Nepal for their potential as soldiers for the British Indian army.[12] He was adamant that Himalayan ethnicities like the Khas, Gurung, and Magar embodied superior traits to those of the plains, where religious taboos (especially those of castes) were thought to interfere with soldierly duty. In the decades before the Rebellion of 1857 (often referred to as the "Mutiny"), he wrote repeatedly of the British Indian army's need for these tribes. His ideas proved prescient, as Gurkhas were instrumental in defeating the mutinous rebellion of 1857–58. But Hodgson looked to curb the "martial spirit" of the tribes for other reasons as well. He worried that if the innate martial spirit of the Nepalis were not marshaled for productive purposes, it would lead to a perpetually unstable frontier for British India. Though Hodgson was expressly concerned with the religious habits (or lack thereof) of the martial tribes, there was no clear antagonism between tribes and "Hindooism" or tribes and castes in his renderings.

Hodgson was, however, very concerned with race and racial origins. One of the more interesting distinctions he relied upon was that between "unbroken tribes" and "broken tribes." "Unbroken tribes" included groups like the Gurungs, Magars, and Khas. They were recognizable, bounded communities—discrete ethnicities, we might say, with traceable sociocultural forms and history. "Broken tribes," on the other hand, were those groups "whose status and condition . . . sufficiently demonstrate that they are of much older standing . . . [with a] remote past too vague for ascertaining."[13] Hodgson depicted broken tribes as on the verge of extinction. They lacked the cultural vitality, coherence, and function of the "unbroken," "martial," "hill tribes" of the region that would become the fancy of both nineteenth- and twentieth-century Himalayan anthropology. Accordingly, Hodgson devoted little time to the broken tribes. They were compromised, "broken" forms of an ideal type—in other words, subjects too "vague" for either scholarly or imperial use.

Hodgson was a pioneer of colonial ethnology, developing its methodologies and taxonomies at a time when the ethnological impulse was more faint and scattered than it would become following the jarring events of 1857.[14] Breaking with the orientalist dispensations of his day, his work bore a distinctly ethnographic imprint. As Peter Pels (1999) has noted, Hodgson shifted the primary object of study from "foundational texts" to "aboriginal bodies." Important to this methodological expansion was Hodgson's reliance on literate upper-caste research assistants to decipher not only texts but also cultural practice. His collaboration with native informants helped establish key paradigms of colonial knowledge production. Hodgson's tireless attention to detail likewise anticipated the empiricist and positivist bents that drove the giants of colonial ethnology like Hunter, Risley, Latham, Dalton, Grierson, and others. As ethnology emerged as a science unto itself from the 1860s onward, many of these figures looked back to Hodgson as a standard-bearer of the ethnological cum colonial enterprise.[15]

Yet Hodgson was emblematic in other ways as well. Read carefully, his work exhibits a classificatory uncertainty that dogged colonial ethnology from the start. Particularly in his distinction between "broken tribes" and "unbroken tribes" we see cracks already appearing in the epistemic foundations of tribal recognition. The distinction of broken and unbroken tribes would reappear in later colonial ethnologies, such as E. T. Dalton's *Descriptive Ethnology of Bengal* (1872), and W. W. Hunter's *Statistical Account of Bengal* (1875), where it was clubbed with designations like "hinduised aborigines" and "semi-hinduised aborigines" to denote groups that belied the conceptual purity of "aboriginal tribes," "hill tribes," and "martial tribes."

Hybridity's corrosion to ideal types—captured here with notions like "broken tribes," "hinduised aborigines," and "semi-hinduised aborigines"— became a source of perennial consternation for the British. But if racial, religious, and cultural mixing provoked epistemic disquiet, it also drove the need for better taxonomies. The disjunctions between life and classification thereby engendered both epistemic concern and innovation. Tellingly, though, the rubrics of Brian Hodgson show tribal recognition to be "broken" from the start.

Hodgson's legacy lives on. Today, his work continues to be cited by the Government of India in its adjudication of Scheduled Tribes (more on this later in the book). Likewise, Hodgson references pepper the ST applications from Darjeeling. Given his history in the hills, this comes as no surprise. Hodgson's migration from Nepal to Darjeeling paralleled the migration of the Nepali laborers' migration to the up-and-coming hill station. That Hodgson did most of his writing on the "hill tribes" while living in Darjeeling must not be overlooked. There is little in his personal papers and collections to suggest how he engaged with his fellow immigrants, either socially or through research. But his work ensured that there would be no dearth of information on these groups when it came time for them to be entered into the ledgers of the ethnographic state.[16] Suffice it to say, at both the local and the national levels, Brian Hodgson was instrumental in shaping the prospects (and problems) of tribal recognition. From these "broken" foundations, I turn now to ethnology's subsequent evolution across India.

THE "MUSEUM OF THE RACES"[17]

Since its founding in Calcutta in 1784, the Asiatic Society of Bengal served as a forum for colonial intellectual pursuits. Its museum and library teemed with oriental curiosities collected from across the British Empire in South Asia. Hodgson alone was responsible for more than 180 submissions. In August 1865, the society's members—consisting of British colonials and high-caste *babus*—held their monthly meeting. Ethnology was at the forefront of their concerns. The Hon'ble George Campbell—himself a judge on Calcutta's high court, an ethnologist, and the soon-to-be lieutenant governor of Bengal (1871–74)—opened the proceedings by hailing ethnology as "the most popular and rising science of the day":

> It seems strange that we should at this moment have in constant and immediate contact with us—working around us daily—men of a race and of languages wholly different from our own—a race certainly among the most

interesting—perhaps the very oldest in the world; and that we should have scarcely any knowledge of them.[18]

Campbell went on to suggest that these unknown races "hand down to us something like what may have been the aboriginal Adam of the human species."[19] In February 1866, he sustained his call for study of these living relics of mankind's past by exalting India as "an unlimited field for ethnological observation and inquiry" and describing his personal efforts to bring "into the field several of the most learned and scientific men . . . to reap this abundant harvest."[20]

A month later, Dr. J. Fayrer, a professor of surgery in the Medical College, captured the imagination of the Asiatic Society with a proposal to hold what he called the Ethnological Congress,[21] which would put on display not cultural artifacts and human crania (the collection of which was already under way), but living specimens curated into "booths or stalls divided into compartments, like the boxes in a theater or the shops in a bazaar." Campbell supported the idea, suggesting that each specimen should be

> classified according to races and tribes, should sit down in his own stall, should receive and converse with the public, and submit to be photographed, painted, taken off in casts, and otherwise reasonably dealt with in the interest of science . . . I hope, I need scarcely argue, that a movement of this kind is no mere dilettantism. Of all sciences, the neglected study of man is now recognized as the most important . . . When we better understand his nature, his varieties, and the laws of his development, we may better improve him.[22]

The members supported the proposal unanimously. The next step was to pitch the idea to the Government of Bengal. Initially, the government responded positively by sending instructions to all commissioners to gather preliminary data for the event.[23] However, that proved the extent of the government's support. The proposal remained under consideration for years, but ultimately the Ethnological Congress was never convened.

It is as a historical *non-event* that the Ethnological Congress reveals the most.[24] As an idea, the proposal illustrates the traction that the "science of ethnology" had gained in the colonial imagination. But as an event that never happened, the Ethnological Congress shows the changing face of liberalism in nineteenth-century India.

Uday Mehta has argued that when reading the ideologues of liberalism in the colonies, "one gets the vivid sense of thought that has found a project."[25] On the ground, that project bore its share of contingency, however. When the Rebellion of 1857 nearly turned the tables on imperial rule, it checked the presumptive logics of colonial liberalism. As Metcalf has noted, the rebellion showed that colonial subjects "did not, in the British view, pursue their own best interests, but obstinately clung to traditional ways . . . [T]he liberal presumption that all men were inherently rational and educable [thus] fell to the ground."[26] For the British, the traumas of 1857–58 forced a re-evaluation of the way liberal thought should (and should not) inform imperial governance.

Importantly, many of the lessons learned were ethnological in nature. That an upheaval as monumental as the 1857 Rebellion could be triggered by a detail so seemingly small as a religious taboo barring sepoys (soldiers) from using cartridges greased with animal lard hammered home to the British the need for greater understanding of their colonial subjects. Following these alarming events, the problem of populations became not just a challenge of liberal governance—as Foucault has framed it[27]—but an imperial mandate, shot through with anxieties about the surety of both colonial knowledge and colonial power. Such were the contingent origins of ethnological governmentality on the subcontinent.

Pitched just years after the dust of 1857 had settled, the Ethnological Congress hailed from a seemingly dated liberalism. Despite their appeals to the "enlightened spirit" of "liberal government" and their promises to study "how far the great varieties of our race are capable of improvement," what the members of the Asiatic Society missed when they proposed their idea to government was the anxiety-ridden *need* for ethnological knowledge. Human difference had shown itself in far more real terms than could be displayed by any "museum of the races." The government would need to respond in kind.

A SCIENCE OF GOVERNANCE

By the late 1860s, the British Raj sought projects of greater utility and rigor. In 1869, W. W. Hunter was appointed director general of statistics and tasked with standardizing the *Imperial Gazetteers* of India.[28] The themes of inquiry were to include: *ethnical*, topographical, agricultural, industrial, administrative, medical, and others. Carrying out such projects, the British relied on educated upper-caste (typically Brahman) informants.[29] These collaborations did much to structure the ways in which difference was known and ruled. The collaborations yielded a curious synthesis of British conceptions of race and Brahmanical conceptions of caste. European theories that Aryan races (epitomized by the figure of the Brahman) gradually spread across the subcontinent, encountering and absorbing darker-skinned aboriginals along the way, fused beautifully with Brahmanical ideals of the varnic caste order and its mythical historical bases. The synthesized view that emerged placed tribes at the margins of a peculiarly Euro-Brahmanical imaginary.

Dalton's statements on "Hinduised Aboriginals and Broken Tribes" in his *Descriptive Ethnology of Bengal* (1872) offer a working example of these interleavings of racial and religious difference. He writes: "In ascribing fanciful origins to the aborigines, the Aryans to a certain extent admitted them into their own families as bastard relatives of their own and of their gods. There is, says Menu, no fifth class from which impure tribes could have been born."[30] In this overlaid British and Brahmanical figuring of the tribe, im/purity thus became dually inflected: racially (as per the British construal) and religiously (as per the Brahmanical construal).

This interplay of British and Brahmanical worldviews generated two interconnected versions of the caste-tribe binary. The first was a synchronic version that held castes and tribes to be diametrically opposed ideal types—"pure fixed and separate antecedents," as Robert Young would say.[31] Socioreligious hybridity was thus seen as a devolution of these pure antecedents. The second version of the caste-tribe binary was diachronic. It held that tribes were inevitably moving toward Hindu assimilation. Hybridity figured here as a unidirectional process—the endgame being a full (but impure) absorption into the Hindu order. Tribes exhibiting the syncretic trace were thus understood to be tribes in transition, or as would become the standard denotation of the late nineteenth century, "semi-hinduised tribes."

These were general frameworks—rules of thumb, as it were. Put into enumerative practice, these logics proved ill-equipped to handle India's dynamic diversity. As early as 1872, when the first (yet partial) census took place, the categories had already become problematic. In his *Report of the Census of Bengal 1872*, Census Commissioner Beverley raised the profound question: "What is a hindoo?" he asked. "What then is to be the test of faith which is to define the real hindoo from the semi-hindooised aboriginal? . . . Without some such test no two men will agree in the classification of numerous aboriginal tribes and castes in India who profess hindooism in some or other of its multifarious forms."[32]

Beverley's intervention seems to be of a most undermining kind. Notably, he does not call for an abandonment of the Hindu caste-tribe binary, rather for a better epistemic instrument—a "test of faith"—to "define the real hindoo from the semi-hindooised aboriginal." What is particularly interesting is the ambivalence of Beverley's intervention. He advocates finding an improved device for identifying populations mired in sociocultural and religious mixture. But the ontology of the "real hindoo" and his perfect other, the "aboriginal/tribal," is not called into question. These pure antecedent pasts remain at large in the murk of India's diversity. In Beverly's view, it is hybridity that is the problem.

Beverley's reflexivity may appear jarring against the backdrop of ethnology's rising credence. But he was not alone. Throughout the 1860s, 1870s, and 1880s, the categories and techniques of colonial ethnology were shrouded in reflexive concern. If projects like the census reified taxonomic difference by projecting hard and fast distinctions onto fluid social processes,[33] that reification was not lost upon those charged with implementing the state's classificatory systems. Neither was the fuzziness of sociocultural life itself. One need only evaluate the extensive reports that attended the decennial censuses to appreciate the disquiet. These reports recorded myriad frustrations of enumerators, administrators, and the occasional European ethnologist as they attempted to map the indeterminate realities of sociocultural life into the rubrics of the colonial state.

These concerns mark a key dimension of colonial rule—and its historiography. To suggest that epistemic discontent was integral to the colonial regime is not to tear down the extant histories of colonial knowledge in India. Rather, it is to fray the genealogy of ethnological governmentality with the agents, anxieties, and sociopolitical contingencies that shaped its development.[34] Uncertainty figures here as part and parcel of colonial knowing. That said, efforts were constantly afoot to shore up the foundations of tribal recognition.

THE EMPIRICIST EDGE

In March of 1885, a Conference on Ethnography of Northern India was held in Lahore. It was not so much a conference as a meeting of three men with "considerable experience in similar enquiries." Present were D. C. J. Ibbetson (director of public instruction, Punjab), J. C. Nesfield (inspector of schools, Oudh), and H. H. Risley (on special duty, Bengal). Several months earlier, Risley had been appointed to oversee a systemic inquiry into the customs and physical characteristics of all castes and tribes of Bengal. The conference in Lahore was to lay the groundwork for that inquiry.

Risley, Ibbetson, and Nesfield sat together for four days. As Risley later explained, "The endeavor throughout was not so much to strike out new lines of inquiry as to adapt the methods already sanctioned by the approval of European men of science to the special conditions which have to be taken into account of in India."[35] The conference yielded a list of 391 questions to guide Risley's study. The published conference proceedings began with a one-page statement titled "Suggestions Regarding Some Doubtful Points of Ethnographical Nomenclature." The statement defined (1) "caste" and (2) "tribe" as the principal social organizations in India—with caste understood as a "community of occupation" and tribe "based upon a real or fictitious community of descent or upon common occupation of territory."[36] These definitions carried little weight in Risley's future work. Despite this brief mention of tribes, the 391 questions that followed focused almost solely on issues of caste. Risley's obsession with caste became a signature of his ethnology.[37] It was undergirded, however, by a more fundamental concern with race—or more specifically, racial origins.[38]

To bolster his acumen, Risley solicited the opinion of esteemed European scholars. Max Müller, Francis Galton, E. B. Tylor, Sir Henry Maine, and Paul Topinard all commented favorably on Risley's plans.[39] Müller provided the most extensive feedback. He began by warning Risley of the dangers of misapplying classificatory terms. With so much of this already happening, Müller lamented, ethnology had "almost ceased to be a true science." He advised Risley to be "afraid of words such as *totemism*, *fetishism*, and several other *isms* which have found their way into the ethnological sciences." Those cautions aside, when it came to race, Müller, was far more encouraging:

> In India we have first of all the two principal ingredients of the population—the dark aboriginal inhabitants and their more fair skinned conquerors . . . Here, therefore, the ethnologist has a splendid opportunity of discovering some tests by which, even after a neighborly intercourse lasting for thousands of years, the descendants of one race may be told from the descendants of the others.[40]

What were these tests to be? How could the ethnologist cut through the din of "neighborly intercourse lasting thousands of years" (read: "hybridity") to trace racial origins? Risley turned to the anthropometry of Drs. Paul Topinard and Paul Broca. He framed the problem (hybridity) and solution (anthropometry) as follows:

> I find myself continually met by the difficulty that people change within a comparatively short time their religion, their language, and their customs to such an extent that there is often no custom that can be safely pointed to as a test of Aryan or non-Aryan descent. In this difficulty it has occurred to me that recourse might possibly be had to measurement of the heads of the different castes.[41]

To Risley, caste was a contagion that tainted the pure forms of the past.[42] Even ethnographic inquiry was likely to be duped by hybridity. As he explained, "The admission of a tribe into the charmed circle of Hinduism results after a generation or two in the practical disappearance of the tribe as such. Its identity can no longer be traced by direct enquiry from its members, or inferred from observation of its members."[43] Risley accordingly proffered anthropometry as the cutting-edge science needed to slice through the indeterminateness of India's masses.

In March 1886, Risley submitted a statement to the government titled "On the Application of Dr. Topinard's Anthropometric System on the Tribes and Castes of Bengal." His hard sell of anthropometry worked. The Government of Bengal approved the proposal and began circulating detailed instructions on the ethnographic techniques *and* bodily measurements that would constitute Risley's study. Anthropometric measurements were to be conducted on jailed prisoners of selected castes. The project was thought to be a great success. Its findings were published as *The Tribes and Castes of Bengal* (1891). From this study, Risley launched a career as the colonial ethnologist cum administrator par excellence.

Risley's racial empiricism ruled the next two decades. His ethnology was without question one of great hubris. Yet it is important to remember that his "science" arose from deeper epistemic concerns. Paradoxically, the more the colonial state pursued ethnologically attuned policies, the more the impossibilities of classificatory precision haunted their enterprise. With a sharply empiricist edge, anthropometry thus became Risley's antidote to these quandaries. Nevertheless, it was *epistemic discontent* that thrust Risley and his heady science to colonial prominence.

PLACING THE TRIBAL

It was never clear for the British how to classify tribes/aboriginals. The first comprehensive census of India in 1881 awkwardly placed "aboriginals" under the heading "Population Classified by Religion," a position that drew immediate concern. Census Commissioner W. C. Plowden called the classification "dubious," explaining that "those whom I have grouped together under this term in the religious classification consist of the aboriginal tribes who, not having been converted to Christianity, or to Islam, or the Hindoo belief, retain, if they have any religion at all, the primitive cult of their forefathers, adoring nature."[44] Plowden further complicated matters by quoting at length Beverley's aforementioned doubts over "what is a hindoo." Despite the indeterminacy of the "Hindoo," Plowden conceded that Hinduism functioned dually as the default classification *and* the dominant reference point against which "aboriginals" were determined.

Ten years later, in the 1891 Census, tribes were again placed in "The Distribution of the Population by Religion" section—only this time, with a different valance. Here they were explicitly associated with the religious category "animism." Census Commissioner J. A. Baines explained: "The rules for enumeration were that under the head of Animistic should come all members of the forest tribes who were not locally acknowledged to be Hindu, Musálman, Christian, or Buddhist, by religion."[45] Elsewhere, the 1891 Census redoubled the concentration on castes, reifying its default centrality to the taxonomies deployed.[46] That Risley's work was beginning to circulate (and was repeatedly cited in the Census Report of 1891) is not coincidental.

Risley himself became census commissioner in 1901. By this time, the census was in its fourth generation, and frustrations were rising over its failing categories. The classificatory rubrics that Risley inherited in 1901 were a mess of residual and emergent ethnological sensibilities. Conceptually, they were incoherent. In practice, they were inconsistent and highly subjective. And yet the scapegoat remained hybridity. Ever the empiricist, Risley wiped the slate clean by proclaiming: "Until physical measurements have been extended to the chief castes and tribes of India, and the results correlated with those ethnographic data which furnish a clue to probable origins, it is impossible to say whether any scientific classification of the population can be arrived at."[47]

With endorsements from the British Association for the Advancement of Science, Risley recommended that additional ethnological inquiries be conducted in conjunction with the 1901 census.[48] As Risley framed it, "The census provides the necessary statistics; it remains to bring out and interpret the facts which lie behind the statistics."[49] To augment the census's typical modes of enumeration, Risley organized a series of additional ethnographic, anthropometric, and photographic inquiries. These endeavors made the 1901 census the British Raj's largest ethnological project to date. Risley eventually published its additional findings in his now famous *The People of India* (1908). Reinscribing the obsession with caste and race, the 1901 census and its subsequent iterations provided a fitting end to ethnology's nineteenth-century development in India.

ETHNOLOGIES OF ILL REPUTE

New currents of thought soon began to erode Risley's empiricist edifice, however. The 1911 Census carried on the practice of "lumping together as animistic" the "aboriginal tribes who have not yet been absorbed in the Hindu social system," but it did so with major reservations. As the census report noted, "The practical difficulty is to say at what stage a man ceases to be an Animist and becomes a Hindu. The religions of India, as we have already seen, are by no means mutually exclusive."[50] Of course, simply recognizing the fluidity of socioreligious life in no way excused census officials from the unavoidable reality that mutual exclusion was, to a large degree, the modus operandi of their classificatory duty. Still, the 1911 Census signaled important changes away from the paradigms of Risley. It instituted a new heading, "Caste, Tribe, and Race." Whereas the previous censuses designated tribes on religious grounds, the 1911 edition defined tribes in terms of sociopolitical structure.[51] This brought the census into line with technical definitions of tribal societies, which were increasingly in use in European and American anthropology. Even once citing Franz Boas, the 1911 Census showed a declining faith in the anthropometric tactics of Risley, Topinard, and Broca.[52] But it did not go so far as to relinquish the presumption of caste and race. Instead, it bent the existing narrative to accommodate emerging anthropological sensibilities—so as to correct and improve these ways of knowing the ethnos.

As of 1921, the categories continued to crumble. "Animism" became "tribal religion." But as soon as that category was created, it was rendered "extremely problematic" on the grounds that it was "misleading" and lacking the standardized precision called for by a census.[53] The census report leveled an analogous critique of the category "Hindu," calling it "unsatisfactory."[54] But while the report expressed interest in ridding the census of "caste" altogether, it maintained that "caste is still the foundation of the Indian social fabric."[55] Like "tribe," its ontology was not in question. The problem was epistemological. In trying to enframe[56]—that is, accurately know and formally classify—these societal "foundations," simplicity proved elusive. For example, the "Caste, Tribe, and Race" header of 1911 became "Caste, Tribe, Race, and *Nationality*" in 1921. But this was fraught with further contradictions, as the primitive tribes listed there were divided into "tribes some of which have racial and others territorial origin."[57] This is to say nothing of the *political* designation of tribes implemented just ten years earlier.

Reading the census reports over the decades, one gets the sense of a classificatory project entangled in ever-tightening knots, with precedent pulling on one end and emerging anthropological paradigms pulling at the other. Making matters more troubling was the fact that census categories were beginning to feed back into the populations in question. Through what Ian Hacking has elsewhere called a "looping effect,"[58] communities began to identify with these classifications and put them to new uses. These emerging politics of recognition forced the British to face the unruly social life of categories that they themselves had largely created.

CONUNDRUMS OF CALCULABILITY

As political representation and governmental provisions were pegged to official recognition, the census took on heightened importance. Census officials were well aware of the consequent maneuvers taken up by majorities and minorities alike to "press for recognition of social claims and to secure, if possible, a step upwards on the social ladder"—to quote the 1921 Census Report.[59] These dynamics put fresh problems to census administrators. Communities were now taking up and repurposing state categories in order to be counted in certain ways and not others. These agendas challenged the presumed at-a-remove relation of the census to its objects of study (in this case, populations, castes, tribes, etc.). The stability of the subject-object relationship—and the putative accuracy of state classification—was thus thrown into question. Timothy Mitchell has noted similar dynamics in colonial Egypt, where the census and other instruments of expert knowledge did not merely represent their objects but also transformed them, in effect making the very "facts that statistics wished to fix far more elusive and difficult to define." As Mitchell notes, "Expert knowledge works to format social relations, never simply to report or picture them."[60] The irony is that the practices of calculability made the populations harder to count.

Census officials saw this and voiced their concerns. Especially as the anticolonial struggle intensified, officials knew full well that since it was the state that formally recognized communal distinctions, so too was it the state that would ultimately be held accountable for its categorical failings. The 1931 Census Report, in this regard, sustained the concerns with reification, but had little choice but to continue on with its enumerative work. Despite the reification and looping effects at hand, the 1931 commissioner lamented, "The census cannot hide its head in the sand like the proverbial ostrich, but must record as accurately as possible facts as they exist."[61]

The government's contextual awareness obtained on other registers as well. Into officials' treatment of tribes crept a growing sense of protectionism. Signaling the structural functionalist leanings to come, tribes came to be seen as isolated, self-sufficient sociocultural groups living in harmony with their environment. The 1931 Census warned of the dangers of disturbing this precious equilibrium: "A tribe living in comparative isolation will usually be found to have developed an adaptation to its environment which within certain limits approaches perfection, an adaptation which may have taken many millennia to accomplish and the breakdown of which may be the ruin of the tribe."[62]

These concerns raised new quandaries. By this point, British census officials had little confidence in the tribal/aboriginal designations. How then was the government to recognize and protect these populations living on the precipice of "perfection" and "ruin"? To deal with this problem, the 1931 Census provided a list of "primitive tribes," but how primitiveness was to be determined remained unclear.[63]

TRIBAL IN/VISIBILITY

Finding a stable form of recognition for these vulnerable populations became more imperative in the decades leading up to independence. Nationalist leaders like Gandhi, Nehru, Bose, Jinnah, and Ambedkar may have converged around the idea of freedom from British rule, but they harbored markedly different ideas of what an independent India should look like. Representing different constituencies with different agendas, these leaders clashed over the terms of inclusion in the nation-to-be. Up for grabs was the very "idea of India"—as Sunil Kilnani has noted.[64] Who would belong? And with what rights, representation, and power? The answers to these questions would guide the trajectory of liberal democracy in India for decades to come.

The interwar years were vital to these reckonings. This was a period that, Anupama Rao has argued, involved a "renewed focus on, and redefinition of, the Political"—one wherein minority recognition became a key concern.[65] The 1930s saw the question of separate electorates for Hindus and Muslims come to a head with the Anglo-Indian Roundtable Conferences. In the first of these conferences (November 1930–January 1931), Dr. B. R. Ambedkar added a demand for separate electorates for the Depressed Classes (otherwise known as "Dalits"; formerly "Untouchables"). Ambedkar's intervention brought the Dalits' plight to the table of late colonial nation-making. The Second Roundtable (September–December 1931) yielded the Communal Award, which promised separate electorates for the Depressed Classes (read: "Dalits"). But dissent quickly emerged within the Hindu contingent. Gandhi, in particular, took issue with the Communal Award on the grounds that it would divide Hindus. He subsequently launched a fast until death in protest. Under great pressure to save the life of the Mahatma, Ambedkar eventually conceded, leading to the signing of the Poona Pact in the Yerawada Jail on September 20, 1932. Instead of separate electorates, the pact established reserved seats for Depressed Classes within a joint electorate. Crucially, the Primitive and Aboriginal Tribes were *not* included as Depressed Classes—so declared the Indian Franchise Committee.[66]

The Roundtables precipitated the Government of India Act of 1935—the final constitution of British-ruled India. The act would see the designation "Primitive Tribes" become "Backward Tribes," but the meaning and implications remained, per usual, nebulous. Importantly, the act redesignated "Depressed Classes" as "Scheduled Castes"—thus putting in place a governmental distinction that would become a centerpiece of postcolonial affirmative action. By achieving this distinction and its concordant rights and representation, Ambedkar and the Dalits pioneered a new politics of minority in India. As Anupama Rao has discussed, their collective action, selective evocation of liberal ideals, and deft reframing of Dalit alterity, transformed India's scattered "untouchable" populations into a new kind of political subject—itself collective, unified, and morally endowed to make powerful claims upon the nation-state.[67]

The politics of India's tribes took a markedly different path. Precisely when minority rights were coming to the fore of public debate, the question of tribes began to slide quietly from view. Where Ambedkar carved out a Dalit alterity for his constituents within (and against) the Hindu order, tribes remained nebulously defined as not-Hindu. Similar to Dalits, they were strewn about the country and vulnerable. But unlike their Dalit contemporaries, they lacked the leadership, voice, and collective action to constitute themselves as a national political subject.[68] And so, as giants like Gandhi, Nehru, Ambedkar, and Jinnah occupied the limelight in their negotiations of a national polity, tribes receded further into the shadows.

If the removal of the tribes from the Depressed Classes dealt a political blow, the 1941 Census sounded the death knell on the category itself. The census commissioner stated in no uncertain terms, "Every census has seen the old nuisance about tribal enumeration and 1941 saw communal activities at their height. The religious return in respect of tribes has never been anything but worthless."[69] The report proceeded to declare the whole inquiry of tribal classification "unsound" and opined that "it was time the whole question was put on something approaching an exact and scientific basis."[70] This was a stark rebuke of earlier taxonomies, but note how the 1941 report refutes tribal recognition on largely the same grounds that Risley had before, and Beverley had before that. It was, after all, similar calls for exactitude, scientific integrity, and the allaying of epistemic uncertainty that propelled those earlier critiques and subsequent innovations to ethnological classification.

The 1941 Census did away with "caste" and supplanted the religious distinction of tribes with a new category: "Community Origin." The report explained, "No opinion has been expressed on whether the number returned as tribes should be considered as assimilated to Hindus or not." Seemingly, then, census officials had finally cut their losses and given up on the problematic dichotomy of Hindu castes versus non-Hindu tribes. Given the stakes, "Community Origin" was deemed a safer, better analytic—not perfect, but nevertheless necessary, considering the tribes' diminishing visibility in the ongoing nationalist debates. The 1941 report framed the vanishing as follows: "With the abolition of caste sorting this year, it was essential to bring the figures for tribes into a community table if they were not to be lost sight of."[71]

Despite the admitted problems with the term itself, "not losing sight of the tribals" was both a moral and an administrative imperative. Along with the protectionist sensibilities mentioned earlier, Sections 91 and 92 of the 1935 act created "Reserved and Partially Reserved Areas" for regions inhabited predominantly by people of "tribal origin." (These would later become the Fifth and Sixth Schedules.) These "tribal areas" were to be placed under the special administration of the governors of the state within which they were contained. Since "tribals" were the logical inhabitants of these Reserved and Partially Reserved Areas for people of "tribal origin," they needed to be counted. Administrative logics alone then precipitated a placeholder category like "community origin." If the government was to grant its ethnic exceptions, it needed its corresponding paradigms of distinction—no matter how fraught they may have been. A short numerical table (XIV) headed "Variation in Population of Select Tribes" was thus added to ensure that these marginalized groups would not vanish from administrative sight completely. This solution marked but the latest compromise in the more broadly compromised enterprise of tribal recognition writ large.

THE TRANSFER OF PARADOX

Refigured as such, this history of a colonial category and its discontents holds important lessons for our understandings of the past and present politics of recognition in India. More broadly, it reminds us of the messy histories that undergird the ethno-contemporary today. From the "broken" foundations of Brian Hodgson, to the heady empiricism of Risley, and through the category's slow but sure demise in the first half of the twentieth century, tribal recognition developed as much through epistemic imposition and hubris as through doubt and uncertainty. Epistemic anxiety figures in this genealogy not as the affective by-product of colonial knowledge production, but rather as integral to ethnology's history in India. Dogged by reflexive concerns and seldom stable, the history of tribal recognition provides a telling window into a categorically unstable knowledge regime.

These instabilities of colonial knowledge cannot be disassociated from the instabilities of colonial power. If the 1857 Rebellion thrust the question of human difference to the fore of the colonial project, the forms of knowledge-power that emerged were themselves uncertain and unstable. The anxiety-producing events of 1857 may have engendered the *need* to classify India's diverse populations into fixed conceptual forms, but that endeavor proved philosophically fraught from the start.[72] The hybridity, dynamism, and sociopolitical savvy of India's peoples complicated matters further—particularly in the run-up to independence when a formidable politics of recognition further unsettled the grounds of classification. The great paradox heading toward independence was that both the stakes of state recognition and its quandaries were escalating simultaneously.

By the final decade of British rule, the colonial state had all but given up on the category "tribe." It had been deemed "worthless," "dubious," and "unsound," and its epistemology lay in shambles. Confidence in the category was at an all-time low. What remained were bits and pieces of classificatory systems torn asunder by paradigmatic transformations in British imperialism and anthropological thought. Decolonization necessarily bequeathed this "imperial debris"[73] to the leaders of independent India—and with it, its inherent contradictions and politics. The transfer of power, in this regard, proved also a transfer of paradox. How India's future leaders negotiated these conundrums would largely set the terms of liberal inclusion in the nation-to-come.

Already, the colonial history of tribal recognition puts some important questions to the present day. How has a category deemed "worthless" and all but abandoned on the eve of independence become such a coveted object of political desire? Or, to be more ethnologically specific: Why the efforts in Darjeeling to exorcize Hinduism's trace? Why the movement to re-present a people through the well-worn tropes of primitiveness, backwardness, and all the rest? To wit, Why the Rock and not Durga? Colonial critique cannot answer these questions—at least not fully. The challenge in assessing the politics of tribal recognition today remains how to keep in view their obvious coloniality *and* their perplexing postcolonial forms. If, as Paul Rabinow has argued, the interplays of the old and the new are precisely what define the contemporary more generally,[74] then sorting through these articulations remains a vital step to understanding the forms of our current moment and their variously inhabited im/possibilities—tribal and otherwise.

The impacts of colonialism on the ethno-contemporary are undeniable. Yet, riddles like Durga and the Rock also challenge us to engage more recent pasts. In postcolonial India, this means taking a closer look at the forging of affirmative action and social justice since independence. Decolonization would see the know-and-rule technologies of liberal governance revamped to uniquely Indian understandings of justice, equality, democratic participation, and difference. From these coordinates would issue a new breed of ethnological governmentality—this one recognizably multicultural, socialist, and Hindu-centric in its designs.

The colonial part of this story told, it is to these dynamics of postcolonial knowledge, power, and policy that this study of the Indian ethno-contemporary now turns.

CHAPTER 3

TRIBAL RECOGNITION

A Postcolonial Problem

IT IS NINE A.M. and the Phulpāti parade of 2006 is about to begin. The Rock is waiting just kilometers away. In any other year, the seventh day of Durga Pujā would be celebrated in great splendor with Phulpāti offerings being made to Durga. In any other year, costumed representatives of the Hindu goddess herself would dance through the parade furiously wielding their knives, symbolically cutting through whatever obstacles they encountered. But today, a different spectacle is in the works. Stretching as far back along Hill Cart Road as the eye can see, thousands have gathered to demonstrate their tribal identities. Following the instructions sent out by the local administration, the public has turned out, bedecked in tribal attire. The pending quests for Scheduled Tribe status and Sixth Schedule autonomy demand nothing less.

The parade is slated to snake through town en route to Chow Rasta, the town square, where the Rock awaits its devotees. Officials do their best to control the unwieldy masses, as last-minute participants swell the ranks. Shamans' drums sound up and down the road, and loudspeakers blare unintelligible instructions. Banners are unfurled. Flags are hoisted. Amid the cacophony, dancers' bodies begin to move ahead of schedule. The crowd surges forward in anticipation.

Standing on a gravel pile along with half a dozen others, I watch the scene grow increasingly chaotic as the officials struggle to hold back the parade until everything is in order. About fifty meters back stands a cluster of young girls and their mothers. The girls, who look to be between the ages of eight and ten, are wonderfully dressed up, with saris of deep red hues. They sparkle in beautiful gold jewelry. Their black eyeliner is applied thick and heavy, an overindulgent beautifying touch befitting the year's big event.

Suddenly, the people in front of the girls begin to move. This is it. The parade is setting out. Not more than ten paces in, though, the girls suddenly come face-to-face with a man in a tweed suit. He stands forcibly in front of them, putting space between these young women and those in whose footsteps they were following. The official begins shouting something at the girls' mothers, waving his hands about. It is hard to make out what he is saying, but his face expresses clear disapproval. The mothers begin to step sideways, not in the direction of the parade. The girls look up to their mothers, eyes wide with confusion. From where I stand, I can only imagine what is running through their heads: What is happening? Who is this man? Why is he holding us up? Why is Mother stepping out of the parade? There is no time for questions, though. The mothers grab their daughters' hands and pull them out of the parade. The suited official continues waving his arms, haranguing the women as they scurry across the grimy railroad tracks, away from the tribal parade. The gap in the parade quickly sutures itself, and the man in the tweed suit disappears as quickly as he appeared. Spectators around me are outraged. "This is such a political thing," I hear them quip, infuriated by the official's treatment of the Phulpāti revelers. The women and daughters, for their part, escape to behind the gravel pile where we are standing—safely out of the limelight. Meanwhile, the parade marches on without them, leaving mothers to explain to their crestfallen daughters that they have been banished for being too Hindu.

. . .

I did not know these women, but I did know the man who expelled them from the parade. I knew him well. He was Ram Bahadur Koli, the executive officer of Darjeeling's Department of Information and Cultural Affairs (DICA). Early in my fieldwork, my research assistant Eklavya—ever the fixer[1]—introduced me to Koli, believing that as a public intellectual and tribal activist, he might share some of my anthropological concerns. Eklavya was right. Koli and I soon struck up a relationship. From the start, the diminutive Koli struck me as humble and generous. His public stature changed soon after we met, though, when political supremo Subash Ghisingh recruited him into the local administration to bolster the bids for tribal recognition and autonomy. Suddenly, Koli became a politically appointed bureaucrat with a mandate to make Darjeeling tribal. This, as we saw, required sometimes uncomfortable cultural interventions.

During fieldwork, I spent considerable time with Koli and his DICA colleagues as they planned and carried out their latest spectacles. Throughout 2006 and 2007, their work filled the streets with vivid demonstrations of tribal identity—at once mystifying and compelling the public into action. Backed by the considerable resources of Subash Ghisingh and the GNLF-controlled local government, DICA figured centrally in the tribal movements at hand. Its work, however, became increasingly controversial. Still, Koli and his staff pressed on. Making Darjeeling tribal was what they had been brought in to do. It was, as Indian bureaucrats like to say, their "duty."

POSTCOLONIAL KNOWLEDGE, POWER, AND POLICY

Koli's encounter with the young women illustrates how prescriptions of tribal difference were pressed upon the people of Darjeeling. These impositions put a decidedly postcolonial face on the history covered in Chapter 2. There is no denying the coloniality of tribal recognition in India. But as I mean to show, the postcolonial era has brought important changes to its operations—and operatives. These changes bear directly upon those who do and do not fit the mold of the recognizably tribal subject—crestfallen daughters included. This chapter turns attention to these permutations of ethnological governmentality in the postcolony. With compliments to earlier studies of "colonialism and its forms of knowledge,"[2] here I ask what happens to knowledge, power, and policy *after* independence. This requires tracking the changing faces and persuasions of the ethnographic state from the twilight of the colonial period into the present day.[3]

Another way of framing this problem is to ask the following questions: How did the massive anthropological apparatus of the British Raj transform into the world's largest affirmative action system? How has the much-maligned category of the *tribe* become a beacon of social justice? How do we get from the categorical uncertainties of colonial ethnology to the imperious cultural interventions of Ram Bahadur Koli and DICA? Or more poignantly, what are we to make of the mothers and daughters left standing by the road?

The trajectory of tribal recognition neither stopped nor started with decolonization. It did, however, change. In the 1940s, India's modernist elites assumed positions and powers previously unavailable to them under the British. With a new nation in the offing and the colonial state still largely intact, these newly empowered legislators brought with them their own ideas of who and what would constitute an independent India. The debates spawned an Indian liberal order that would push tribes to the margins of a uniquely Hindu-centric imaginary.

India's first constitution laid the groundwork for affirmative action measures that became hallmarks of Nehruvian socialism. Among these were specific provisions for tribal populations. By 1965, when the official criteria for ST status were established, tribal recognition had assumed a fixity and hubris eclipsing its colonial antecedents. Throughout the 1970s, the government continued to allocate more and more resources to the development and welfare of tribal populations.[4] These provisions attached lucrative incentives to formal designations of "backwardness," "primitiveness," "cultural distinctiveness," etc.—thereby offering redress for generations of marginalization. Consequently, the demands for recognition grew. The escalation has been particularly pronounced following India's embrace of economic liberalization in the 1990s, as marginalized minorities have scrambled for purchase amid the turbulence of economic reform. The Mandal Commission controversies of the early 1990s, the subsequent flare-ups over proposed hikes in reservation quotas, and today's increasingly violent protests for tribal status punctuate the charged circumstances of affirmative action. All the while, the rising demands continue to strain a government that is struggling desperately to square its socialist past with the prospects of a neoliberal future.[5]

These circumstances constitute a specifically Indian quandary of late liberalism, fraught with questions about how the state can possibly manage the myriad claims of collective difference and rights made possible by the anti-colonial triumph, while sacrificing neither its sovereignty nor India's global economic ascendency.[6] Amid these conditions of late liberalism, tribal recognition has emerged as a decidedly postcolonial problem demanding postcolonial solutions.

This chapter picks up where the last chapter left off: with the question of what happens to tribal recognition *after* colonialism. To address the question, we must look beyond the administrative history of tribal recognition and into the actual practices and persuasions of governance in India. On this front, I join ethnographers like Akhil Gupta, Thomas Blom Hansen, Finn Stepputat, and Mathew Hull in turning the lens of anthropology upon the agents of the postcolonial state in South Asia.[7] But here and in the chapters to come, I work to take the initiative a step further. Ultimately, if we are to appreciate what happens to tribal recognition after independence, we need to expand the scope to consider the politics and experiences of those the postcolonial state purports to govern—in this case, Darjeeling's aspiring tribes.

Ethnopolitical operatives like Ram Bahadur Koli and the Department of Information and Cultural Affairs (DICA) complicate matters in productive ways. Technically, DICA was part of the Darjeeling Gorkha Hill Council and thus part of the local government. From this position, however, it functioned as the de facto anthropology wing of the GNLF—the party in control of the region. One of Koli's main tasks was to coordinate the various bodies of civil society into a unified tribal whole—as we saw with the ethnic associations lined up for the tribal parade. In this configuration, the ostensible lines between civil society, political society, and the state begin to look very blurry. Charting these dynamics, we may find recourse in the thoughts of Antonio Gramsci, who asks us to consider civil and political society as but parts of the state and its corresponding forms of hegemony. Both are, as it were, "trenches" in the war of position over who sets the terms of power, politics, and life itself.[8] For Gramsci, the critic's task is to interrogate the powers by which operatives impress upon the masses particular forms of knowledge and social order.

How, in other words, did leaders like Ram Bahadur Koli persuade people to fall into ethnological line? And what happened when they did not?

As Gramsci would have anticipated, political authority, class, expertise, and the threat of violence all were instrumental in the actualization of Darjeeling's tribal turn. How exactly these movements took hold of the body politic remains a decidedly ethnographic question that I shall return to later. But moments like Koli's ejection of the young women from the parade also pry open heavier historical questions about colonialism's burdens on the present. What possibilities has ethnology's checkered history in India bequeathed to the contemporary? What constraints? And how are communities, like those of Darjeeling, working within these received grids of ethno-intelligibility to attain rights, solidarity, and social justice?[9]

There is little doubt that the postcolonial state has extended many of the know-and-rule logics of its colonial predecessor. The administrative continuities notwithstanding, what are we to make of the hard fact that "native" agents like Koli and his fellow leaders are brandishing these erstwhile colonial paradigms with such force? This is to say nothing of those born-again ethnics who continue to "find themselves" in these vestiges of ethnology's past. At present, the dividing lines between governance, taxonomies of difference, and community lifeways are breaking down—and being renegotiated—in newly generative ways. Amid these dynamics, the "native point of view" begins to look less essentially native and more fundamentally hybrid, innovative, and positively *post*colonial. In India, we are long past the point at which neat lines can be drawn between native (emic) and governmental or academic (etic) renderings of difference. This emic-etic bleed, in fact, has become a signature condition of the ethno-contemporary on the subcontinent and beyond.

Navigating these circumstances, the ethnographer carries a responsibility—and capacity—to search out the experiences of those who dwell within and beyond these regimes of recognition. Part of this humanizing project, however, must be to understand those who set the terms of difference and its recognition in the first place. These include the drafters of India's constitution, the operators of its massive affirmative action system, and the culture makers of its subsequent politics, Subash Ghisingh and

Ram Bahadur Koli included. As I aim to show, getting to know *their* history and *their* work is vital to understanding not just those running the show, but also those left standing by the side of the road as the proverbial parade marches on.

With these scenes of the Indian ethno-contemporary in mind, let me restart this history of the present by asking first when—or rather, with whom—the postcolonial begins?

THE ANTHROPOLOGY OF DR. B. R. AMBEDKAR

The Cultural Research Institute (CRI) is a vacuous government building on the outskirts of Kolkata.[10] Inside this mildewed monolith, Scheduled Tribe applications (including those from Darjeeling) flutter incessantly beneath the paperweights that pin them to the bureaucratic table. In the CRI's stairwell hangs a lone portrait of Dr. B. R. Ambedkar—the pioneering Dalit activist and "architect" of the Indian Constitution. Disproportionately small, the portrait seems too modest to preside over the happenings of the department, but it is there nonetheless, hanging quietly on a barren concrete wall.

It is telling that Ambedkar's image would bedeck the CRI's stark interior. On the one hand, as the chairman of the Constitution Drafting Committee (1947–49), Ambedkar oversaw the formation of India's affirmative action system. The constitutional provisions for Scheduled Castes and Tribes, and the ethnic-based autonomies guaranteed by the Fifth and Sixth Schedules, established the government's credence as the Archimedean arbitrator of political identity. Thanks to these measures, government operatives like the anthropologists of the CRI now wield extraordinary powers of recognition. On the other hand, Ambedkar's activism for the Depressed Classes (Dalits) established key paradigms for minority politics across South Asia.[11] His steadfast critiques of caste inequality, his calls for positive discrimination, and his tactics of mobilization became exemplary for minorities seeking rights and social justice. Marking his legacy, similar portraits of Ambedkar hang on the walls of caste and tribal welfare organizations in Darjeeling and throughout India. Reading Ambedkar as bureaucrat and activist, we may accordingly learn a great deal about the history of minority politics and liberal democracy on the subcontinent.[12] Reading Ambedkar as organic anthropologist, we may learn even more.

Ambedkar was a luminary of acute, if problematic, ethnological sensibilities. Though he maintained that positive discrimination should draw its impetus from disadvantage, not difference,[13] his attacks on Brahmanism continually ventured into sociocultural terrain to critique the logics through which Hindus castigated the "untouchable" Dalits. Anupama Rao has eloquently demonstrated the ways in which Ambedkar created an antagonistic alterity between high-caste Hindus and Dalits, so as to establish the moral grounds for equitable rights and representation.[14] Ambedkar's attempts to carve a distinctive Dalit identity out of the Hindu fold famously drew the ire of Gandhi. Faced with the Mahatma's hunger strike (discussed in Chapter 2), Ambedkar eventually caved on the issue of a separate Dalit electorate. Nevertheless, he remained steadfast in his declarations of a radical alterity between Dalits and Hindus. The alterity became a linchpin for the formation of the collective Dalit subject.

There was another kind of alterity lurking in Ambedkar's worldview, however. By his own admission, Ambedkar's politics virtually disavowed the so-called tribal or aboriginal peoples of India. Ambedkar justified this by proclaiming: "The Aboriginal Tribes have not as yet developed any political sense to make the best use of their political opportunities and they may easily become mere instruments in the hands either of a majority or a minority and thereby disturb the balance without doing any good to themselves."[15] Tribes, he averred, were "not as yet" ready to be responsible citizens in the world of liberal democracy. Ambedkar's phrasing calls to mind Dipesh Chakrabarty's critiques of the "not yet" historicist logics through which particular peoples have been relegated to the "waiting room of history."[16] Only here, historicist and ethno-logics worked hand in glove to structure Ambedkar's modernist vision of India. Tribes lacked the credentials of properly modern subjects. As "primitive," "backward," and not-Hindu, they became the negative against which Hindu modernity defined itself. Figured accordingly, tribes were not only Hinduism's other-beyond-mention, they were modernity's.

While Ambedkar the bureaucrat eventually steered in special constitutional provisions for tribal development, his ethnological sensibilities were emblematic of liberal thought on the subcontinent. By excluding tribes from ostensibly universal democratic rights, Ambedkar extended liberal contradictions emanating from deep within the colonial past. As Uday Singh Mehta and others have noted, liberalism in the colonies drew a stark line between those ready for "universal" rights and those not. Mehta explains this *anthropological minimum* as follows: "The exclusionary basis of liberalism . . . is so not because the ideals are theoretically disingenuous or concretely impractical, but rather because behind the capacities ascribed to all human beings exists a thicker set of social credentials that constitute the real bases of political inclusion."[17] Throughout the colonial period, these exclusionary logics proved axiomatic to a *false liberalism* wherein certain forms of difference were admitted into the hallowed domains of democratic citizenship, while others were not.[18]

As we see with Ambedkar, this history of liberal exception extended into the postcolonial era. Tribes became the anachronous, "backward" other against which modernity framed its advance. Such logics of the "savage/tribal slot" have carried across the postcolonial world,[19] but it is particularly striking in the case of Ambedkar, otherwise a hero of the downtrodden. That India's most strident spokesman for the disadvantaged could so easily push the tribals from the pale of political rights bespeaks the ethnological underpinnings of India's then-nascent democracy. Elsewhere, Ambedkar sounded wary of human classification and its political consequences.[20] But as bureaucrat and activist, he clearly trafficked in the business of classificatory distinction. In both capacities, ethnological prejudices snuck in the back door of Ambedkar's view of India unannounced, yet silently shaping the imagination and policies of an embryonic nation-state.

Ambedkar was not alone. His fellow architects of India harbored similar dispensations—both stated and unstated. Once the anti-colonial struggle was won, these nationalist leaders cemented many of these persuasions into the laws and policies of the Nehruvian state. In a Gramscian framing, these middle decades of the twentieth century would see a *war of movement* morph into a *war of position*, wherein the state became a repository of class power and its corresponding forms of knowledge.[21] On these terms, decolonization ushered in a veritable changing of the guard—and with it, a changing of the terms by which difference (tribal and otherwise) would be recognized and governed.

Eventually, Ambedkar and India's modernist elites turned to affirmative action and governmental care as the antidote to the tribals' "backwardness," but only after intense—and exceptionally telling—negotiations.

THE CONSTITUENT ASSEMBLY DEBATES

India's Constituent Assembly was first convened on December 9, 1946. Nearly three years later, on November 26, 1949, its 207 members finally settled on the first Constitution of India. The debates over this three-year span ranged from banal deliberations regarding the letters of the law to fierce ideological (and often personal) attacks over who and what constituted India. The Constituent Assembly, in these ways and many others, was a crucible of the modern nation-state. Venturing an anthropological reading of its debates, particularly those dealing with positive discrimination, we can begin to glean the persuasions of a conspicuously Hindu-centric liberal order that would set the terms of tribal recognition and its politics going forward.

On September 5, 1949, the assembly met to finalize the details of the Fifth Schedule, a constitutional measure to ensure special forms of governance for designated tribal areas. Professor Shibban Lal Saksena initiated the debate by proclaiming, "The existence of the Scheduled Tribes and the Scheduled Areas are a stigma on our nation just as the existence of untouchability is a stigma on the Hindu religion. That these brethren of ours are still in such a sub-human state of existence is something for which we should be ashamed."[22]

A. V. Thakkar questioned the tribals' capacity for self-rule on accounts that they were "too shy." He went on to say, "Therefore the more *we* are able to know of these tribes the better it is for the country as a whole and to assimilate those tribal people as fast as *we* can in the whole society of the nation as *we* are now" (italics here and throughout this section are mine).

Biswanath Das questioned, "What are we doing now? We are creating another virus, a racial virus in Tribal Councils, Scheduled Areas, and the rest. Sir, why not save the country from the troubles arising from the

distinctions between adibasis [tribals] and nonadibasis [non-tribals]?
. . . As long as you keep recognizing such terms, you keep on fanning
difference."

The following day, the assembly members shifted their attention to
the Sixth Schedule, which dealt with tribal areas in Assam and other
states of the Northeast. The debates got personal. Kuladhar Chalisa of
Assam began, "If you see the background of this Schedule, you will find
that the British mind is still there. There is the old separatist tendency
and you want to keep them away from *us*. You will thus be creating a
Tribalstan, just as you have created a Pakistan." Chalisa's history was not
off base. There was a long record of exceptionalism for "aboriginal," "frontier," and/or "backward" areas and their populations. Antecedents of the
Fifth and Sixth Schedules include: the Scheduled District Acts of 1874;
The Government of India Act of 1919 (Sec. 52–A(2), which established
Backward Tracts; and The Government of India Act of 1935 (Sec. 91 &
92), which demarcated Excluded and Partially Excluded Areas. The Fifth
and Sixth Schedules would extend this history of exceptionalism by declaring particular regions "tribal areas." The granting of ethnic-based sovereignty alarmed some members of the assembly, however. Brajeshwar
Prasad opined, "To vest wide political powers into the hands of tribals is
the surest method of inviting chaos, anarchy and disorder throughout the
length and breadth of this country."

R. K. Chaudhari concurred and took the critique a step further by
accusing Ambedkar, who was presenting the draft under consideration,
of "wanting to perpetuate the British method so far as the tribals are
concerned. *We* want to assimilate the tribals."

Rev. Nichols Roy of Assam at this point intervened: "I myself being
a hillman know what I feel. It is said by one honourable gentleman that
the hill tribes have to be brought to the culture which he said was 'our
culture,' meaning the culture of the plainsman. . . . You say, "I am educated
and you are uneducated and because of that you must sit at my feet." That
is not the principle among the hill tribes. When they come together they
all sit together whether educated or uneducated, high or low. There is that
feeling of equality among the hill tribes in Assam, which you do not find
among the plains people."

This infuriated Chaudhari, a high-caste Hindu: "Why do you make propaganda against *our* people? Do *we* not dig earth in our villages and raise houses? Why do you vilify *our* people?"

Roy quipped back, "I am telling facts!"

Kuladhar Chalisa commanded Roy, "Please withdraw your remarks!" His objection was not sustained by the president, at which point Ambedkar tried to steer the conversation back on track by stating, "I am speaking of Assam and other areas for the moment. The difference seems to be this. The tribal people in areas other than Assam are more or less Hinduised, more or less assimilated with the civilization and culture of the majority of the people in whose midst they live. With regard to the tribals in Assam that is not the case. Their roots are still in their own civilization and their own culture."

But the hotheaded Chaudhari was not done. He retorted, "Is the Honorable Dr. Ambedkar entitled to make insinuations against *us*?" This was a seemingly out-of-bounds personal attack on Ambedkar. We should remember here who Ambedkar was: a steadfast critic of Brahmanical oppression; a leader of the Dalits; and himself a Dalit chairing a diverse, predominantly Hindu Constituent Assembly. The spat died down soon thereafter, but not before revealing the prejudices and presumptions that shaped the policies in question. The Sixth Schedule was finalized the following day: September 7, 1949.

As Rev. Roy, the self-proclaimed "hillman" from Assam, pointed out, the issue here was as much about the "tribals" as it was about the majority, the de facto "we," against which they were being defined. Who was the "we" that should be ashamed of their "sub-human tribal brethren"? Who was the "we" that found offense to the comments made by Roy (a "hillman") and Ambedkar (a Dalit)? In short, who had the right to claim the first-person of the nation? This was the subtextual issue undergirding the public discussion of how best to govern the tribes.

Despite its often-heated debates, the Constituent Assembly bore a recognizably liberal bent. The modernist sensibilities of India's nationalist leaders are well known.[23] What is remarkable in these debates are the ways in which these leaders wove modernist and Brahmanical persuasions into a discernibly Hindu-centric liberal order. Hinduism became the unmarked center against which marginality would be defined—Muslim, Dalit, tribal, etc. If the dichotomy of Hindu castes versus tribes dates back to the colonial period, with decolonization that alterity became re-institutionalized in a notably different demographic and political context.

Take, for instance, what happens to hybridity in these debates. Once the bane of colonial classification, hybridity suddenly gets proffered as a proactive solution to tribal backwardness. Recall Chaudhari's "we want to assimilate the tribals," and Thakkar's preference "to assimilate those tribal people as fast as *we* can in the whole society of the nation as *we* are now." For these Hindu elites, hybridity was no longer an epistemological problem. It was a sociopolitical process to be encouraged, a way of centripetally pulling tribes in from the forested margins toward an appropriately modern, Hindu center. So claimed the proponents of assimilation. Those of a more protectionist leaning saw ethnically attuned governance as necessary for the survival of the tribes—vulnerable as they were to the encroachments of modern life. Outside the Constituent Assembly, these assimilationist-versus-protectionist debates came to be represented by two eminent social scientists of the day. Advocating more-assimilationist policies was Indian sociologist G. S. Ghurye. Championing special protections for tribals was the British-born ethnologist Verrier Elwin, who, over the course of his career, became both a citizen of India and its most outspoken protector of tribal culture.[24]

The Ghurye-Elwin debates spanned decades. Those of the Constituent Assembly unfolded in a matter of days. In the end, the Constituent Assembly's policy solutions effectively split the difference between assimilation and protectionism. Affirmative action for Scheduled Tribes would assuage the integration of these groups into the national mainstream. The Fifth and Sixth Schedules would grant them the autonomy to preserve their unique ways of life.

Tribal recognition thereby became a centerpiece of affirmative action. Where the British had all but given up on the category, Ambedkar and his modernist peers resurrected the category and made tribal peoples a target of postcolonial governmental concern. These epistemic recuperations were neither wholesale, nor could they have been. The classificatory schemas bequeathed to Ambedkar and his colleagues were anything but coherent. They represented a smattering of ideological and epistemic fragments— *imperial debris*, as Ann Stoler might have it.[25] Coherent or not, the state's classificatory system was under duress. The politics of identity had intensified considerably in the run-up to independence, as communities vied for representation in the nation-to-come.[26] Re-administering difference accordingly became both a responsibility and an opportunity for the leaders of independent India. That the epistemic remains of tribal recognition were re-gathered and institutionalized the way they were should come as no surprise given the context of these decisions—and *who* was making them. The war of positions notwithstanding, the decisions made would set the terms of difference and its rightful recognition going forward.

TRIBES BY LAW

Legalizing identity is, by definition, a fraught affair.[27] In 1949, when the Indian Constitution was in its final drafts, the Ministry of Home Affairs sent orders to all provincial governments to prepare lists and information on Scheduled Castes, Scheduled Tribes, and Other Backward Classes.[28] It was imperative that the lists be finalized before the 1951 Census so that the designated groups could be counted and thus begin receiving the advantages laid out for them by the newly ratified constitution.[29] These inquiries produced the first list of India's Scheduled Tribes in 1950.[30] Nowhere did any of these legal proceedings mention the criteria by which tribes were to be recognized.

Nehru's government invested considerable resources in the tribal problem. Intellectually, it called upon the Anthropological Survey of India (est. 1945) to sustain its research on tribal peoples. The ASI's task was to educate the public about India's diverse peoples through a variety of projects and publications. Administratively, Nehru's government doubled down on the state's engagement with tribes. By 1953 the commissioner for Scheduled Castes and Tribes was advocating for the establishment of research institutes across the country, to be manned by social anthropologists and devoted to the study of ST communities. In West Bengal, this took the form of the Cultural Research Institute (CRI), founded in 1955, and Tribal Research Institutes (TRIs) in other states.

"The STs have been pushed back to the jungles and the hill areas and have been altogether neglected both by the Government and the society for centuries," the commissioner explained. "The STs will naturally take more time in coming up to the level of the SCs in their assertion of their rights, and therefore, Government help and encouragement are very necessary in the initial stages."[31]

With no criteria for ST recognition on file, the tribes' relationship to Hinduism remained unwritten. The opposition obtained only in the designations "Scheduled Castes" versus "Scheduled Tribes." But key concerns were beginning to distinguish the government's tribal attentions. Chief among these was the growing emphasis on culture, vulnerability, and backwardness. Vulnerable and unique, tribal culture required preservation. Isolated and backward, tribal welfare required governmental intervention in the form of development. Representing protectionist and assimilationist leanings respectively, these were two sides of the newly minted coin of affirmative action.

Almost as soon as the first list of Scheduled Tribes was created in 1950, however, problems began to arise. By 1953, members of parliament were convinced that the original list excluded groups that were deserving of ST and SC status. Further complications arose with the creation of new states throughout the 1950s—and in particular the States Reorganization Act of 1956. Since SCs and STs are recognized on a state-by-state basis, redrawing state lines meant re-enumerating those that were eligible for affirmative action. A multitude of constitutional orders soon followed to keep pace with these shifting political boundaries.

The logistical problems were met with broader concerns about the irrationality of the lists themselves. A rash of complaints eventually convinced legislators that action was needed. In 1965, the federal government passed a resolution to revise the lists of Scheduled Tribes and Scheduled Castes in a "scientific and rational manner."[32] Justice B. N. Lokur was appointed to chair an advisory committee to, once and for all, put tribal recognition on solid ground. The committee—comprising Lokur (from the Ministry of Law), A. D. Pande (Home Affairs), and N. Sundaram (Backward Class Welfare)—traveled the country, talking with bureaucrats, activists, and anthropologists. They reviewed the cases in more than 800 communities, fielding innumerable petitions for inclusion along the way. The committee members quickly realized the profundity of their task. Not even social scientists, they realized, had any clear definition of a tribe. How then was this three-person committee of bureaucrats to solve this problem? Not surprisingly, the committee began to back away from the challenge of "scientific" enumeration, claiming "it was just not possible." The scope for revising the list in a "rational and scientific manner," they insisted, was "limited."[33]

In the end, they settled on the following five criteria for inclusion in India's List of Scheduled Tribes: (a) indication of primitive traits, (b) distinctive culture, (c) geographical isolation, (d) shyness of contact with the community at large, and (e) backwardness. The Lokur Committee presented these criteria in a rather understated way. (They were buried in a single paragraph of the committee's final report.) Nevertheless, these became *the* criteria for tribal recognition. As of 2015, they remain the standard by which tribes are measured.

The work of the Lokur Committee became a watershed moment in the history of tribal recognition. By fixing the criteria as they did, this three-person team capped the convoluted history of tribal recognition, effectively smoothing over the uncertainties and epistemic messiness of earlier renderings. In the process, the Lokur Committee rendered tribes in far more rigid terms than their predecessors had. These developments open up important considerations of not so much colonial, but rather *post*colonial, knowledge, power, and policy.

It is a telling antinomy that in this era of increasing globalization, hybridity, and intercultural flow, the postcolonial state insists upon "cultural distinctiveness" and "geographic isolation" in such pristine terms. The suturing of culture to primitiveness, shyness, and backwardness likewise summons the logics of an earlier anthropology, which academics now tend to shun. Per these terms, tribes are to be culturally pure, socially inept, and anachronistic—as though perfectly sealed off from the murk of modern life. As one might expect, these criteria pose considerable difficulties for communities struggling to fit themselves into the straitjacket of tribal recognition. For communities like those of Darjeeling, for which transnational migration and hybridity are a fact of life, meeting these ethnological demands has proven especially impossible.

But as the people of Darjeeling and others have come to know, there is more to achieving ST status than demonstrating compliance with the state's written norms. These criteria are only policy, after all. In practice, myriad other ethno-logics enter into the reckoning of tribal difference. None of these are more decisive than the assumptions of a radical alterity between tribes and Hinduism. In subsequent chapters, I show how these assumptions inform the real-time practices of the ethnographic state. But already it is worth considering how these written and unwritten criteria shape the lives and politics of those vying for this designation.

To examine these issues requires crossing back over the interface of tribal recognition—from the policies of the postcolonial state to the politics of those seeking its care—to explore *who* was making Darjeeling tribal and *how*. Of concern are the leaders of the tribal turn and the sometimes imperious ways in which they impressed tribal identity upon their people. Here we encounter some notably different (but nevertheless associated) operations—and operatives—of knowledge and power in the postcolony.

CULTURAL AFFAIRS

In 2006, Darjeeling stood on the brink of tribal autonomy. Subash Ghisingh had signed the agreement to bring the Sixth Schedule to the hills. But with the bill yet to advance to parliament, he was leaving nothing to chance. Throughout the year, Ghisingh retooled his administration to prove the region's tribal identity. Ghisingh let ethnic associations handle the bids for ST status and affirmative action. He personally would direct the movements for autonomy. Together, they would make Darjeeling tribal—thus bringing the people the rights, autonomy, and belonging they desired.

Ghisingh tasked the Department of Information and Cultural Affairs (DICA) with engineering the demonstrations necessary to persuade the Indian government—and the people of hills—of their tribal identity. Since the department was technically a part of the local government, Ghisingh could funnel funds directly to its accounts. All the department needed was a proper expert to run it. In the summer of 2006, Ghisingh found his man: Ram Bahadur Koli.

Koli came from humble beginnings. As a member of one of Darjeel-ing's Dalit communities and a recognized Scheduled Caste, Koli was a stranger to neither discrimination nor affirmative action. From an early age, he showed a keen interest in the social welfare of his people. His activism spawned a deepening interest in anthropology and politics. Eventually, Koli achieved a midlevel administrative post in the local gov-ernment. But a series of missteps in the 1990s estranged him from the ruling GNLF, forcing him and his family to move to Delhi. Nearly a decade later, the tribal turn brought him back.

By the early 2000s, Koli was publishing essays in the local papers on the cultures, customs, and histories of Darjeeling's tribes. Given the tribal movements afoot, his writings found a growing audience, and he quickly earned a reputation as a resident expert. During this time, he continued his activist work, channeling his growing fame toward the welfare of Dar-jeeling's Dalits (Kamis, Damais, and Sarkis), but with one key difference. He believed these groups should be recognized as Scheduled Tribes, not Scheduled Castes (a status they had enjoyed since the 1950s). With other Dalit leaders, Koli formed a new ethnic association, the Gorkha Janajati Ka.Da.Sa Sangh, with this goal in mind. The proposed move from SC to ST status provoked considerable controversy within these communities,[34] but such were the times.

It was in his role as an activist that I first met Koli. My research as-sistant Eklavya knew Koli through their earlier activism for Darjeeling's underrepresented minorities. With Eklavya's introduction, Koli and I found instant rapport. Our anthropological sensibilities were markedly different, but soon we were swapping articles and research ideas. That was when Koli got the call to join Ghisingh's administration. He subse-quently welcomed Eklavya and me into DICA's offices as "old friends," affording us an inside look at the administrative makings of tribal culture.

Koli took to his post as executive officer with great vigor. For a man with a difficult past, it was as much an honor to be allowed into Ghis-ingh's mystical inner circle as it was to be rewarded for his ethnologi-cal expertise. The plush office, administrative staff, chauffeur and car (an SUV no less, the ultimate sign of power in the hills), and a modest bu-reaucratic salary only sweetened the deal. Koli now had the kind of power he had always craved. He would accordingly let no detail go unnoticed in the realization of tribal Darjeeling.

Koli's job was clear: to engineer tribal culture for all to see. The DGHC's coffers and menacing GNLF cadres at his back ensured he had ample resources to do so. Koli was joined in his work by a rather motley crew of artists, bureaucrats, activists, and others that constituted DICA's staff. Their projects ranged from coordinating cultural shows at local tourist destinations to the orchestration of massive tribal spectacles that took over Darjeeling Town for days.

At first, it seemed as though Koli could do no wrong. With Ghisingh pulling the strings and affirmative action and autonomy in the offing, the public showed up in force to DICA's events. Koli used this time to further his studies and connections with other tribal movements—particularly in the Northeast, where there were important lessons for Darjeeling.

FIGURE 3.1 *DICA Organizes the Tribal Masses*

Enjoying the rare opportunity to deepen his research and put it directly into political practice, Koli sailed through his first months on the job.

In 2007, his work became more difficult. With Ghisingh remaining coy on the Sixth Schedule's details, the public was growing suspicious of his tribal ploys. More and more people began questioning whether tribal autonomy and its ethnological mandates were right for them. The mounting criticism naturally fell upon the shoulders of Koli and his staff. And the job soon began to wear on Koli in visible ways. As the cultural spokesman of the GNLF, his name was no longer appearing in the papers as the purveyor of ethnological insight, but rather as the defender of a fabricated, increasingly bizarre tribal orthodoxy. Koli's tryst with power had put him at the center of a political maelstrom. His health declined rapidly, as did his enthusiasm for this particular brand of anthropology. Increasingly when I visited his offices, I would have to make my way through hawkish journalists hovering about, awaiting an audience with Koli to find out what Ghisingh and his administration were cooking up next. Months into his tenure, Koli admitted to me how bad it had actually gotten: Ghisingh had installed a one-way telephone line straight into his office. Orders were coming from above and there was little that could be said otherwise.

I came to know Koli as a kind and sensitive man. It pained me to watch the ill effects that this work was having on him and the people of Darjeeling. Koli's ascendance to power may have been swift, but he was not unlike many of the other ethnic leaders I was working with. Like them, he was committed to the welfare of his people. Like them, he believed in a return to the "authentic cultures and customs" that had been "lost" in the course of modern life. The revitalization of tribal identity, the purification of religious practice, the dress codes, and the general compulsions to conform were all in his people's best interests. Having ascended from his humble beginnings, Koli, like so many others, saw it as a moral duty to help his people rediscover their tribal identities. That moral imperative was hard to deny. But so were its sometimes-austere actualizations.

As I watched all of this, Koli's work struck me as a particularly clear, but crude, articulation of knowledge-power—certainly more crass than the subtle mechanisms of subject formation that Foucault trained us to see.[35] But they were operations levied upon the population nonetheless.

Framed in this way, Koli and DICA's story fits well within the history of ethnological governmentality sketched over the last two chapters. But if their work was connected to a colonial past, these operations and operatives of ethnological knowledge-power were markedly different than in the heydays of Hodgson and Risley.

To see these agents as but the latest in a long line of ethnologist-bureaucrats says nothing, of course, about how the people of Darjeeling did—and did not—comply with the tribal prescriptions on order. Such a reading also passes all too easily over the economic and political gradients through which these mandates made their way down from the policies of the postcolonial state into the work of Koli and DICA and then further still, into the lives of Darjeeling's constituents. As has become common, the leaders of these tribal movements appealed to national and international discourses of indigenous rights, affirmative action, and justice to support their cause. But they also called upon local political power and their own class superiority to forcibly set the terms of ethnopolitical mobilization in the hills. With very few exceptions, these tribal movements were led by educated male elites who maintained clear ties to Darjeeling's political parties. That Koli had the backing of Subash Ghisingh and the GNLF is not insignificant. For the everyday citizen, that affiliation alone meant that falling out of step ethnologically could mean falling out of sway politically—a dangerous proposition in the hills. What was morally worse, individual transgressions were said to undermine the greater community's chance of achieving rights and much-needed advantage. With multicultural governance providing the carrot and party cadres wielding the stick, consent and coercion thus combined into a particular kind of late liberal compulsion.

Not that this necessarily led to compliance. Quite the contrary. For Koli and his DICA colleagues, forcing the unruly lifeways of Darjeeling's people into the neat and tidy box of the tribe proved a difficult, if not impossible, task. And yet their work—and the tribal turn more generally—hinged precisely on that possibility. Suffice it to say that when it came to making Darjeeling tribal, seldom did things go according to plan.

Here it is worth returning to where we began: with the beginning and the unexpected end of the tribal parade.

THE END/S OF GOVERNMENTALITY

The parade's participants were growing restive. With shamans' drums reverberating up and down the procession, people were beginning to dance and march in place. The Rock was waiting just a few kilometers away. And it was Phulpāti, one of the year's biggest celebrations! The ethnic associations had done their part. Thousands were lined up under their respective banners, adorned in resplendent tribal attire. With Koli and his staff corralling the masses, everything seemed in order. Whereas just a mile down the road, the Darjeeling Police Unit (under the aegis of the Government of West Bengal) was sponsoring its annual Phulpāti celebration replete with Brahmans and sacrifices to Durga, these facets of Hinduism were banned from DICA's tribal parade. Transgressors were being forcibly removed—even children, as we saw.

Having done all it could, DICA unleashed the parade. With rumbling drums and dancing bodies, the parade of tribes began its boisterous march through town on its way to Chow Rasta, where the Rock awaited its devotees. The tribal parade arrived at Chow Rasta late in the morning. Jeeps with loudspeakers blaring and GNLF banners flying overhead led the way. Shamans bedecked in full ritual attire followed the vehicles, leading countless troupes of ethnic performers and thousands of marchers past an equally impressive crowd that had gathered along the route. The parade inched its way slowly toward the center of Chow Rasta, where a performance area had been cordoned off. It was here that tribal culture was to be displayed for all to see. The Rock, meanwhile, sat dumbly on the stage above.

Just minutes after the tribal parade arrived, however, the bagpipes of the Darjeeling Police Marching Band announced the approach of a second parade—this one originating from the Hindu celebration put on just down the road from where the parade of tribes had begun. The numbers of this Hindu parade paled in comparison to those of its tribal counterparts, but the thunderous roar of the marching band, accompanied by the iconically enraged idols of Durga, made for a formidable foe. The clashing sounds of bagpipes, drums, and loudspeakers gave the confrontation an even more frenetic feel. Tourists and locals alike jockeyed for position to witness the clash. I, for one, found a perch atop a concrete pillar, clinging to a lamppost for balance.

With people scrambling for position, the scene grew increasingly chaotic as the crowd surged this way and that. For a moment it was unclear
how exactly the encroaching parade would proceed. Then something peculiar happened. DICA officials jumped forth to manage the showdown.
Holding their arms out wide, DICA's staff quickly put themselves between the Hindu parade and the audience. At first glance, it seemed as
though they were trying to help their rivals. But as the officials struggled
to keep separation between the crowd and the encroaching parade, their
intentions were laid bare: they were acting as human shields to hermeti-
cally seal off the Hindu parade from the masses. If the Hindu parade was
to enter the carefully contrived space of the tribe, it would necessarily do
so as matter out of place—at once dangerous and an abomination to the
order of the day.[36]

DICA's officials were grossly overmatched. As Durga, leading the
Hindu parade, cut away her obstacles and the giant sling of offerings
known as the Doli followed her, the crowd surged forward. Suddenly
individuals began darting out from every direction, tossing offerings into
the Doli and diving under the sling to receive the cherished blessings of
Durga. The audience erupted in cheers, as individuals flitted back and
forth across DICA's ill-fated barriers, faces beaming. The crowd pressed
in more and more, cheering on their fellow revelers, as more and more
individuals took their chance and made a break for the Doli. Amid the
clamor, DICA's officials did not relent in their efforts to maintain distinction. Their arms outstretched, they sidled along with the enemy parade as
it made its way slowly through the throng. The parades—one ostensibly
tribal, the other ostensibly Hindu—slid through and around each other
like water and oil, their distinctiveness penetrated only by the desires and
the unruliness of the masses.

The scene epitomized the times. In doing so, it offers important lessons about the functions and limits of ethnological governmentality. First,
we see here the divisive potentials of ethno-logics that stress cultural distinctiveness, purity, and absolute alterity. In this regard, the water and oil
separation of these two parades—one tribal, the other Hindu—illustrates
what happens when rigid concepts of difference are forced upon the contingent, garrulous lifeways of contemporary subjects. Second, we might

also note that it was not so much policy as people who were mandating these absolute separations. What is remarkable in this case is that DICA's workers were not merely mandating the radical distinction between tribes and Hindus, they were quite literally becoming that boundary. Their outstretched arms and ultimately futile attempts to corral the masses serve as a timely reminder that it is not knowledge itself that carves up social worlds. It is people—in this case, operatives vested with considerable socioeconomic and political power.

Third, and crucially, we see here that the human element cuts another way. This clash of parades, in this regard, tells a very different story—that of the imminent failure of late liberal recognition to shape communities in its own image. Just as it was people that created the barriers between these distinctive parades, it was individuals and communities that broke through DICA's human barriers to place their offerings in the Doli. Celebratory, contingent, and alive, these were the practices of a syncretic tradition generations in the making. Despite Koli's planning and tireless attention to detail, DICA's ethno-logics were no match for the vibrant lifeways of the hills—especially not in this moment of holiday effervescence.[37]

READING THE ETHNO-CONTEMPORARY

From this one event, we can read two stories. The first is that of ethnology's extraordinary salience in the politics of modern India. The second is that of a people whose ways of being have never quite fit the molds of the day. The first is a story that stretches from the practices of colonial ethnology, through the structures of the postcolonial state, and into the bleeding edge of twenty-first-century struggles for rights and recognition. This is the story of ethnological governmentality—or what we might see as an administrative history of ethnology and its gradual seep into the world it studies.[38]

The second story is of a different order, but no less important. This is the story of resilience, contingency, and the appreciable failure of late liberal recognition to capture the realities of sociocultural life. Amid these frayed ends of ethnological governmentality, the question becomes not only how knowledge-power shapes contemporary subjects, but also how it does not. The latter pushes us to think beyond governmentality to those ways of being that refuse and/or survive these grids of late liberal intelligibility.

Ultimately, the anthropology of the ethno-contemporary needs both of these stories.[39] At our current juncture, they beckon each other in unprecedented ways. Combining these concerns, we can venture fresh questions about how the colonial past does and does not shape the post-colonial present; how ethnological prescriptions are foisted upon marginalized communities; and how these groups are consequently turning these norms back upon the state—and themselves—to remake their politics and their worlds. These are the dynamics of reproduction, emergence, negotiation, and recombination that define the ethno-contemporary. Read both ways, these scenes from Darjeeling are best understood as but the latest permutation of ethnology's complicated history in India—itself contingent, moving, and transformative.

Eerily old but also new, ethnology's uncanny returns here and elsewhere continue to pose meaningful challenges and opportunities for anthropology, the postcolonial state, and communities themselves. Precisely for these reasons, they call for ongoing historical and ethnographic attention. In the spirit of the latter, I turn now to the pivotal events of the Ethnographic Survey of 2006, wherein Darjeeling's aspiring tribes would attempt to prove their tribal identities to the anthropologists of the Indian government. At this signature interface of the ethno-contemporary, ethnology would return anew to render the proverbial encounter of anthropologist and tribes proverbial no more.

CHAPTER 4

INTERFACE

Encounters of the Multicultural State

IN JULY OF 2006, the Government of West Bengal announced that its anthropologists were coming to Darjeeling to verify the identities of ten communities seeking to become Scheduled Tribes of India.[1] The team from the Cultural Research Institute (CRI), itself a subsidiary of West Bengal's Backward Class Welfare Department, would arrive in just over a week. A formal Ethnographic Survey would commence upon the team's arrival. Among the communities I was working with in Darjeeling, the news brought excitement and concern. This was the moment of truth they had been waiting for. But the timing caught them off guard. Whereas others seeking tribal status had waited years—even decades—for their moment in the ethnographic spotlight, the state's anthropologists would be in Darjeeling in a matter of days.

No doubt Darjeeling's pending autonomy as a tribal area had something to do with it. Subash Ghisingh, at this point, had Darjeeling on the cusp of Sixth Schedule status. But amid all the backdoor dealings to bring this form of autonomy to the hills, the numbers were proving tricky. The Sixth Schedule was meant for regions with tribal majorities. As of 2006, only 32 percent of Darjeeling's population was recognized as Scheduled Tribes. The sudden Ethnographic Survey, it was believed, was geared toward changing that number, thereby tipping the demographic balance in favor of tribal autonomy.

The CRI team arrived on July 18, 2006. That day, they held a closed-door meeting with local ethnic association leaders to outline the week's proceedings. Each group was to take the anthropologists to a "model community" of the association's choosing, where they would be given one day to prove their tribal identities. The ethnographic data would be recorded, brought back to Kolkata, and cross-checked against the written materials furnished by the applicant groups, as well as against available scholarly and governmental literatures on the groups in question. The CRI would then draft an official ethnographic report that would be circulated through the government, where it would play a pivotal role in determining whether or not these groups would be conferred ST status. Having been briefed, the ethnic leaders had only one more thing to decide and that was which group would be studied when. They drew straws.

At eight p.m. that evening, a small van slipped out of town to begin an arduous journey through heavy monsoon rains. The road went from bad to worse as the van drove through the darkness, slowly making its way to a remote corner of the district. Inside rode several leaders of the Lekh Hitkari Ethnic Association (LHEA).[2] They were on their way to the distant village of Laharā Gāũ, the "model community" they had selected for the next morning's ethnographic survey. (The Lekh drew the short straw.) With precious little time to prepare, the LHEA's central offices in Darjeeling Town had already relayed the news to the branch leaders in Laharā Gāũ. Preparations were therefore under way when the van finally pulled into the mountainside hamlet. Together, these leaders and the villagers of Laharā Gāũ would work through the night preparing for their moment of recognition.

Meanwhile, back in Darjeeling Town, a prominent Lekh intellectual woke at five a.m. to put the final touches on a memorandum that his organization planned to submit along with its ethnographic presentations. The document bore the title "A Prayer for Inclusion of All the Unit Tribes of GORKHA Tribal Community into the Scheduled Tribe Status—with a fresh set of proofs and the causes why this should be done." Written on behalf of not only the Lekh but all "left-out" (read: "non-ST") communities of the hills, the thirty-page "fresh set of proofs" called upon native and Western anthropologies, colonial ethnologies, and census data to bolster its claims. It furthermore cited a litany of ancient texts (including the Mahabharata and the Puranas) to trace out the primordial tribal history of these groups. Blending anthropology, history, and a dose of political vitriol, the document claimed definitively, "The Gorkha community as a whole [and thus the ethnicities within it] has been and is a purely tribal community having a definite tribal, socio-cultural, and distinct tribal ethnic background." Failure to recognize the left-out communities as Scheduled Tribes would thus be a "great political blunder and a constitutional crime"—one that would lead to "inevitable unrest" and "chaos" in the hills. Affecting liberal ideals, the memorandum put the onus of recognition squarely on the state's shoulders:

> So, now your honourable self has the duty to properly represent our community's worthiness to fulfill all the criteria to be constitutionally scheduled as a Tribe. So that the people will not lose the faith in the government but get strengthened in the belief that our government is the one who gives impartial and equal opportunity to all the people and the citizens of the country, specially so to the sons of the soil and is truly working along the lines of fulfilling the just dreams and the rights of the citizens of India.

The memorandum finished by "anticipating a prompt and just decision and action from your side on this burning and seriously sensitive matter."

Minutes after eight a.m., I arrived at the Lekh's cramped offices to find the author of the memorandum seated amid an array of open academic books, scribbling final revisions. Despite the urgency of the situation, the memorandum was not yet complete. His colleagues welcomed me in whispered *namastes*, letting me know he was not to be disturbed. The frantic pace at which he worked belied the smooth figure he cut with his fine suit and tie, slicked-back hair, and sleek laptop bag at his side. His eyes darted from one book to another, cross-referencing sources, then back again to the memorandum. Beads of sweat began to stand up on his nose. He made a slight change. Someone checked the clock. It was getting late. If he and his colleagues were to make it to Laharā Gāũ in time, they needed to leave immediately. And so, with time running out, the intellectual waited for the whiteout to dry, then penciled in one last citation.

Minutes later, three suit-clad men hurried from the office, their memorandum in tow. Knowing that I was an anthropologist, they had invited me along for the day, so I did my best to keep pace as they navigated their way through the crowded bazaar. We found their hired van idling nearby and quickly climbed in to begin the same arduous journey their colleagues had made the night before. As the van sputtered out of town, the men inside could only hope that their written representations corresponded with the preparations being made in Laharā Gāū. The day demanded a perfect similitude between what their memorandum said and what their people did. Everything had to be in order. They *would* be tested.

Somewhere along the same road, the government anthropologists were making their way toward the same model community, armed with clipboards, criteria, questionnaires, and considerable power. With them in their governmental jeeps and us in our little van, it was hard to tell who was in front of whom on this monsoon-beaten road. Having sweated out the final draft of their memorandum and completed their eleventh-hour preparations, the Lekh leaders nevertheless believed they were one step ahead of the anthropologists. Time would soon tell.

TOWARD A META-ETHNOGRAPHY

This chapter examines what actually happened when the government anthropologists climbed down from their jeeps to verify the tribal identities of Darjeeling's "left-out" minorities. There on the ground of state ethnography, anthropologists, ethnic elites, and everyday subjects—each individual with his own agenda, understanding, and capacity—met one another in a markedly uneven field of ethnographic practice. What ensued was a spectacle of epic proportion and considerable consequence.

Here, I take as my "object" of analysis this encounter—this interface—of aspiring tribes and government anthropologists. Venturing an ethnography of state ethnography itself, I ask how classificatory moments like the Ethnographic Survey deploy, demand, and ultimately instantiate the norms and forms of a particular multicultural order. This question takes us to the heart of this classificatory moment and beyond, where ethnologics of the tribe continue to rework community life in new, sometimes troubling ways. Figured here as emblematic of the ethno-contemporary more generally, the Ethnographic Survey affords an acute site through which to probe the ever-evolving collusions of ethnological thought and late liberal statecraft.

Yet something else stirs in this encounter of anthropologists and tribes. At this interface, we catch glimpses of the innovative tactics with which communities are renegotiating the structures—and epistemologies—of late liberal governance. Studied ethnographically, this singular event opens into broader considerations of the kinds of difference that are possible—and legible—amid these regimes of recognition. What kinds of politics, sociality, and subjectivity are gaining traction in this age of ethnological normativity? What are not? And crucially, what are the dynamics of these determinations? These questions may seem too big to search out in the stilted space of the Ethnographic Survey. Certainly these concerns ripple far beyond the event itself. But we must also remember state ethnography's centrality to the management of diversity in India. As I intend to show, classificatory moments like the Ethnographic Survey function as key mechanisms in broader processes of exclusion, inclusion, affirmation, and denial. Precisely for these reasons, they offer unique opportunities for taking up these bigger questions of the ethno-contemporary.

Methodologically, this requires analysis not from one side or the other, but rather across the ethnographic interface itself. To cross over this interface is to see this encounter as just that: an encounter. Turning attention to state ethnography in this way, this chapter works to fill an important gap in our understandings of the politics and real-time practices of recognition in India and beyond.[3] Crossing-over here affords a timely means of rethinking the proverbial encounter of anthropologists and tribes—and perhaps, too, the assumed veracity and power of ethnography more generally.

Toward that end, it is worth recalling a mandate from anthropology's past. Long ago, Franz Boas preached to his students the importance of questioning what the researcher brings with him/her to the study of the Other. The imperative has since been rearticulated many times over in the various "reflexive" turns of the social sciences. But in thinking about the Ethnographic Survey, it is worth asking whether, at our current moment, we might profitably flip the script on Boas's directive to consider *what the studied bring with them* to the table of ethnological reckoning. To understand the dynamics of scheduling tribes, venturing such an analogue, I believe, is imperative. Let me then turn to the anxious events leading up to the arrival of the government anthropologists in Darjeeling. These last-minute preparations reveal many of the hopes, expectations, and strategies that the aspiring STs of Darjeeling brought with them to the Ethnographic Survey. Many pertained specifically to this classificatory moment; others hailed from deeper histories.

EMERGENCY MEETING

News spread quickly that the anthropologists were coming. Just over a week before their arrival, word was sent from Kolkata that a spot-visit was in the works. Two days before the research team was to arrive, the leaders of the respective ethnic associations convened an "emergency meeting" to determine the most effective strategy for being studied. The session was held under the aegis of the Gorkha Janjati Manyata Samity (GJMS)—the Gorkha Tribal Recognition Committee—an umbrella organization recently formed to represent the collective interests of the applicant communities. The GJMS being without an actual office, the meeting got off to a scattered start, with ethnic leaders roaming the grimy halls of the Old Supermarket Building in search of others. I made my way into one of the offices where several leaders had gathered. Removed from the view of others, they promptly requested that I provide whatever information I could on their ethnic group. Such academic renderings they hoped could be put to use in their representations to the government. Having already shared some of my earlier work on their contemporaries in Nepal, as well as a bibliography of academic sources, I told them there was little else I could provide. Clearly, though, they wanted more out of their affiliation with me.

Having parried their pleas, I ventured back into the halls. Soon clusters of men in dapper tweed coats, three-piece suits, and polished shoes formed in various rooms where small talk, rumors, and old-boy jokes flowed freely. Eventually, we were let into a nearby language institute, where the twenty-five or so ethnic association leaders took their seats at rows of tables typically used for pupils. To start, the general secretary (GS) welcomed those present, framing their purpose as follows:

> As we all know, the members of the CRI are coming to Darjeeling and will be conducting an inquiry with all the communities regarding their culture, traditions, etc. So since the CRI is coming I would like to say how we should present ourselves to them and what are our tribal traits. What should we exhibit, what we ought to present: this is what I would like to discuss today. It will be neither easy nor as simple as we think. It has to be deliberated and presented very cautiously.

After his introductory remarks, the GS turned the floor over to two high-ranking local government officials who, not incidentally, were also active in their communities' bids for ST status. The first, Mr. Ram Bahadur Koli, the recently appointed executive officer of Darjeeling's Department of Information and Cultural Affairs (whom we met earlier), explained how his delegation had lobbied for the government's attention at various departments in Kolkata. "We told them, 'You have the files of all the communities with their demands for tribal status. These submissions must be gathering dust, so please bring them out from your shelves and come and make spot-inquiries.'"

A second official followed with important advice:

> There is one other very important thing: that is the Hindu dharma or our being Hindus. We have spoken about that earlier too and whether the Hindu dharma has been imposed on us or not. Birth, death, and ceremonies, we need to prove our *adivasi* traits in these three things. In this regard whatever little we have studied and what we know, we will have to present this. This is the opportunity for the communities to do their best. Our effort should be to score a goal in the first match!

With collaborative zeal, the ethnic leaders thus set to discussing where the CRI team should be taken, what rituals should be shown, which traits should be concealed, and how best to engage with the anthropologists. Requests were made for the leaders to reconvene every evening to compare notes and formulate strategies accordingly. After an hour of deliberation, they began finalizing their list of "model communities." As the secretary went down the roll eliciting each community's final decision, someone piped up to suggest that each ethnic group have backup locations in mind, should the anthropologists demand a sudden change of course. Silence. The mere mention that the CRI team might want to see something other than the carefully chosen and equally well-prepared model communities drew stunned, worried looks. For several seconds, no one spoke a word. Eyes glanced from face to face searching for answers. Finally, the GS broke the silence. "Well, in that case we will fail!" he erupted. "We ask them to go to one place and then they choose to go to another. In that case we will not be able to fulfill their criteria." It was a sobering moment for everyone in the room.

Later, the GS struck upon more deep-seated anxieties, cautioning the leaders on the details of self-ascription. Under no circumstance were research subjects to use the term "Nepali" as a self-signifier. In Darjeeling, the term is used solely in a sociolinguistic sense (not as a national indicator). Yet it was feared that if community members were to self-identify as Nepali, they would be considered foreigners (as they have often been throughout their history in India). Similar groups applying for ST status had been told, "If you are Nepali, then go back to Nepal," the GS reported:

> Thus, what we are trying to say is the word "Gorkha." But then, they are trying to tell us that the Gorkhas are followers of Hinduism [and thus castes, not tribes]. Therefore Nepalis are foreigners and Gorkhas are Hindus. . . . They are calling this a "diplomatic process." But they are trying to make this Gorkha word a failure, so that it won't fulfill the tribal criteria. This "diplomatic process" will also become their policy to divide us. . . . Tomorrow, if we are destroyed, the entire Gorkha community will be destroyed. And this is what they want! The GJMS was formed by the beliefs, will, and understanding of all of us to stall the black days of the future for our community. For our tribe! For the entire hills! We have a moral and social responsibility to do this! [extremely animated]

That the GS would end with such an impassioned, firebrand flourish was typical of his character. In an earlier political life, he had fought as the commander of a guerrilla unit of the Gorkhaland National Liberation

Front (GNLF) during the 1980s agitation for Gorkhaland. Now, he was leading a newfound tribal politics. Having served on the front lines of both of these struggles—one a violent subnationalist movement, the next a decidedly more legal affair—the GS, like so many others, was deeply invested in the quests for rights, recognition, and autonomy. His anxieties regarding the CRI articulated pervasive antagonisms between the people of West Bengal and Darjeeling. Often rendered through geo-racial paradigms of "plainsmen" versus "hill people," the antagonisms stem from decades of internal neo-colonization of Darjeeling, most viscerally rehashed in the memories of the 1980s when military and paramilitary forces of the Government of West Bengal were involved in many of the atrocities of the Gorkhaland Movement. That Darjeeling remains within West Bengal is, for many, a painful reminder of these histories of domination.

For the GS and others, it was not an insignificant feature of the Ethnographic Survey that the civil servants adjudicating their claims were themselves Bengali. That subject-position alone was seen as an egregious imposition of irony—one that re-aggravated feelings of injustice at the very moment when positive discrimination offered a modicum of historical retribution.

BUREAUCRATIC DESIGNS, ETHNOGRAPHIC PRACTICES

Facing the growing demands for ST status, it is telling that the Indian government would turn to the truth-revealing capacities of ethnographic inquiry. The current modalities of recognition call for the verification of five official criteria for Scheduled Tribes: (a) indication of primitive traits, (b) distinctive culture, (c) geographical isolation, (d) shyness of contact with the community at large, and (e) backwardness.[4] These criteria evince familiar intercalations of classical ethnological tropes and liberal statecraft.[5] Following the critical concerns of Charles Taylor and Elizabeth Povinelli, we may see how these requisites of recognition effectively prefigure the community forms eligible for social justice. Tribal certification, in this sense, functions as an acute subtype of recognition—the acuity of which is bound up in the hyper-prescriptive logics of verifying predetermined criteria.

The cunning at hand exceeds the formal criteria and policies of scheduling tribes, however. In other words, it is not only through the *formal* designs of multicultural governance that the postcolonial state impresses upon minorities its ethno-logics. Equally, it is through the *contingencies* of ethnographic knowledge production itself. State ethnography involves practices that surpass the official designs of tribal recognition, as well as contingencies of a more affective register. Precisely because they are face-to-face encounters, classificatory moments like the Ethnographic Survey elicit powerful articulations of hope, desperation, and victimhood. These affective elements are in many ways necessary,[6] yet they find an awkward place within the processes of ST recognition—even as they shape actions on both sides of the encounter. To account for these unwritten contingencies, one has to look to the actual practices and interpersonal dynamics of state ethnography.

Interestingly, nowhere do the formal procedures for scheduling tribes specify how exactly the five criteria are to be verified. That is left to the expert designs of government anthropologists themselves. Prior to their arrival in Darjeeling, the CRI team drew up their own list of ethnographic guidelines (presented below). This juxtaposition illustrates the mushrooming complexity of tribal recognition as it moves from bureaucratic design to ethnographic practice. The CRI's guidelines chart a

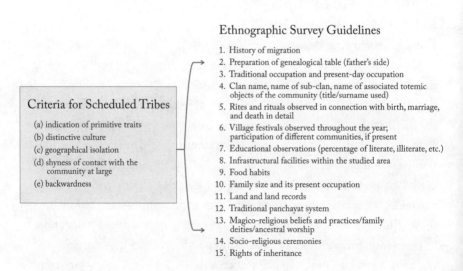

Ethnographic Survey Guidelines

1. History of migration
2. Preparation of genealogical table (father's side)
3. Traditional occupation and present-day occupation
4. Clan name, name of sub-clan, name of associated totemic objects of the community (title/surname used)
5. Rites and rituals observed in connection with birth, marriage, and death in detail
6. Village festivals observed throughout the year; participation of different communities, if present
7. Educational observations (percentage of literate, illiterate, etc.)
8. Infrastructural facilities within the studied area
9. Food habits
10. Family size and its present occupation
11. Land and land records
12. Traditional panchayat system
13. Magico-religious beliefs and practices/family deities/ancestral worship
14. Socio-religious ceremonies
15. Rights of inheritance

Criteria for Scheduled Tribes

(a) indication of primitive traits
(b) distinctive culture
(c) geographical isolation
(d) shyness of contact with the community at large
(e) backwardness

FIGURE 4.1 *Formal Criteria vs. Ethnographic Guidelines*

research agenda clearly in excess of the task of verifying the five official criteria. Points 13 and 14 on "magico-religious beliefs" and "socio-religious ceremonies" are especially noteworthy, as they seemingly contradict the stated policy that "religion is no bar to becoming tribal" (more on this later). Already, though, these pre-field preparations show cracks in the rational, "secular" project of positive discrimination. What may be said then about the dynamics of the encounter itself?

A DAY IN THE FIELD

The Ethnographic Survey began early on the morning of July 19, 2006. For the Lekh, as we saw, it began even earlier. To the relief of the Lekh leaders with whom I was riding, our little van beat the anthropologists' jeeps to the site. Somewhere on the road behind, their diesel engines were droning toward us. But for a moment at least, the LHEA leaders could assess the preparations made by their forerunners the night before. By the looks on the faces we met, it had been a long night coaching the locals.

FIGURE 4.2 *The Subject Community*

It was therefore with measured anticipation that the CRI anthropologists arrived at this distant hamlet. The "village community," which was actually an assemblage of residents from around the area, greeted the team in a mixture of tattered clothes and festival attire—men to one side, women to the other. Ethnic association leaders immediately garlanded the anthropologists, as the crowd swarmed around them. Over the cacophony, the leaders did their best to convey their plans to the researchers.

Meanwhile, the community sprang into action, transforming Laharā Gāũ into an ethnological lollapalooza. Before the anthropologists could get their bearings, they were whisked away to a "jungle house" a kilometer up the road. There, a treacherous footpath led to a modest house, where a man lived with his small garden, chickens, and several head of cattle. The owner wore traditional attire, brandishing a large *khukuri* (Nepali knife) in his waist sash. But as the anthropologists began investigating his home, he spoke hardly a word. Instead, suit-clad ethnic leaders—many

FIGURE 4.3 *Performing Daily Life*

of whom the man had never met—conversed in Bengali (a language he could not speak) with the researchers about the particulars of this "jungle house." The leaders' animated explanations quickly began to fill the hitherto blank pages of the CRI's notebooks.

Upon their return to the village proper, the research team found troupes of young women singing folk songs and milling grain (see opposite). The men, for their part, concentrated on the ritual next up on the docket: the *goth-pujā*. Here, the anthropologists were led to a manure-floored cowshed, where a local shaman had set up a small shrine. Smoke billowed under the low-hanging roof, as anthropologists stooped to have a closer look. Again it was loud, so ethnic leaders had to shout their explanations into the ears of the anthropologists. Several researchers tried to engage the shaman directly, but because they did not speak Nepali, and he spoke neither adequate Bengali nor Hindi, their conversations were translated by ethnic leaders. With nearly a dozen people crammed into the shed, the scene grew all the more chaotic as a group of adolescent boys began circling the cowshed with bows and arrows, howling savage cries into the thick monsoon skies.

A brief meal was then served by the women of the village. This quieter time afforded ethnic leaders the opportunity to convey additional information. Having sampled the local fare and fielded a barrage of native ethnological opinion, the anthropologists announced that they would break into two teams. One team would commandeer a house to conduct interviews; the other would follow the course of planned demonstrations. To translate, interpret, and otherwise mediate the locals' interviews, the Lekh's foremost native intellectual stayed behind to help in whatever way possible. The rest of us began a long hike up the mountain to a cave where drums had already begun to sound. The magnitude of the spectacle was just beginning to set in.

As we walked up the trail, the aforementioned general secretary of the left-out communities pulled me aside. Now that we were out of earshot of the CRI team, it seemed he needed to get something off his chest. "Towns," he began, "to fulfill this tribal criteria, this is a ridiculous thing. You know Hegel? Hegel said man has reached the heights of civilization. But now look at us! We are going back to the cave!"

It was an honest, if awkwardly timed, assessment. For him, the fact that his community had to be "backward," "primitive," and all the rest in order to progress through the channels of positive discrimination was a paradox so glaring that it could not go unacknowledged—at least not between the two of us. Nevertheless, he knew full well that if his community were to join the lauded national mainstream as STs, they would have to satisfy modernity's demands of anachrony. Given our less-than-private location, I felt compelled to stymie this line of critique before others could hear. I quickly assured him that the irony was not lost on me either. My acknowledgment seemed to satisfy him. So he grabbed me by the arm and we once again scurried up the trail together—to where else but the cave where his community was to prove its tribal identity.

The hillside into which the cave was etched was far too steep to accommodate the hundred-plus spectators gathered for the show. Space was nevertheless made for the anthropologists, the Lekh's cameraman, and me to be privy to what was about to occur: the Masta/Diwali Pujā.

FIGURE 4.4 *At the Mouth of the Cave*

Inside the cave three shamans danced in full regalia, barefooted, with their drums in hand. Their bodies shook to the syncopated rhythms and their eyes rolled back in their heads as they chanted their sacred texts in the signature cadence of Himalayan spirit mediumship. With anthropologists clinging to the rocks trying to get a better view, suddenly a charcoal-colored goat appeared from the crowd. The shamans and their attendants quickly circled around it, focusing their intention. The drums intensified and their dance became wilder. Within seconds, the *khukuri* was raised overhead, coming down mercilessly on the goat's outstretched neck, sending its decapitated head bouncing down the hillside. Several men immediately hoisted the still-writhing torso into the air, and up to the lips of the shamans, who voraciously drank the spewing blood. Three times this scene played out as charcoal-colored goat after charcoaled-colored goat lost its life to the spectacle. Eventually the tour moved on, with the shamans continuing their trance in their now blood-speckled gowns.

FIGURE 4.5 *Shamanic Showings*

Next up was the farmhouse, where various primitive tools were assembled for viewing. But this was no static exhibition, for soon a full-fledged exorcism got under way. The rite of *moch marne* began just outside the house where a woman, said to have undergone a miscarriage, was huddled over a hole dug in the ground. Above the hole hung an upside-down chicken (still alive); in the hole lay the skull of a dead dog. On the porch behind her, another shaman had assembled a small shrine. With hundreds of villagers surrounding them, the anthropologists rushed to record the details of the ritual before the final act was completed. The shamans' cadence soon quickened, though, and in one fell swoop, the chicken was beheaded, falling atop the dog's skull. Villagers suddenly hurried in to kick and stomp dirt into the hole before the evil spirit could escape. Others carried the woman upstairs, where she would lie ill until the researchers were gone.

Following these swift events, the anthropologists once again toured the home, documenting the various artifacts laid out before them. Meanwhile, one of the researchers slipped away to a bench on a nearby path to set up an impromptu interview session with several of the village men. Relying on an ethnic association leader to translate, he drew questions from a printed form, as each interviewee dutifully provided their particulars (name, occupation, education, etc.). During the forty-five minutes or so it took for the researchers to gather their information, women occasionally (and somewhat begrudgingly) stepped forth into the courtyard to dance for the cameras and wandering ethnographic eyes.

Their performances were a bit lackluster, so the men took it upon themselves to recapitulate the performative zeal with a spirited round of *deusi khelne*—a call-and-response song and dance that engulfed the anthropologists with a parting taste of festival time in the hills.

Having completed their respective tasks, the two teams of researchers reconvened for a late-afternoon lunch hosted by the Lekh. Only the CRI research team, ethnic association leaders, and other VIPs were invited inside. The fare was abundant, savory, and whenever possible indigenous, except of course for the bottles of Royal Challenge Whisky which sat atop the tables. (It was safely assumed that the local hooch, a powerful concoction known as *raksi*, would be too biting for these government

FIGURE 4.6 *Dancing for the State*

men from the city.) The anthropologists, citing official duty, refrained from partaking of the whiskey. Others, like myself, lacked such an easy out and submitted to the Royal treatment.

The meal marked the end of a pivotal day for the Lekh. By the time we emerged from lunch, most of the locals had returned home. The CRI team was subsequently escorted down the hill to where their jeeps waited to take them back to Darjeeling Town. With the sun making a welcome monsoon visit, the general secretary, several others, and I stuck around to unwind and revisit the day's events. For everyone, it seemed a great relief that the CRI team was gone and that the study was over. Eventually, we made our way back to the road, where our vehicles were waiting. Just before we left, several of the ethnic association leaders huddled with a dozen or so local men—most of them branch representatives—to give a final word on their performance. The leaders from Darjeeling Town expressed great thanks for the locals' efforts, and while they could not prophesy the fate of their ST application, they were unanimously satisfied with the day's events. With only the occasional hiccup, their strategy had been executed to virtual perfection.

And with that, our vehicles started up, and we pulled away from the remote hamlet of Laharā Gāū. For the Lekh, their moment to shine was complete. As for the anthropologists of the CRI, their ethnographic obligations had only just begun. Come morning, they would begin anew with another study of yet another community seeking inclusion in India's list of Scheduled Tribes. Such were the demands of tribal recognition.

THE POLITICS OF ETHNOGRAPHIC MEDIATION

As was made spectacularly clear by the Lekh, the people of Darjeeling and the CRI team each arrived at this interface with their own ideals of the tribal subject and how s/he was to be known. For the communities under investigation, the perfect representation promised nothing less than ST status. It was therefore for "the good of the community" that ethnic leaders controlled who was spoken to and what was said. More often than not, these elites simply spoke on behalf of the locals, effectively displacing their voice at the very moment they held them up as exemplary tribal subjects.

Feeding the anthropologists carefully crafted statements, ethnic leaders constantly peered over the researchers' shoulders to be sure the data were being properly recorded. Misunderstandings were to be avoided at all costs. Vagaries were to be combed over or otherwise explained away. At times, the taking of field notes was an openly collaborative affair; at others, a contentious tussle over a basic aspect of ethnographic knowledge production.

The anthropologists, for their part, harbored their own desires for what they would call the "real" subjects of tribal ethnography. During and after their fieldwork, they frequently spoke in the lofty idioms of "knowing the essence of the field" and "getting in touch with the flavor of the ethnos." Despite their romantic ideals, the government anthropologists were well aware of the strategies of mediation at hand, and thus perennially frustrated by the stilted nature of their field. On several occasions, the CRI director quipped to me that "nothing was raw; everything was cooked." Months later, another team member similarly vented: "You went

FIGURE 4.7 *Monitoring and Mediating Ethnographic Data*

there. You saw it. It was all arranged for us. They led us in. We only met the people they [the ethnic leaders] wanted us to meet. And they had told them [the villagers] what to say. So what could we do?"

Contending with these politics of ethnographic (im)mediation was tiring.[7] The researchers clearly resented ethnic leaders' steering their gaze this way and that, mediating everything from their interactions with research subjects to the anthropologists' lunch—itself the most exquisite tribal cuisine. Yet despite their efforts to circumvent these tactics of mediation, the CRI team necessarily relied on ethnic leaders as ethnographic liaisons. What became unmistakably clear was that the politics of the moment were operating precisely at the epistemological level. All parties were acutely concerned with *how* the community was to be known. But this was no free epistemic field. Instead, the ways in which the community was to be known, shown, and adjudicated were over-determined by the rigid conceptual frameworks of ST certification itself. The mandates of ethnological compliance created constraints and opportunities for all parties involved.

At the center of these tactical negotiations were the residents of the model communities. They had been chosen by the "big men" (*thulo mānches*) of the ethnic association and placed under the looking glass of the Indian state. There, they were made the consummate tribal examples— the real types, as it were, to confirm the ideal type.[8] Yet many were only vaguely aware of the terms of their appearance. When I returned to Laharā Gāū a year later, the residents were uncertain when asked why the government officials had come to study them. With about twenty of us crammed in a room to watch videos I had brought with me of the survey, my research assistant, Eklavya, broached the subject:

> Eklavya: So what were they taking the information for?
>
> Older Man: It could be that we are the backward community.
>
> Eklavya: You mean an Other Backward Class [an official designation]?
>
> Older Man: No, not the OBC . . . ahmmmm. . . . What is it called? . . . ahmmm . . . tribal . . . for the tribal!
>
> Towns: And for the tribal, what does a community have to be or have? In other words, what are the criteria for being a tribal?
>
> Older Man: For becoming tribals . . . we cannot say.
>
> Eklavya: So they didn't tell you what the requirements were?
>
> Older Man: No, they didn't tell us anything. Even if they did, they might have only told our big shots.
>
> Eklavya: [to the group] So you all don't know what it takes to be tribal?
>
> [to which two middle-age women respond in frustration]
>
> Woman A: We are tiny, insignificant little bugs [*bhusunā*]. We wouldn't know!
>
> Woman B: We were told, "You should do all of these things." So in one day we brought all of these things from our houses and did it. Right?
>
> [to the group for affirmation. they affirm]

I was familiar with the interleavings of class and the politics of ethnic representation that this conversation articulated. Yet I left this interaction particularly struck by the woman's comment about she and her fellow villagers being "bugs" (*bhusunā*), removed from the know of tribal recognition. This seemed a most telling statement of subalternity. Thrust into the ethnographic spotlight, yet kept in the proverbial dark, these

FIGURE 4.8 *An Ethnic Leader Narrates an Exemplary Tribal Subject*

individuals had been called upon to sing, dance, and perform their rituals, but they were not to speak.[9] Neither, so it seemed a year later, were they to fully grasp the terms and ramifications of their performance. As they themselves said, "We are tiny, insignificant little bugs [*bhusunā*]. We wouldn't know!"

In contemplating these dynamics, we might profitably recall Kirk Dombrowski's point that "the articulation of a particular cultural vision requires the indirect, often unwilling cooperation of some whose role may be simply to drop off of the ethnographic radar."[10] Only, in the context of legal recognition, we may conversely ask: Just what kinds of subjects must appear on the ethnographic radar, and through what hierarchies of representation do they arrive there? Quite clearly, the exigencies of tribal recognition play upon and induce significant intra-community politics of representation.[11] The residents of Laharā Gāū, in this regard, lend a valuable subaltern voice to our understandings of these representational hierarchies. Comments like "we are bugs" expose the actual experiences of these dynamics of appearing and disappearing, speaking and not speaking, which attend legal recognition and its prescriptions of difference. And they do so in telling terms.

POLISHED GOATS, HYBRIDITY, AND THE NATION

The tactics of the studied created innumerable difficulties for the CRI team. Getting to the bottom of such obviously stilted affairs became a nearly impossible task. Several months after the survey, the director and I were sitting in his office in Kolkata discussing these issues when he guided my memory back to the first day of the survey when the charcoal-colored goats were sacrificed. "Most of those things we saw that day were arranged," he told me:

> I touched two of the goats, and when I looked at my fingers, there was black stuff on my fingers. So what they had told me was that you had to sacrifice black goats. But you see, [leaning toward me and lowering his voice as though revealing a secret] they couldn't find any perfectly black goats. So they had to put shoe polish on the goats. But you see a goat, when it is naturally black and one that is made to look black, they don't look right! [erupting in laughter]

That aspiring communities would go so far as to polish a goat is remarkable. The Lekh's application said that the goat should be black, and so it was made black. In this rather Baudrillardian moment,[12] the simulacra of the ethnological word came to precede its referent. The beheading of a *black* goat was subsequently held forth as a metonym of the Lekh's unique culture. It signaled, as the criteria would have it, "cultural distinctiveness." The gruesomeness of the rite further connoted "primitiveness," "backwardness," "animism," "savagery," "nature-worship," and other qualities of the tribe, as it has been popularly construed in India and beyond.

Chicaneries like the polishing of goats challenged the CRI team's expertise. Their bureaucratic duty, after all, was to verify—empirically—the state's criteria. To cross-check their findings, the team turned to secondary sources like colonial ethnologies, census data, and academic anthropologies. The available literatures were limited, however. From time to time, the CRI even floated the idea of making a surprise visit to Darjeeling to check the facts. This triggered panic-inflected rumors in Darjeeling that such a visit was imminent. Ultimately, though, it never happened.

Further difficulties arose with the issue of hybridity. Given the classificatory requisites of scheduling tribes—articulated most pointedly by the criteria of "cultural distinctiveness" and "geographic isolation"—traces of sociocultural mixture were deemed problematic by both sides. For the communities under investigation, the problem was especially acute. Since migrating to Darjeeling, they had "lost" (*harāyo*) many of the distinctive cultural, linguistic, and religious traits of their ancestors and contemporaries in Nepal. Paradoxically, these were precisely the kinds of traits that they needed to show the anthropologists.

These conundrums of transnational heritage arose with affective force. As these groups looked to Nepal to furnish the stuff of recognition in India, they ran the risk of confused nationality. Beyond just avoiding terms like "Nepali" and "migration" around the anthropologists, some groups went so far as to deny any sort of historical links with Nepal whatsoever. These revisionist histories claimed these groups were "sons of the soil," Darjeeling's original inhabitants. The claims to autochthony were dubious at best. And they often undermined the credibility of the community in the eyes of the anthropologists. But given the Gorkhas' anxieties over belonging in India (discussed in Chapter 1), it is easy to see why the CRI's probing of the groups' cross-border histories struck a nerve. The CRI researchers dug through these histories primarily in hopes of discovering the communities' tribal origins (more on this in a moment), but the communities under investigation feared more-exclusionary designs. Though overindulged, their fears were not entirely unfounded.

Many days after the survey, the director and I were discussing why it was necessary to explore the transnational history of these groups. He began by telling me that "all the peoples of Darjeeling are immigrant peoples."

To which I responded, "Do you think that will hurt their chances of becoming STs since their ancestors were immigrants and have origins in Nepal?"

"Maybe."

I continued, "Because I know there is a lot of insecurity in Darjeeling about being labeled as immigrants. But if India is a relatively young country, and they were all in Darjeeling when the nation was formed, then . . ."

The director cut me off before I could finish. "No," he told me, "India is a very old country. It's just our geographic borders have shifted recently." The comment and tone caught me off guard. In no way was he denying Indian citizenship to the people of Darjeeling. That was clear. But his statement evoked an all-too-familiar breed of primordial nationalism. To say "India is a very old country" skated blithely over the rocky decades of the twentieth century through which British India became not one but two (and later three) independent nation-states. His ethnocentric, ahistorical statement seemed to invoke an imagined community of India from which minorities who actually *had* histories—and transnational ones at that—might be easily excluded. For the people of Darjeeling, managing their histories of migration and hybridity was thus a legitimate concern in their attempts to become Scheduled Tribes *of India*.

For the government anthropologists, hybridity was a different sort of problem. As we saw in Chapter 2, hybridity has dogged government ethnology since the colonial days—particularly the blurry lines between tribes and Hindu castes. This remains the case today. How then did the

CRI anthropologists get around this problem to fulfill their classificatory duties? While observing the survey, I could not understand the apparent fixation with seemingly trivial empirical details—be they etchings on a bamboo stick or the names of each herb used in ritual practice. To my eye, these details had little to do with the five criteria being checked. But to the government anthropologists, they served a different analytic purpose. By way of a curiously allochronistic logic,[13] these details were understood to be vestiges of a community's pure tribal past—a past hidden in the present, yet revealing the community's true identity.[14] As the CRI director put it: "To see their tribal origin, you have to study the minutiae, the very detailed differences." An attention to detail, in other words, was the key to unlocking the classificatory riddles of hybridity.

One afternoon in Kolkata, I pressed the CRI team on this issue. "As anthropologists whose job it is to classify people," I asked them, "how do you deal with the question of mixture?" The director responded:

> Yes, this is a very relevant question for our work. Well, there are two things. The first is: To what extent the tribal characteristics have been maintained as yet in the current culture? And the second is whether these groups also maintain a position in the caste system, in the general Hindu caste system. In other words, whether there is a relevant hierarchy that we maintain, whether this is applicable.

More so than his empiricist presumption that evidence of tribal origins was hiding in the details of current culture, the director's response is notable for his use of the first person: viz—the issue of whether the communities of Darjeeling maintained the kind of "hierarchy that *we* maintain." The anthropologists with whom I was speaking (as was the case with the entire eight-person team) were predominantly of upper-caste Hindu descent. Was the use of the first person "we," then, a subtle indexing of a Hindu identity from and against which tribal alterity was being rendered? The ensuing discussion would suggest that it was. As the conversation turned to the Gorkhas' history, this issue came up again.

> Director: [Within their history], there are dual religions in place, the Brahmanical and the tribal. The Great Tradition and the Little Tradition.

> There was religious assimilation, but due to lack of proper institutional support, a proper cultural assimilation couldn't take place. It was, if I may say so, not a proper assimilation.
>
> Amit: Yes, they are trying to make their own Great Tradition with this Gorkha identity . . . as though it's a form of Hindu practice. [Previously] they have been saying, "Let us all be known as Gorkhas to become part of the Hindu fold." They think that it is to be boiled down as a melting pot, but it doesn't work like that *here*.

Note how the talk of the Great versus Little traditions marks Hinduism (or the "Brahmanical") as the established center against which tribal alterity (or lack thereof) is being judged. Consider also the concluding statement: "It doesn't work like that *here*." The deictic "here" tacitly marks Kolkata—home of the Hindu "we"—as the orthodox center of ethnological distinction. Such statements casually deny Gorkha identity and its constituent ethnic groups on the grounds that they violate the norms of the ethnographic first-person and *his* homeland. Presumptions of purity and the nation thereby informed tribal recognition in subtle, but powerful ways.

These were not official rulings. They were off-the-cuff renderings of difference. In Gadamerian terms,[15] such *prejudices of understanding* may be said to be part and parcel of the ethnographic enterprise, broadly speaking. Here, though, they take a more pointed form. It is precisely through these subjective dimensions of knowledge production that state ethnography often smuggles back into the equation many of the prejudices that positive discrimination is designed to mitigate. Wittingly and unwittingly, government anthropologists animate tribal recognition with moral sensibilities that continually exceed its formal bureaucratic—purportedly "secular"—designs. State ethnography, in turn, comes to function as an instrument of what Corrigan and Sayer have termed *moral regulation*: "a project of normalizing, rendering natural, and taken for granted, in a word 'obvious,' what are in fact ontological and epistemological premises of a particular and historical form of social order."[16]

The use of the first-person, deictics, and off-the-cuff distinctions offers subtle clues to these ideological underpinnings. Other evidence is less subtle. Documents obtained from the federal government in Delhi rejected one community's application on the following grounds:

> Though [the community] had tribal origin, with the passage of time and due to their contact with exogenous people and their contacts with the Hindu tradition, they are gradually assimilating into the Great Tradition. It will be then a retrograde step if they are included into the list of Scheduled Tribes.[17]

Echoing the logics of the "Great Tradition," its vested teleology, and associated assessments of hybridity, the statement recapitulates the prejudices hinted at earlier—albeit with far more authority. The cracks in the secular project of scheduling tribes, in this instance, extend to far higher levels of government. Especially amid the escalating politics of tribal recognition, these systemic contradictions only weaken the already strained credibility of India's affirmative action system. These contradictions issue from and contribute to what is now widely seen as India's "crisis of secular nationalism"—a crisis colored by resurgent communalisms and incessant demands on an overburdened, inconsistent, and programmatically partial state.[18]

SUPPLICATION

Several days into the Ethnographic Survey, the CRI director and I struck up our first conversation about our shared craft of anthropology. With his team scattered about the village conducting interviews and documenting the ritual accoutrements of the local *jhankri* (shaman), we finally had a moment to get to know each other. Our conversation didn't last long. A messenger soon arrived, summoning the director to an important meeting. Not wanting to abandon our discussion, he invited me along.

The messenger led us down a trail to a one-room schoolhouse where two well-dressed ethnic leaders waited. They greeted the director nervously, and then had a quick word with the teacher. Seconds later, she and her students filed out of the schoolhouse, leaving us to find our places at child-size tables. The ethnic leaders had an agenda. But the director immediately launched into a lecture on state anthropology in India—clearly a continuation of the conversation we had begun just minutes before. In English, he explained:

> You see the type of anthropology that you practice in America and the type we are doing here in India, there is something different there. Ethnography is about capturing the minutiae of culture . . . In America, or the UK, there are all the great writers there, whether it is Margaret Meade or Malinowksi. [The ethnic leaders nod along, unsure of where this lecture is leading.] What we do as anthropologists is we are specialists in observation, so we observe these things. . . . You know, participant observation like Malinowski! But here we cannot do this. We have been given petitions from these hill communities and we have been sent here to perform studies, so how can we do participant observation? Like these rituals and things that you have laid out for us today [turning to the ethnic leaders], you see these are just duplicates of culture. They are not the original culture. [The ethnic leaders try to interject, but he speaks over them.] They are duplicates! They are not the original forms of culture. [He becomes argumentative, as the ethnic leaders again try to claim otherwise.] No . . . You see this is not original . . . The only way to know what is the original is to do participant observation and stay with a community for some time. Like Malinowski . . . These groups submit these petitions to the government, and then the files come to us and we have to go out into the field to observe these groups. So what is the role of the anthropologist? He is not an administrator or a politician. He is an advocate. We are advocates for these groups . . . [a thoughtful, agonizing pause] . . . if the criteria are fulfilled.

"But sir, we are a vanishing tribe," one of the leaders pleads desperately.

"No! I don't agree," the director replies sternly, "This term 'vanishing tribe' should be taken as a derogatory term. You are not vanishing. Your population is not decreasing. How can you say you are vanishing?"

The leaders struggle to find ground to stand on: "We have been so oppressed. Look at me, I have graduated with a degree in mathematics, but I am the first and only one in my whole family who has done this."

"Yes, he is the exception," the other adds.

The director listens, cigarette in hand, shaking his head. He acknowledges their economic condition but tells them, "If you can light the fire of aspiration in your people, you will reap the fruits in the form of your children, and your tribe will not vanish . . . The main function of your association should thus be to motivate people. You have to do the role of the catalyst."

Their appeals grow more desperate. "Let me express our experiences here in Darjeeling. He and I, we *are* doing the role of catalyst, but we have been oppressed—economically and by population. So we are thinking that you can help save our community." The director continues smoking, shaking his head, denying them. "You are our savior! You are not our inspector," the ethnic leader begs, his hands pressed together in prayer position.

"No!" the director retorts. "I am not a man to be prayed to!"

.   .   .

The conversation had taken a dark turn. The meeting ended awkwardly soon thereafter. On the way out of the schoolhouse, I caught a last glimpse of the ethnic leaders. They looked devastated. Their special meeting had gone terribly awry. As the director and I climbed back up the hill, he seemed especially irked. "Sometimes so much is said," he confided in a winded voice. "Perhaps I have said too much, but ahhh . . ." giving it a shrug and carrying on up the trail.

In the remaining days of the survey, I witnessed the director countenance several similar scenarios. Ethnic leaders constantly wanted to have a private word with him, constantly wanted to pull him away from his research to persuade him by other means. Both artful and heartfelt, these demands were difficult to manage. They tugged on sensibilities that belied the prescribed formalism of state ethnography. And while such pleas were ventured and received with visible discomfort, both sides frequently appealed to emotional registers, as we saw with the leader's "We have been so oppressed . . . You are our savior" and the anthropologist's "We are advocates." These articulations of desperation and care may be integral to the calculus of recognition,[19] but they fit uncomfortably within the classificatory moment itself. Hence the director's agonizing pause before his qualification, "if the criteria are met." Hence the regret-tinged "sometimes so much is said . . . Perhaps I have said too much."

These affective exchanges offer a nuanced picture of late liberal governance. We see here a decidedly human face of the postcolonial state contending with the poignant demands of its citizens. Importantly, the ethnic leaders' supplications were just part of their multidimensional appeal to the ethnological and moral sensibilities of the Indian state. Figured as an emblematic moment of Indian *political society*, this testy schoolhouse encounter epitomizes the contingencies with which governmental agencies like the CRI, as Partha Chatterjee would have it, "descend from the high ground [of universal rights, equality, and ethnological ideals] to the terrain of political society in order to renew their legitimacy as providers of well-being and there to confront whatever is the current configuration of politically mobilized demands."[20] Shot through with power and persuasions of multiple kinds, here again the Ethnographic Survey proved to be an interface in the truest sense of the word.

IMPLICATED

I was, of course, present. And like it or not, I often stood in as the face of Western, academic anthropology. This subject-position introduced its own contingencies into the encounter. I have little doubt that my presence threw a wrench into the ethnic leaders' plans to convince the director of their community's tribal worth. Certainly, I brought on the director's contentious lecture. As often happened in my research, my professional identity instigated the performance of anthropological ideals—only this time it was not the stuff of ethnic song and dance being performed, but instead a powerful narrative of expert identity.

Anthropology's implications in these circumstances run deep. It is not surprising that the histories covered in the previous two chapters found their way into this signature moment of the ethno-contemporary in Darjeeling. Take, for instance, what occurred in the final moments of the Ethnographic Survey: Having made it through their day of study—again involving shamanic rituals, caves, and lengthy interview sessions—the Molung community was about to bid farewell to the CRI team. Some thirty or so members of the model community stood back as the CRI team prepared to climb into their jeeps. Since I had caught a ride with the team, I too was about to climb aboard, when the president of the

Molung ethnic association stepped forward from the crowd. There in front of the audience—the government anthropologists on one side and the local community on the other—he grabbed my hand in a protracted, unrelenting handshake. "So, Dr. Townsend," he said to me, but for all to hear, "having seen the demonstrations of all the different communities, what do you say about our performance here?"

All eyes were on me, just as he intended. Standing there, his hand still clutching mine, it was clear that he wanted my expert opinion. More than that, he wanted the authoritative endorsement of a Western academic anthropologist verifying that, yes, his community was tribal. From the corner of my eye, I caught a glimpse of the CRI anthropologists. They too were keen to hear my response. I was in a difficult position. How was I to support the Molung's quest for the recognition and rights they needed without endorsing—and being folded into—a system in dire need of critique? Realizing my compromised situation, I scrambled for a diplomatic answer.

"Well, in my opinion, I think the format is somewhat unfair to everybody, including the anthropologists and communities like yours," I said.

Seeing that I was being elusive, he responded, "Well, just what *is* your opinion then? What do you think?" . . . still gripping my hand, unwilling to let go.

"Well, having seen the others I would say that you have done well for yourselves, and that your community has done a good job today."

Realizing he was not going to get the definitive answer he wanted, he cracked a smile and began shaking my hand vigorously, saying, "Okay, thank you very much, sir, thank you very much," seemingly parlaying my response in his community's favor.

Finally, he released my hand and I turned away, eyes down, embarrassed by the expectations put upon me, and disappointed by my inability to help the people who were staring at me, awaiting some authoritative claim to bolster their case. As I turned, the anthropologists quickly diverted their attention away from me—as though they hadn't been watching. Somewhat ashamed, I made my way toward the vehicles and bid *namaste* to the local community before climbing into the back of the jeep—itself a compromised position.

As we rolled away, the CRI team began to poke fun at the situation I had just endured, laughing about how I had been put on the spot. The ribbing seemed to be an expression of their growing familiarity with me and perhaps an inclusion of me into their group. I feigned good humor until the jokes trickled off, and then settled in for what was to be a long ride home. Unlike the morning's ride with these civil servants, itself filled with excitement to be crossing over the lines of tribal recognition, the return trip left me only with the somber task of coming to terms with my own illusions of staying above the fray of this always already anthropological circumstance. Each of us, so it seemed, had a role to play—and historical burdens to bear—at this interface of the ethno-contemporary.

THE ARTIFICE OF ETHNOGRAPHY

The Ethnographic Survey proved a pivotal encounter of a people and the state. Yet there is more to observe in this meeting of anthropologists and tribes than just the extended collusions of ethnological thought and liberal governance. The actual dynamics of this encounter alert us to new developments on the horizons of ethnopolitical becoming. The tactics deployed by Darjeeling's aspiring tribes—the repurposing of governmental categories, the politics of mediation, the affective supplications, etc.— show the inventive means by which marginalized communities are renegotiating their place in the nation-state. We catch important glimpses of the political possibilities and impossibilities that adhere to these regimes of recognition—as well the socialities and subjectivities that animate these forms of state-sponsored multiculturalism. The questions here concern what kinds of difference count in this late liberal order, what do not, and what are the forces tipping these scales of inclusion and exclusion, affirmation and denial.

In India, state ethnography directly informs these reckonings. Ethnology's governmental history (charted in previous chapters) bears heavily upon these operations. Yet when we move beyond the formalism of scheduling tribes, we gain new understandings of how tribal recognition works and how its ethno-logics are actualized in and through these encounters with the multicultural state. For all parties, the contingencies of ethnographic practice afforded a crucial space of maneuver—for Darjeeling's aspiring tribes, a cunning tactics of concealing, revealing, and turning back the state's ethno-logics upon itself; for government anthropologists, the articulation of *prejudices of understanding*, only some of which have a place in the written policies of the state. In these throes of classification, ethnological governmentality and its moral regulations of difference took a decidedly human face and found decidedly human objects. But these, of course, were not objects at all, but rather people with transformative ethnological capacities, strategies, and desires. Precisely as an interface, then, the Ethnographic Survey offers telling portrayals of the ethno-contemporary in India.

But perhaps we shouldn't get so carried away by this classificatory moment and its theoretical promise. Whether we slow it down and scrutinize the interface in real time, or speed it up and see it as part of a longer trajectory of identity politics in Darjeeling, the Ethnographic Survey may not be what it originally seemed. Even at the point of study, key players doubted its veracity. The general secretary of the left-out communities called the survey a *dekhāwati*, a drama, an "eyewash." The CRI director similarly griped that it was all "cooked," not "raw." Yet both men committed themselves—and their respective tribes—to this moment in earnest. What, then, are we to make of this apparatus—this artifice—of state ethnography? What are they?

If the charged dynamics of the Ethnographic Survey are any indication, a great deal should be made of it. In this regard, it is not merely the stakes, magnitude, or genuineness of this spectacle that grabs the attention, but rather the undeniable compulsion to participate. This compulsion invokes Derek Sayer's point about the performative nature of state power. As he notes, "Individuals live in the lie that is 'the state' and it lives through their performance... What is demanded of them is only—but precisely—performances."[21] The point spans the ethnographic interface. Whether we are talking about the director, the general secretary, or the various other subjects who constituted this moment, the suspension of critique functioned as a prerequisite to being part of—and playing one's part in—this theater of ethnographic reckoning. Though less graphic than the savage rituals that colored this encounter, here we find perhaps the most compelling evidence of recognition's ambiguously coercive/consensual power.[22]

That power, however, proves categorically uneven in its designs, implications, and compulsions. Government anthropologists and well-intended ethnic leaders may have dominated this struggle for the ethnographic truth, but there was always someone else in the frame. Thrust into the gaze of the postcolonial state—and there made impossibly central but silent, past but present, ideal but real—was the purported tribal subject. There s/he was made the ethnological example—the sublime object of recognition's desire. This was the figure—or figment—upon which this whole moment turned. In this phantasmatic subject rested the hopes of a people and the presumed veracity and power of state ethnography itself. In the crosshairs of the state, recognition's tautologies would not—and could not—be denied. The circular logics were too perfect. The stakes were too compelling.

Alas, becoming tribal requires a good deal more than compliance with the designs and desires of the postcolonial state—as the people of Darjeeling would come to learn. In spite of all that went into this classificatory encounter, at the end of the day, it remained only one moment in a much more complicated *process* of tribal recognition. Now that the Ethnographic Survey was complete, the files and fate of these "left-out" communities were about to enter into another realm of governance—this one bearing its own forms of technocratic knowledge, power, and politics.

CHAPTER 5

SOFT SCIENCE IN HARD PLACES
Government Anthropologists and Their Knowledge

ON JULY 27, 2006, the much-anticipated Ethnographic Survey of Darjeeling drew to a close. The ten communities under investigation had done all they could to convince the government anthropologists of their tribal identity. No one knew whether it would be enough to bring Scheduled Tribe status to these groups and tribal autonomy to the region, but the communities had done their best. All they could do now was wait.

For the government anthropologists, the survey was nothing short of exhausting. The slippery terrain and equally slippery informants were difficult enough. The journalists and television cameras only made matters worse. By the survey's end, tempers were running short and some of the researchers' health was failing (heart troubles). It was trying work, to say the least. Yet despite it all, these civil servants had also done their best. Now with their bags packed and field notes safely stowed, they climbed into their jeeps for one last ride through the Darjeeling Hills. A three-hour trip to the plains below took them to New Jalpaiguri, where they caught the night train back to their homes and offices in Kolkata.

RECOGNITION FROM THE INSIDE OUT

This chapter shifts attention to the lives and work of government anthropologists.[1] It follows the CRI team and the files of Darjeeling aspiring tribes back to Kolkata and beyond in order to understand the inner workings of today's ethnographic state.[2] These bureaucratic procedures are a vital part of tribal recognition and its politics. They determine the conferral of Scheduled Tribe status, as well as the experiences of those vying for it. A study of the Indian bureaucracy—and in particular, its anthropologists—is therefore indispensable to understanding how affirmative action works and how its ethno-logics impact minorities in need. The chapter accordingly mobilizes the anthropology of bureaucracy to examine the governing procedures that shape the ethno-contemporary in India.[3] Turning the ethnographic lens upon government anthropologists and their knowledge, it interrogates tribal recognition from the inside out.

The journey from Darjeeling to Kolkata was one I came to know well. Traveling to Kolkata for archival work, I became a frequent visitor to the CRI's offices in the months and years following the Ethnographic Survey. What began as a chance encounter among anthropologists in the field gradually developed into more meaningful connections. My experiences with the team emerged as a methodological complement to my work with Darjeeling's aspiring tribes. I spent many afternoons whiling away the time in the CRI's offices, sipping tea, and trading stories. These experiences gave me an inside look at the people, processes, and politics of tribal recognition. Watching these civil servants write up their work and defend their findings, I came to a greater appreciation of the quandaries of being a government anthropologist. Their quandaries mapped to those of late liberalism more generally. The CRI team faced impossible challenges: on the one hand were the demands of minorities desperate for governmental attention; on the other were the burdens of manning a massive affirmative action system that was under-resourced, over-stretched, and riddled with contending forms of expertise and politics. The team's work was under constant attack from technocrats who questioned the value of their soft science. The difficulties of fieldwork, in this case, were matched only by the team's struggles to advance ethnological knowledge through an increasingly technocratic state.

Amid the banality of the average workday, my discussions with the CRI team frequently turned to Darjeeling's aspiring tribes and their files. Gradually, the anthropologists started opening up to me about what was going on behind the scenes, both in their offices and in the higher echelons of government. It became clear that the files were tangled up in a politics of difference that was operating well above the CRI team. There was more in the offing, after all, than just ST status. Regional autonomy and a possible end to Darjeeling's violent history of subnationalism were also at stake. Government anthropologists, in theory, played an integral role in this calculus of tribal recognition and autonomy. In bureaucratic practice, however, the CRI team was largely shut out of the decisions being made. The jettisoning of their expertise angered the team, and they frequently vented their frustrations to me—another anthropologist who might understand.

By sharing their lives and work, these civil servant anthropologists offered me an inside look at the processes and paradoxes of tribal recognition in late liberal India. One cannot deny the colonial antecedents. As the CRI's director once told me with a wry grin, "Anthropology in India is a colonial product. And we are its subjects. But we don't mind." That said, these anthropologists are part of a far larger governmental apparatus comprising contending political agendas, technocratic dispensations, and bureaucratic constraints. These conditions introduce a number of difficulties into the scheduling of tribes, which affect both the government anthropologists and the communities they study. Indeed, these conditions frequently translate into one community's success and another's failure in attaining ST status. Along the way, they fundamentally alter how minorities understand and experience the postcolonial state.

Scholars have grown increasingly interested in minorities' struggles for recognition and social justice. From James Clifford's groundbreaking study "Identity at Mashpee" in the United States to Elizabeth Povinelli's work in Australia and Charles Hale's in Latin America, the courtroom has been a key site for examining processes of legal recognition.[4] But the courtroom is not the only site where difference, recognition, and rights are adjudicated. The reckoning of tribal difference in India typically happens deep within the technocratic corridors of the state—far from the public's eye. Shadowing civil servants offers a way into these corridors and a method for understanding how social justice is administered. Adopting this technique, I take a page from the exemplary work of Akhil Gupta, Mathew Hull, Thomas Blom Hansen, and Finn Stepputat to shed some light on these less well-known inner workings of postcolonial bureaucracy in South Asia.[5] Humanizing and disaggregating the state, as

Gupta argues, is a prerequisite to understanding its (dys)functionality.[6] My interface-based approach works to extend this line of critique one step further, so as to consider how the internal procedures of affirmative action translate into the lives of those who do—and do not—fall under its ambit of recognition.

The need for this type of study is particularly acute in India, where, despite the attention to its colonial predecessor, the functioning of today's ethnographic state remains under-explored.[7] The inattention obviates crucial considerations of the policies, politics, and actual people that shape tribal recognition *within* the Indian government. Heeding broader calls for ethnographic engagement with civil servants,[8] here I ask what those who work the front lines of affirmative action might teach us about the growing problem of tribal recognition in India. I do so through those who know the problem best: government anthropologists.

Let me begin by examining the inexorably social nature of recognition and state knowledge production more generally.[9]

PRODUCING STATE ETHNOLOGY

Once the CRI team returned to Kolkata, a new phase of recognition began. Now that fieldwork was done, the team set about writing the official report that would be the basis of the "left-out" communities' ST applications going forward. Having observed the Ethnographic Survey, I was keen to know how the team would reconstruct the "truths" from the "facts" of the spectacular event.[10]

The writing of the report proved a social affair. Soon after the survey, the CRI sent forms to the ethnic associations of the groups in question, demanding extensive information, including: population distribution; marriage, divorce, and widowhood rates; literacy, occupation, and income figures; and a range of other demographic metrics. The "census form," as it came to be known, engendered both difficulty and opportunity for these groups. On the one hand, it called for data that neither local knowledge nor governmental records could provide. On the other, it transferred the onus of enumeration back onto the communities themselves—effectively enabling them to tailor their demographic profile to meet what they guessed to be that of a proper tribe.

Ethnic leaders and politicians convened urgent meetings to discuss how they should fill in the "census form." I was invited to attend several of these sessions. At one of the meetings—held in the plush offices of Ram Bahadur Koli at Darjeeling's Department of Information and Cultural Affairs—a high-ranking official explained that the local block development offices (BDOs) did not have the required information on these groups (since they were not already STs). Nevertheless, if the ethnic leaders were clever, they could have the BDO stamp the forms, thereby giving the appearance that the figures were official. With this plan in place, the conversation then shifted to how these groups should answer specific questions. Everyone agreed that under no circumstances should they write that they were Hindu. Regarding education and economic status, one leader opined, "We should be 95% backwards, at least!" Then jokingly, "What does this term 'illiterate' mean anyhow?" His joke elicited laughter, but also hinted at the doctoring of information that was to occur later in the offices of these ethnic associations.

Having formed a collective strategy of sorts, the ethnic leaders adjourned to tackle their respective forms. For groups that had previously endeavored to enumerate their local populations, only minor tweaking was required to fill out the government's form. Others used what little census information could be derived from local voter registration lists and then added an estimated population growth rate to arrive at current numbers. Others simply made up numbers to match what they perceived to be the appropriate profile. During one of these doctoring meetings, I pulled the communities' newly appointed demographer aside after he had presented his figures to association leaders. Having heard him lament the "technical difficulties" of understanding the "census form" and filling out its fields, I was curious to know how he had gone about ascertaining the required information. "So, were you going village to village?" I asked.

"No, I was just doing the math," he told me. "We just had to make the numbers work out perfectly"—the implication being that the numbers were largely fudged. His number-crunching served his community well; the government accepted the information. Others weren't as careful. When government statisticians caught the inconsistencies in the figures, the forms were sent back to the communities for further correction. Their profiles of backwardness literally did not add up. The CRI duly noted the lack of honesty.

Trust figured prominently into these reckonings. Throughout 2006 and 2007, delegations from Darjeeling made numerous trips to the CRI, bringing books, essays, memorandums, and various other persuasions to bolster their cases. These face-to-face exchanges made a difference, but not always in intended ways. The CRI researchers came to know certain ethnic leaders as pushy and full of cunning, whereas others were respected as earnest and helpful intermediaries. Some cases were flagged as problematic, not because the community did or did not conform to the criteria of Scheduled Tribes, but because of their leaders' questionable tactics.

The government anthropologists were wary of, but largely reliant on, the information provided. With only one day of fieldwork per community, the team had limited ethnographic data to work with. While they turned to governmental and academic literatures to cross-check the submitted materials, they couldn't possibly verify all the evidence presented to them. From time to time, the CRI expressed interest in returning to Darjeeling for additional fieldwork, but their resources did not permit a follow-up visit. The ethnographic portions of the report were therefore written solely on the basis of one day of fieldwork per group. Given the paucity of empirical data, the auto-ethnological essays, books, and documentaries submitted by the groups enabled the CRI to draft a more robust report.

The official Ethnographic Report, once complete, was a sprawling document of more than two hundred pages, comprising both qualitative and quantitative data. Because there is no template for these reports, the CRI was left largely to its own designs to present its findings. A short introduction described the nature of the study. Each community was subsequently allotted one chapter. The descriptions borrowed heavily from the materials written and submitted by the communities. The chapters contained discussions of classic ethnological topics like rites of birth, marriage, death; religious beliefs and practice; dress; material artifacts; language. Appended to these descriptions were tables compiled by the statistical division of the CRI, enumerating metrics such as population, average income, education levels, and literacy rates. Much of this quantitative data was gleaned from the aforementioned "census forms."

The report took a year to complete. In the fall of 2007, it was finally sent to the Writers' Building (West Bengal's state capital) for processing. Now that it was a "policy matter," as the CRI members liked to say, the file was "out of their hands." The institutional travels of these cases, however, were just beginning.

BUREAUCRATIC CIRCULATIONS

By design, the CRI's report would embark on a convoluted bureaucratic journey taking it from Kolkata to New Delhi and into the highest reaches of government. Moving from ministry to ministry and desk to desk, the files would cross numerous thresholds of technocratic expertise and power. How they crossed those thresholds would determine the outcome of the cases under consideration. Mapping these bureaucratic procedures, we may consult Mathew Hull's recent work on the postcolonial state in Pakistan.[11] Tracking the social life of documents within the government, Hull underscores the analytic value of attention to both the production *and* circulation of governmental documents. In that spirit, the figure below maps the typical path of a successful ST application.

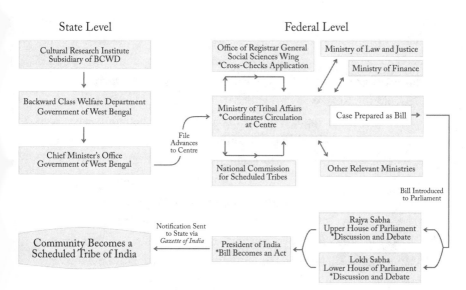

FIGURE 5.1 *Bureaucratic Path of an ST Application*

Anthropologically speaking, ST cases face their biggest test in the Social Sciences Wing of the Registrar General of India (RGI), located in New Delhi. The RGI's social scientists cross-check the report against available literatures on the community in question. These literatures often date back to colonial ethnology. As one of the RGI social scientists explained to me during an interview in Delhi:

> Before independence, there were these reports, because when they were taking the census, there would be supplemental ethnological enquiries. Like back in the 1890s, there was the *Tribes and Castes of Bengal*, published by, published by . . . [a searching pause] . . . His name was Risley. Yes, Risley. And there you will find very detailed ethnographic information on all of these groups . . . What we do is try to see if these groups were traditionally tribal. Because nowadays you will not get that level of primitiveness, so what we do by consulting these literatures is to see the traditional tribal characteristics. So the question is: At that time, were they primitive tribals?

The Risley he recalled was none other than the H. H. Risley discussed in Chapter 2—the consummate colonial ethnologist qua bureaucrat. The fact that the work of Risley and many other nineteenth-century ethnologists continues to inform the process of tribal recognition shows the residual coloniality of these proceedings. And while the RGI social scientists purport to be looking only for *past* primitive characteristics, their actual rulings often contradict this claim by insisting upon *present* primitiveness (more on these allochronistic judgments in a moment).[12]

Should the RGI or any other department along the way find problems with a community's application, the file may be returned to the state level, at which point the CRI/TRI will conduct further inquiries and/or revise their earlier work. The file then is circulated through the system again. If it fails for a second time, the case will be terminated. From start to finish, the process takes years, often decades, as files are lost, found, shelved, scrutinized, passed over, and passed on. The bureaucratic life of these files bespeaks the state's technocratic complexity and its seemingly interminable temporality. This protracted temporality—what I call the *bureaucratic durée*—delays the administration of much-needed rights and benefits. In the process, it only further frustrates the minorities in question. *Waiting for the state* figures here as endemic to the politics of tribal recognition in India—and a signature condition of late liberal governance writ large.[13] It is how recognition "works."

For communities, navigating the process requires patience and political agility—typically in realms from which these groups have been marginalized. Take, for instance, the Tamangs of West Bengal, who achieved ST status in 2003. Spearheaded by the All India Tamang Buddhist Association (AITBA) headquartered in Darjeeling, the Tamangs relied on extensive auto-ethnological research to bolster their case. Tamang leaders and CRI members alike spoke of the excellent rapport and outstanding ethnographic performances during their application process. Still, the Tamangs realized that more was required. Throughout their twenty-two-year struggle for ST status, the Tamangs sent seventy-seven delegations to Delhi alone, augmenting these efforts with hunger strikes, underground political networking, and the lobbying of multiple agencies at the Centre and state levels. Despite their perseverance, it took a final push from the chief minister of Sikkim to bring ST recognition to the Tamangs of neighboring West Bengal. These tactics illustrate the political patience and wherewithal necessary to attain ST status. Performing the "tribal slot" is not enough.[14]

For aspiring tribes, the ability to wait out the bureaucratic durée is essential. To borrow a term from Elizabeth Povinelli, "endurance" proves vital to the attainment of recognition and rights.[15] Aspirant minorities must learn to deal with the state's constant deferral and delay. Frustrating though they may be, these are the conditions through which the state comes into existence—and is experienced—as an arbiter of difference and social justice. These technocratic complexities and consequent temporalities are best understood not as by-products of bureaucratic sprawl, but rather as operative modes of state power itself. They are the circumstances that marginalized minorities must endure if they are to count in the eyes of the state.

INTERNAL DEBATES

Government anthropologists and ST cases move in realms that are crosscut by contending forms of expertise. As files circulate through the state, they meet with often radically different epistemological orientations.

CRI anthropologists may claim that once they send their report to the Government of West Bengal, it is "a policy decision" and thus "out of their hands." But the reality is that government anthropologists must constantly defend their knowledge throughout the entire process.

For example, in July 2005, the RGI–Social Sciences Wing found problems with two of the CRI's ST cases. The files belonged to two communities of Darjeeling who had applied for ST status in the 1990s (much earlier than the "left-out" communities surveyed in 2006). Nearly a decade after these cases were initiated, the RGI in Delhi decided to return the files to the CRI in Kolkata with fourteen points that needed to be addressed. Among these were concerns over the following: the dubious autochthony of the groups; evidence of religious, economic, and cultural change since the days when they were "nomadic pastoralists, hunters, and shifting cultivators"; their lack of isolation in Darjeeling; the presence of modern amenities such as radios, televisions, and cinemas; and the aforementioned opinion that their "gradual assimilation into the Great Tradition" meant that it would be "a retrograde step" to recognize them as STs. Contrary to what one of their members had told me, clearly the RGI was looking for more than just *past* primitiveness.

Naturally, the CRI anthropologists were upset to have their work returned to them as unsatisfactory, but they addressed each point in earnest. Drawing from their ethnographic research, the CRI's formal response contested many of the RGI's claims. Conceptually, where the RGI cited Dalton (1872), the CRI called upon twentieth-century anthropologists like Malinowksi, Dube, and Pignede, along with a lengthy bibliography of others, to challenge the RGI's expertise. "Assimilating into the Great Tradition does not mean the eradication of Tribal characteristics," the CRI wrote. "The question of retrogression . . . is perhaps value loaded and bias." Like good ethnographers, the CRI marshaled firsthand evidence to support their claims that the communities fulfilled the five ST criteria. Having laid out their case, the CRI closed with the "hope, [that] considering all the above points with empathy, the authority would agree with the recommendation of the State Government to include [these communities] as the two new Scheduled Tribes of the State of West Bengal."[16]

I highlight this dispute between the RGI in Delhi and the CRI in Kolkata to illustrate the ethnological discrepancies *within* the postcolonial state. These disagreements between governmental bodies call to mind Philip Abrams's reminder that "the state is a unified symbol of an actual disunity."[17] Hansen and Stepputat have similarly noted the postcolonial state to be "amorphous and bereft of any unifying and encompassing rationale."[18] Extending this line of critique, the dispute between the RGI and the CRI brings to light what we may see as *partialities* of the Indian state. My double entendre is intentional—with *partiality* denoting (a) the Hindu-centricity of this "secular" multicultural order (namely, the talk of the "Great Tradition" and retrograde steps) and (b) the fragmented, incoherent, and incomplete nature of the state itself. What is remarkable in this instance is how these *partialities* work together to delay and deny rights to minorities. Suffice it to say, these communities learned the hard way about the prejudices and irrationalities through which affirmative action is conferred and denied.

Both the CRI and the RGI–Social Sciences Wing are staffed by anthropologists and social scientists. Ostensibly, then, they would share an epistemological affinity. Yet, despite their allied expertise, here we see each challenging the other's knowledge. If agencies this closely aligned have troubles with agreement and mutual intelligibility, what may be said of the epistemological differences that ST files must span as they circulate through the branches of government that are not oriented toward the social sciences?

As files move from one department to another, they cross into different technocratic camps, often defined by different epistemological commitments. The expertise of one agency may be vastly different from that of the next agency. ST files face the daunting challenge of spanning these *expertise gaps*. Such gaps have become commonplace as the postcolonial state expands its technocratic repertoire. As Hansen and Stepputat have argued, "The practices and sites of governance have also become more dispersed, diversified, and fraught with internal inconsistencies and contradictions."[19] What I am calling expertise gaps is one example of these internal inconsistencies. And while they contradict the purported rationality of state bureaucracy,[20] they remain part of the technocratic evolution of modern governance itself. The irony, of course, is that this internal dissonance ac-crues in the name of an ever-specialized "science" of government. Exper-tise gaps, nevertheless, are instrumental to recognition's (dys)functionality. As we saw during the classificatory moment itself and then again in the RGI's ruling, they are sites where individual agents and agencies imbue the state with their own biases and partialities. In subtle but important ways, these partialities enable the ideological functioning of the state.[21]

For the CRI, the challenge goes beyond establishing mutual intel-ligibility between contending technocratic camps. It requires defending the very craft of ethnography itself. The experiences of anthropologists suggest mixed results at best.

THE POLITICS WITHIN

Late in 2007, I was spending an afternoon at the CRI when the direc-tor updated me on the cases from the 2006 Ethnographic Survey and its subsequent Ethnographic Report: "These policy makers have their own political issues. So it [the Ethnographic Report] is in their hands now. They have not done anything with it. It is difficult because all these ethnic associations come here and pressurize us . . . But it is the bureaucrats at the Writers' Building that have it."

"Yes." Amit, another CRI anthropologist, concurred. "The local bu-reaucrats have their own political games they are playing."

This was fifteen months after the Ethnographic Survey. Why had the report not been sent to the Centre (Delhi)? Everyone assumed the delay was tied to Darjeeling's pending bid for tribal autonomy. As the Sixth Schedule bill neared parliament in 2007, questions were emerging about the suitability of this form of autonomy for Darjeeling. Recall that the region was only 32 percent ST, far short of a tribal majority. It stood to reason that conferring ST status upon the ten "left-out" communities could make or break the deal. With the report inexplicably held up at the Writers' Building, the CRI members assumed the cases were ensnared in other forms of multicultural governance—in a higher-level management of diversity. But they couldn't know for sure. With decisions being made behind closed doors, nobody could rule out the possibility of a secret deal either springing tribal recognition and autonomy or rejecting both outright. As I plied them for information, it became clear that even government anthropologists could not acquire information beyond certain thresholds of knowledge, policy, and power. Such were the difficulties of both studying, and being agents of, the state.[22]

Being excluded from these decisions pained the CRI team. Typically, they directed their ire at "policy makers" in the Writers' Building who made decisions with little understanding of the groups in question. What was worse, these "policy makers" seemed to have little appreciation of anthropology and the ethnographic method. As Amit explained, "You see the real problems arise when they want us to create data to fit their decisions. Because that is what they do! They want us to go up there and take our surveys and they want us to provide reports that fit their politics."

I pushed Amit and the director for a more specific example. They spoke of a superior within the Government of West Bengal who had recently won his post despite lacking any formal training as a social scientist. Aping this figure of technocratic otherness, the director explained:

> He even said so himself: "This anthropology is not like aviation. It is not a skill." So he goes up there and visits a community and within ten minutes just by looking at someone says, "Yes, he is a tribal. . . . so make the report and make them tribal. What's the problem? It's as easy as that." That really happened! He really did that . . . So they just want us to provide the data for their policies, so actually this whole process is just a hoax! That's what it is!

A hoax—it was a potent choice of words. I had always thought more along the lines of an "ethnographic ruse" or at least a "state performance." Ethnic leaders in Darjeeling preferred "eye-wash" or *dekhāwati*. In weighing the director's words, it was difficult to ascertain the degree to which "hoax" referenced the difficulties of fieldwork or the challenges he and his staff face as purveyors of a soft science in the hard places of governance. Knowing him as I did, and considering the earlier parts of the conversation, I sensed that all of these factors were fueling his frustration. To serve under a bureaucrat who so clearly lacked appreciation of the nuances of ethnographic knowledge production, one who could chide, "This anthropology is not like aviation. It is not a skill," was an affront to the CRI's expertise and the director's identity. Indeed, as soon as the word "hoax" left the director's lips, Amit cried out, "This is an identity crisis for us. An identity crisis!"

The director simply closed his eyes and began rubbing his temples in agony. "I am just so scared for the discipline these days. Because all the bureaucrats . . . [long pause, eyes still closed] . . . To be quite frank with you, at this point I am just counting down the days until my retirement."

Having served the Government of West Bengal for thirty-two years, the director was slated to retire in March of 2011. Knowing that he had a sick wife at home and had recently been passed over for promotion, I sensed the anguish in his words. With the conversation exhausted of emotion, we called it a day and started to gather our things. As several of the CRI members and I began our respective bus journeys to various corners of Kolkata, the director, like he did every day, began his long commute home. A jam-packed bus ride across town, then a forty-five-minute train trip, and finally a five-kilometer bicycle ride would take him from the concrete monolith of the CRI to the village he called home.

IN THE STATE'S MEANTIME

The director and Amit give voice to those who man India's massive administration of difference. Inflected with care and frustration, their testimony bespeaks their personal quandaries and those of late liberalism more generally. It is not only government anthropologists, however, who must navigate the postcolonial state's complexity. Marginalized minorities bear the biggest brunt. Examining affirmative action from the inside out, it is worth asking how communities manage the government's inscrutability and endless delays? How do communities in need endure the bureaucratic durée? And what happens in the meantime?

These questions return us to Darjeeling's categorically unstable politics. The state's complexity and corresponding temporality engendered profound difficulties for the people of the hills. Sending delegations back and forth between Darjeeling, Kolkata, and Delhi exhausted aspiring tribes of already limited financial resources. Keeping track of their files proved nearly impossible. Ethnic elites called upon whatever governmental contacts they could in Kolkata and Delhi, but they had little success in finding anyone who could make a difference. When these leaders returned to Darjeeling, they faced the unenviable task of explaining to their constituents the confounding status of their files. Frequently, their news contradicted previous updates. This eroded the credibility of these leaders, whom many looked up to as the educated elites that could get things done in places like Kolkata and Delhi. Ethnic associations pleaded for patience, but their constituents inevitably grew frustrated with the lack of progress. With discontent on the rise, new factions formed, promising better tactics and better results. These organizational fissures worked their way down into daily life, where dividing lines were drawn between those who opted for new leadership and those who believed in staying the course with their original leaders.[23]

The state's intractability did more than exhaust communities of material resources. It exhausted them of energy. The ability to wait out the state—to *endure* the conditions of late liberalism, as Povinelli puts it[24]—proved essential for seeing the ST bids through *and* for maintaining social unity along the way. Endurance was in limited supply, however. As the cases wore on, political enthusiasm gave way to *exhaustion* and varying degrees of frustration. Some groups channeled their frustration into a steely resolve to carry on. Others grew impatient and began looking for political alternatives, often splintering communities in the process.

These interplays of endurance, exhaustion, and frustration define the politics of the unrequited. While the exhausted may fade from view, the frustrated tend to make their case known in increasingly pronounced ways. Violent outbreaks in Assam (2007) and Rajasthan (2007–2010) over unrequited claims for ST status underscore this point.[25] Especially since India has embraced economic liberalization, unrecognized minorities increasingly find themselves on the outside looking in. Privatization and the influx of foreign capital have established new opportunities and, with them, new definitions of success across India. Education and the access to capital have become all the more imperative for realizing these new visions of the good life.[26] The desires and anxieties of the unrecognized only grow as they watch their ST neighbors take advantage of the educational quotas, employment reservations, better loan rates, and various other entitlements guaranteed to Scheduled Tribes. For groups who see themselves as equally deserving as their ST neighbors, the discrepancies breed palpable resentment. Paradoxically, affirmative action—a governmental strategy for leveling the playing field—becomes then a source of communal tensions.

Importantly, many of these tensions stem from the state's bureaucratic procedures. Darjeeling offers a case in point. Consider the chronology: In 2005, West Bengal, the federal government, and Darjeeling's GNLF signed an agreement declaring the Sixth Schedule to be "the full and final solution" to the question of ethnic-based autonomy in the hills. In 2006, West Bengal sent the CRI to certify Darjeeling's ten "left-out" communities. The accelerated timing suggested that the government was fast-tracking the cases to give Darjeeling a tribal majority—thus ensuring a logical passage of the Sixth Schedule bill. Enthusiasm for becoming tribal, at this point, was at an all-time high. But the weeks following the survey soon turned to months, and months to years, and still there was no word on the ST files that would make or break the deal. With politicians, ethnic leaders, and even government anthropologists unsure of the files' whereabouts, the make-or-break cases seemed to have slipped into governmental limbo.

The opposition meanwhile dug in. Madan Tamang of the All India Gorkha League led the critiques throughout 2007, claiming that Ghisingh and GNLF were selling out the people's desires for Gorkhaland with their hollow promises of tribal autonomy. Prominent intellectuals convened a "Citizens Social Forum" to scrutinize the plans and make their concerns public. Doubts began appearing in the op-ed sections of the local papers and gradually in the chatter of the streets. As 2007 wore on, participation in the GNLF's tribal spectacles began to wane, portending categorical changes to come. And still there was no word on the files in question.

Through it all, the state showed a remarkable ability to hide behind its mask, seldom revealing its inner workings and thereby leaving a people and their demands in the lurch.[27] The critical question is whether this was coincidental or, in fact, instrumental to the way late liberal governments handle difference—a way of wearing down and wearing out communities and their politics.[28] Dangled but never conferred, ST recognition has since remained a card that the Indian government can—and does—play in its dealings with the fluctuating demands for subnational autonomy in Darjeeling. The degree to which ST recognition serves the purposes of counter-insurgency remains an open question.[29] One thing, though, is clear: the possibility of tribal recognition remains a source of imminent power over a people still longing for their rightful place in the nation-state. Befitting these operations of late liberalism, the cases of Darjeeling's aspiring tribes remained, as of early 2015, "pending."

RETHINKING TRIBAL RECOGNITION

In the years I have known the CRI team, they have expressed perennial frustration with the system of recognition they implement. Their grievances range from the difficulties of their fieldwork and their checkered relations to policy and politics, to broader questioning of affirmative action in India. They are not alone in their concerns. By all accounts, the system is over-burdened, under-resourced, and severely out of date. At present, the Indian government finds itself ill-equipped to handle the hundreds of Scheduled Tribes already on the books. This says nothing of the estimated one thousand more that are demanding recognition. Meanwhile, the politics of tribal recognition continue to intensify.

Amid these circumstances, critiques are gaining ground at the national level. In 2006, a draft document titled "The National Tribal Policy for the Scheduled Tribes of India" was circulated to government officials and related civil society bodies inviting comment. The draft openly acknowledged the burdens put upon the state for ST recognition. Point 21 reads: "There is an increasing clamor from many communities to get included as STs . . . Adding new communities to the list reduces the benefits that can go to existing STs and is therefore to be resorted to, only if there is no room for doubt." Finally and crucially, the draft stated: "The criteria laid down by the Lokur Committee are hardly relevant today . . . Other more accurate criteria need to be fixed." The draft, in this regard, offered much-needed reflexivity. But in many ways, it retained the problematic epistemic tendencies of its colonial and postcolonial antecedents. It said nothing of what such "fixed" criteria would entail, but presumably they would remain of a similar ethnological register.

More-radical changes were suggested by the Chopra Commission in its ruling on the Gujjar case of 2007. Responding to ST-related violence across Rajasthan, the Chopra Commission opined "that a national debate should be initiated on the existing norms for according ST status to any community. It should impress upon the Centre that certain criteria should be abrogated as they had become outdated." It further suggested, "Current norms should be replaced by quantifiable criteria which will be relevant in the present context. The new criteria must withstand judicial scrutiny, thereby enabling future commissions or committees appointed by the government to examine the issue with exactness and reliability."[30]

These calls for reform are promising, but they perpetuate an empiricist bent to tribal recognition extending far back into the colonial period (see Chapter 2). Given those troubled histories of classification, one can only wonder what these new criteria capable of "withstanding judicial scrutiny" might look like. What kinds of "exactness and reliability" did the Chopra Commission have in mind? While these initiatives advocate an obvious need for change, what they fail to acknowledge are the technocratic complexities and epistemological differences that constitute today's postcolonial state. Finding a singular form of recognition to satisfy these contending expert persuasions will be difficult, to say the least.

As of early 2015, no changes had been made to the ST criteria. Amending the procedures or venturing a more radical overhaul of the system will be difficult. The strongest resistance may well come from existing STs, and those who aspire to this status. The quests for tribal recognition, it is worth remembering, are imbued with powerful senses of hope, entitlement, and identity. Shifting the terms of positive discrimination will inevitably unsettle a host of vested interests. Causes and calls for a timely rethinking are nevertheless at hand.

THE ANTHROPOLOGIST AND THE BUREAUCRAT

In 2013, I traveled to Kolkata to meet with the now-retired director of the CRI. This was the anthropologist who, in the heat of the ethnographic moment, told me, "I am not an administrator. I am here for the research. It is part of my blend." And this was the bureaucrat who managed the CRI and its often-compromised position within the Indian government.

It had been some years since the director and I had met. Now that he was retired, I was curious to hear his thoughts on a career on the front lines of tribal recognition. He arrived at our meeting looking plump and at peace. When I commented on his "healthy" appearance, he explained he had gained some weight since retiring in 2011. That last year on the job, he lamented, had put considerable strain on him and his body. Now life was a little more peaceful, a little more "healthy," he admitted, flashing his wry grin.

With the tea poured and the air-conditioning evaporating the perspiration from his long journey from his village to downtown Kolkata, we settled in for the afternoon. The conversation began as so many of ours had, with the director comparing our respective brands of anthropology. "Well, you see in anthropology," he began, "there are two aspects, the ideological and the practical. In some places, like for you, you might be able to bring these together, to mix these, but we cannot do this in India. Here in India, where politics dictates everything, bringing these two together will not be possible." This was not the first time I had heard him frame the constraints of being a civil servant anthropologist in comparison with academic anthropology. The inability to conduct long-term field studies like Malinowski had done; the inability to get in touch with the "flavor of the ethnos"; the constant politicking within the government; the checkered fate of anthropology in these hard places of the state: the themes he recounted were familiar from years past. But as our conversation went on, his reflections took a more retrospective and remorseful tone than before.

Gently, I pushed him to talk about the Ethnographic Survey of 2006 and all the complications that followed. Unlike in years past, this time he singled out particular individuals within the government—his superiors— who he believed were ultimately calling the shots on the ST cases in question. At the time, everyone knew the cases were bound up in the bid for Sixth Schedule autonomy, but reading the tea leaves of the "policy makers" was difficult from his position. "So we were getting the drops [squeezing his fingers together as though squeezing an eye dropper], the *diktats*, coming down as to what to do," he explained. He went on to recount being summoned to a high-ranking official's office and told, "You just give the reports as we tell you. You do not have the power to determine the whole picture." This was nothing the director did not already know. It was, however, a biting statement of the anthropologist's subordinated place in the greater politics at hand.

Looking back on 2006, the director reasoned that he and his team had been sent to Darjeeling merely to "pacify all the groups demanding ST status." It had all been an "eyewash," he opined. West Bengal had never planned on recommending these groups for ST status—no matter what the CRI had written in its official report. The director's words were inflected with a bitterness that had not waned since his retirement. Yet his retrospection was in certain ways different from what I had heard from him in earlier interviews. When I checked my notes from 2006 and 2007, I found that the director had then explained that his superiors in the West Bengal government had told him, "So make the report and make them tribal."

The contradictions were telling, especially when we consider that perhaps they weren't contradictions at all. Perhaps West Bengal did intend to "make them tribal," thus facilitating the implementation of the Sixth Schedule as a "full and final solution." Or perhaps it really was just an "eyewash" from the start. It was difficult to know. What was clear was that the political circumstances in Darjeeling changed. The years following the Ethnographic Survey of 2006 would see Darjeeling go through yet another violent shift in its terms of ethnopolitical mobilization—a categorical upheaval that I discuss in Chapter 7. That this shift would prompt a change in the way the state worked to manage subnational difference and its politics in this volatile corner of the country is not only plausible but probable. Whatever the case, ascertaining the state's original intentions in 2006 seemed somewhat moot and impossible in 2013. Still, this all weighed on the director heavily.

I asked if it had left a bad taste in his mouth. "Yes, it left a negative impression," he told me. He was largely unable to reflect upon his career as an anthropologist without its accompanying bureaucratic baggage. Recalling the policy makers who issued the *diktats* and gave him the "drops," he complained, "There are these men—the physicists, the chemical engineers—who are up high. So they say it will be this and this. And I have tried to tell them the anthropological perspective. But these men, just because they have I.A.S. [indicating Indian Administrative Service] after their name and are so high, they say, 'What is this?'" Such were the lingering frustrations of being a civil servant anthropologist.

As we got up to smoke a cigarette, the director shared with me his deepest regrets—namely his inability to help the communities he had studied. All his efforts—the fieldwork, the drafting of the reports, the managing of their demands, the meetings with their delegations, the tireless defense of ethnography itself—had been for nothing. "In my heart, I feel sad for these groups. Because I tried; I really tried. And we have done the schooling, the training, the knowledge. And we have the techniques, the techniques of identification. And I tried my best to help them, and *they deserve it*, they really do, I have tried to help them, but . . ." He could say no more. He didn't need to.

This was the anthropologist in him speaking—a researcher who, at the end of the day, retained his commitment to the people with whom he worked, and who was willing to critique power when and where it needed to be critiqued. Backed by a lifetime of experience on the front lines of recognition, the director, in these terms, offers a fitting and final testament to the inner workings at hand.

With these bureaucratic considerations in tow, I turn now to recognition's effects—and affects—among the people of Darjeeling.

CHAPTER 6

REFORMING THE SUBJECT
The Effects and Affects of Recognition

IN A DIRT-FLOORED SCHOOLHOUSE on the local tea estate, fifteen Tamang villagers have gathered for their monthly ethnic association
meeting. It being Sunday, the day of rest on the plantation, their neighbors are likely down the hill watching the week's soccer match, or perhaps
tucked away in a watering hole sipping locally made *raksi* (liquor). Yet,
as they do once a month, these Tamangs have made their way from surrounding villages to deliberate the nuances of Tamang culture (*sanskriti*)
and its ongoing revitalization. Inside the small corrugated-aluminum
building the men and women sit at crudely fashioned wooden desks too
small for adults. At the front of the classroom, facing them, sits an older
gentleman wearing a pin-striped suit, a pressed cotton shirt, and polished
leather boots. He is an elite Central Committee (CC) member of the
All India Tamang Buddhist Association (AITBA). Periodic visits to local
branch meetings such as these are an integral part of AITBA's apparatus of ethnic mobilization. Stretching across India and beyond, AITBA's
structure, political wherewithal, and cultural acumen have made it the
flagship organization of ethnic rebirth in the hills.

Though visibly uncomfortable, the CC member commences the meeting
in business-like fashion. It mustn't run late. His car and driver are waiting.
As is standard, he begins with a formal introduction. Once he is finished,
however, protocol is thwarted as the local members raise complaints about

AITBA's recent political entanglements. For the past year (2006), Darjeeling's political leader Subash Ghisingh (himself a Tamang) has accused AITBA of dividing the greater Gorkha community through AITBA's go-it-alone movements for ST status and ethnic uplift.[1] This has cast the organization's members into an awkward relationship with the ruling GNLF. The CC member tries to stifle the villagers' complaints, but they quickly segue into other concerns about the organization's austere cultural regulations and the presence of a rival faction known as the Tamang Buddhist Gedung, founded on more-lenient cultural principles. Not coincidentally, members of Ghisingh's GNLF founded this rival faction. It therefore posed a cultural *and* political alternative to AITBA's orthodox ways.[2]

The CC member tries to appease his audience by stressing the importance of a unified political and cultural front. He and his organization speak from experience. It took them two decades to secure Scheduled Tribe status for the Tamang community.[3] Their quest included tireless protests, hunger strikes, and extensive lobbying in Delhi, Kolkata, and beyond. At home, it also included extensive cultural engineering programs to revitalize the "pure" (*suddha*) and "original" (*maulik*) form of Tamang culture. These tribal makeovers focused on the elimination of Hindu elements from sociocultural practice. Popular Hindu holidays like Durga Pujā (Dasain/Dussehra) and Diwali were banned.[4] Violators were ostracized and, in some cases, even fined. To advance the rediscovery of Tamang culture, AITBA sent ethnographic delegations to Nepal, started language programs, supplied authentic Tamang dress, and produced a variety of ethnic media promoting Tamang identity. These cultural endeavors were linked to an array of social programs to improve the health, financial, and educational conditions of the Tamangs. Most importantly, AITBA delivered Scheduled Tribe status in 2003.

As the CC member pontificates on political and cultural solidarity, he makes a strong case. To paraphrase: *For unity, Tamangs must have one culture. This is precisely why the association has implemented such strict rules as to what is proper cultural practice. Those who are still unsure of Tamang religious practice, language, script, tradition, attire, festivals, and folk culture may refer to the plethora of DVDs, books, magazines, and notices put out by the association documenting what it means to be a true Tamang. Who is it,* he

asks, *that has brought ST status to the people? Who has re-awoken Tamangs'
sense of identity? What has the Gedung, the rival association, accomplished?
They are but a small local faction. We are All-India! We are international!
Who brought thousands of Tamangs from all over the world to Darjeeling for
the International Tamang Convention (December 2005)? Look, this man here*
[gesturing to me] *came all the way from America for this great event! Culture should be a source of pride, not tension, he reminds them. May we thus set
our differences aside.*[5]

The conversation carries on for some time, ultimately ending with
the CC member's standard invitation for the villagers to bring their concerns to the central offices in Darjeeling Town. They express doubts as
to whether they will be given an audience. Then, realizing the meeting is
running overtime, the branch leaders take charge, shifting the group's attention to local matters. The CC member recedes from the conversation.

On the local docket: an invitation from their Gurung neighbors to
worship in the Gurungs' new *gomba* (monastery) in Bidhuwā Busti. The
gomba has been in the works for years as a showpiece of the Gurungs'
corresponding Buddhist revitalization. Now that it has been officially
opened, the Gurungs have invited their Tamang neighbors to worship.
But among these Tamangs, the gesture is met with skepticism and sar-
casm. Responding to the invitation, a spry seventy-year-old gentleman
pipes up, "So they have built their own Gurung *gomba*. This is all very
good. But what? They bring in Tamang *lamas* [monks] to do Gurung
pujās and then invite us, the Tamangs, into 'their' *gomba*? Before, the Gurungs weren't even using *lamas!*" He smacks his knee to punctuate the
joke. The more-authentic-than-thou reproach elicits considerable laughter among the group.

The meeting goes on for another hour or so, covering a variety of local
issues. The moment the meeting adjourns, the CC member quietly grabs
his coat and sneaks away. The locals, for their part, stick around to chat
before beginning the steep walk back to their villages.[6]

.   .   .

Ethnic associations—commonly referred to as *samājes*—were instrumental to Darjeeling's tribal movements. Straddling the line between civil and

political society, these organizations served as key intermediaries between everyday citizens and the state. They were sites where the ethno-logics of tribal recognition were negotiated, repurposed, and disseminated to a variety of ends. Importantly, associations like AITBA were not just in the business of representing their members. They were in the business of reforming them.

In this chapter, I turn attention to these reformations of the tribal subject—with a specific focus on their social, subjective, and affective impacts. Throughout the 1990s and 2000s, the tribal turn spawned sweeping sensations of ethnic rebirth. But these movements also induced a host of unforeseen, untoward dynamics that significantly reworked the contours of life and politics in the hills. Engendering hope, confusion, and new forms of ethnic consciousness, the prospect of becoming tribal paradoxically divided communities, even as it gave birth to new kinds of political subjects and possibilities. Thinking through these formative tensions, here I take a closer look at the effects and affects of this calculus of late liberal becoming.

These embodied transformations remain a vital—but less understood—dimension of the ethno-contemporary. Be it in the struggles of indigenous peoples for recognition, the commercial branding of ethnic culture, or communities' promotion of their native heritage, anthropologists are only now beginning to get a sense of how the ethno-logics of such endeavors feed back into communities' understandings—and feelings—about themselves.[7] Instances like AITBA's branch meeting offer insight along these lines. Even at what would seem to be the consummate site of ethnic reform, we see tensions in the ranks. The political entanglements, the resistance to imposed orthodoxies, the gradients of class, power, and expertise, and the social nature of the gathering signaled key facets of the tribal turn—and the ethno-contemporary more generally. The Tamangs, in this regard, present a case study of recognition's impacts on the marginalized. Their two-decade struggle for ST status proved successful in 2003, but AITBA's programs have not abated. The organization has powered on with its agendas of ethnic uplift, revitalization, and reform. Still, even for the most committed members, these efforts have proven politically, socially, and subjectively fraught.

This chapter ventures a more phenomenological look at the ambivalent experiences of becoming a twenty-first-century tribe. Understanding how contemporary ethno-logics take hold of the body and the body politic requires working both with and against conventional understandings of governmentality and modern subject formation. A variety of factors figured into the remaking of the tribal subject in Darjeeling—none more pivotal than the mysterious ways in which conceptual forms (like tribe) enter into the corporeal worlds of experience. This interplay between the *conceptual* and the *experiential* was the linchpin of becoming tribal. Unfolding in the most intimate spaces of life, this dialectic of conceptual and experiential forms engendered myriad outcomes. Some were desirable; others were not.

My project in this chapter is to shine some light on the experiential dynamics by which communities variably take up, take on, and take off ethnological paradigms to refashion themselves and their futures. In doing so, I mean to push considerations of sociality, subjectivity, and affect to the fore of scholarly engagements with the ethno-contemporary. What are the effective and affective stakes of these (re)turns—tribal and otherwise?[8] What happens when a descriptive endeavor like ethnology becomes prescriptive? And how do communities and normative ethno-logics rework one another in the process? To gain some traction amid these slippery questions of the ethno-contemporary, it is worth returning to the Tamangs' branch meeting of 2006.

BEYOND GOVERNMENTALITY

With the meeting adjourned, several Tamangs and I begin a long walk down into the tea estate. As we descend past the *momo* (dumpling) shops and liquor stalls that line the steep road, our numbers dwindle until it is just me and my friend Pemba, an ardently born-again Tamang. Pemba has invited me to accompany him as he makes his rounds. We pass through Bidhuwā Busti, where we both live, and on through the tea weigh station where the average workday ends for many of our neighbors. Leaving the "coolie lines" of Bidhuwā Busti, we plunge into the geometric greenery of the tea fields below. Strolling down the steep road, Pemba points out a footpath that leads to his natal village. He explains to me that his home there was razed during the Gorkhaland Agitation of the 1980s. This was the trauma that initiated the tailspin of his life, which culminated in alcoholism, unemployment, and his failings as a father. And it was Buddhism and his rediscovery of Tamang culture that saved him and gave him the *ujyālo* (brightness) of his being today.

Down we walk, past the factory where the tea is processed before being shipped to the international auction houses of Kolkata.[9] Down we walk, into villages tucked into the forested wastelands of the estate. Down into different degrees of poverty. As we descend, Pemba stops along the way to share with Tamang friends and families the main points of the meeting. He speaks with remarkable eloquence and passion, yet as he disseminates the niceties of AITBA's brand of Tamang culture, all traces of the dissent that colored the meeting drop out of his narrative. His phrases and tenor are uncannily like those of the Central Committee member. Time and time again we stop to say hello to fellow Tamangs. Time and time again, Pemba relays AITBA's message before heading farther down. The repetition gives these informal conversations a deliberate bent. Thus, we carry on.

Down to his parents' home, a porous thatched hut, standing wearily on a small plot of level ground. Pemba invites me in. I step inside, only to accidentally see his mother's withered body, shirtless and bent from years of plucking in the fields. His father, wracked by years of alcoholism, sits, toothless, on a bed in the back corner of the hut watching our embarrassing encounter. We are unexpected guests. So we continue on. Down, through forests dotted with Hindu *mandirs* (temples). Down, past the weekly soccer game, the PA system blaring a crackled play-by-play, as six-man teams try to keep the ball in play on a miniature field etched into the steep hillside. As we skirt the field and the hundreds who have gathered to cheer their boys, a wayward kick sends the ball vanishing over the field's edge. The game breaks while the ball is recovered, so we proceed. Down through a mostly Tamang village, their prayer flags flying atop their homes. Down past the Tamang *gomba* built by a resident *lama* in 1951.[10] And down to the newer, more extravagant one built by AITBA in 2000.

Like the Gurungs' *gomba* in Bidhuwā Busti, the Tamangs' Dinchen Tanshi Choeling Gumba stands as a showpiece of Tamang revitalization. Established in September 2000, the seemingly unfinished concrete and corrugated aluminum building sits on a manicured parcel of land overlooking the river valley below. Pemba goes to fetch the caretaker, and soon a middle-aged woman emerges from her home and shuffles across the courtyard, keys in hand, to open the door. As the heavy door creaks open, Pemba launches into an unsolicited lecture on the vitality of Tamang culture. Once again, to paraphrase: *For hundreds, if not thousands of years, the Tamangs have followed their own original form of Buddhism. We are highland people of the Himalayas,* he tells her, *and living high in the mountains we have retained the purest forms of our culture and religion—this, despite the tireless oppression of Hindu rule. Today, we are reviving this pristine culture. Like last year, when hundreds came to this very temple to celebrate our very own Tamang new year. We call it Lochar . . . etc.*

For ten minutes he rhapsodizes. It is difficult to tell whether his speech is directed at me or at the woman who has graciously opened the temple for us. Standing there in the door, echoes of the CC member reverberate through my mind as Pemba waxes on about Tamang unity, their achievements, the details of authentic Tamang culture, the history of AITBA, etc. My attention slips. Meanwhile, the woman stands speechless, trapped on the threshold. Uncertain whether she is the target of his persuasion or whether I am, she is unable to either come or go. She casts a furtive glance in my direction, as though desperate for some kind of freeing interlocution. I can offer no respite, because I am implicated in this articulation. There is no doubt that my presence as an anthropologist is egging Pemba on. Yet to whom he preaches is unclear. His thoughts stream on in what seems to be an almost automated delivery, one after another, fact after so-called fact. As he rambles on, the woman continues to nod, hapless. On the receiving end of this cascade of identity-speak there is little we can do but wait for it to reach its own denouement.

·   ·   ·

Narratives like Pemba's were rampant in Darjeeling. The imperatives of cultural distinctiveness, singular identity, and its rightful recognition were backed by the Indian government's prescriptions of tribal difference. That communities like the Tamangs would take to ethnology to recoup and represent their tribal selves made sense. It afforded, in Partha Chatterjee's words, a way "to give the empirical form of a population group the moral attributes of a community."[11] But these were not just any communities in the making; they were *tribal* communities, ethnologically and morally deserving of the state's recognition, rights, and care. For aspiring STs, representing the self in discernibly ethnological ways was politically necessary—as we have seen. That said, it is these "moral" and experiential dimensions of tribal becoming that concern me here.

In an important rejoinder to recent scholarly emphases on the politics of recognition, Sara Shneiderman has argued for anthropologists to revisit what she calls "recognition beyond politics"—that is, how ethnicity is made, experienced, and affirmed outside the purview of state-based classification.[12] To Shneiderman's point: Narratives of ethnic rebirth in Darjeeling were imbued with feelings that transcended politics and the bids for ST status. As Pemba liked to say, rediscovering Buddhism and Tamang culture gave him the "brightness" (*ujyālo*) of his being. There was more, then, to these movements than the opportunistic pursuit of rights, recognition, and autonomy. As I argued in Chapter 1, these were always also *a politics to belong*. With their programs of ethnic uplift, their refound senses of self, and their newly achieved status as a Scheduled Tribe, Pemba and the Tamangs had credentials to prove their tribal makeover. But this was the story of identity rediscovered, reborn, and recognized. Others were not so fortunate.

The lion's share of Darjeeling's aspiring tribes, at this time, remained unrecognized and ambivalent in their embrace of these new, ostensibly old identities. For every born-again ethnic like Pemba, there were others who rejected such makeovers. Pemba's very neighbors underscore the discrepancies. Just next door to Pemba lived AITBA's local branch president—a similarly ardent champion of Tamang rebirth. Several doors down from him, however, lived Bidhuwā Busti's general village *samāj* president—also a Tamang, but with an outspoken disdain for AITBA's cultural reforms. There were thus two local leaders living in close proximity to each another who had radically different orientations to the tribal turn.

These divergences hold important lessons about the ways that class informed the circulation, but not necessarily the embodiments, of the tribal turn. As we saw at the start, with AITBA's elite ethnic leader preaching to the tea estate villagers, class and expertise played a crucial role in the *circulation* of the paradigms of tribal reform. The same cannot be said, however, of these paradigms' *embodiment*. Within classes and genders, personal orientations to these tribal makeovers were highly uneven.[13] Neighbors and even family members differed markedly in their feelings toward becoming tribal—meaning it was difficult to make sweeping statements about the tribal turn's class and gendered effects.

Between those who embraced and those who rejected the makeovers were many others for whom the project of becoming tribal engendered cultural confusion, sociopolitical division, and angst over who they were and should be. Heeding the call of recognition, some individuals abandoned family tradition in favor of the practices espoused by cultural experts. Others balked at the imposition upon lived practice. Increasingly, neighbors became ethnic others and communities divided internally over who and what exactly constituted authentic culture. Everyday cultural practices suddenly bore significant social and political consequences. No matter where one stood amid these cultural politics, maintaining neutral ground became virtually impossible—lest one have no culture at all.

These dynamics constituted what Alpa Shah has elsewhere termed a "dark side of indigeneity" and its politics.[14] In intentional and unintentional ways, the tribal turn came to rework the terms of not just ethnopolitical mobilization but also everyday life. People were doing things *with* ethnology. And it was doing things *for* them. But so too were late liberal ethno-logics doing things *to* them. How, then, do we balance these positive and negative impacts? How do we reconcile communities' innovative repurposing of disciplinary paradigms *and* their sometimes troubling ends?

Scholars frequently invoke Foucault's notions of *governmentality* and *biopolitics* to explain how modern technologies of governance shape populations, individuals, and life itself.[15] These analytics offer compelling ways to track knowledge-power from the state into communities and individuals. In this spirit, Pemba's relay of AITBA's message from the meeting down into the tea estate illustrates how these tribal movements made their way into daily life. There are, however, limits to what the optic of governmentality can tell us about recognition's impacts. Too often, the Foucauldian reading gets us back to where we started: to the schemas through which populations and their difference are recognized, managed, or otherwise denied. This tells us little of the actual experiences of those who inhabit these grids of ethno-intelligibility. It likewise sheds little light on the ambivalent dynamics by which subjects come into relation with these schemas of the ethnos. We are left wondering how individuals and communities negotiate these paradigms and repurpose them to new ends. If the analytic of governmentality is to follow through on its promise of explaining how knowledge-power shapes the subject, it needs a phenom-enological component. Turning to the contingent everyday realities where the interplays of conceptual and experiential forms unfold, we find some rather telling illustrations of the ways in which people like Pemba are—and are not—finding themselves in these paradigms of the ethnos.

Per the Foucauldian analytic, we might trace a line of ethnological knowledge-power from the Indian government, through the work of civil society bodies like AITBA, and into the body of the born-again ethnic. We might even come to see the "brightness" of Pemba's being as the embodiment of a history of ethnological governmentality with roots extending deep into the colonial past. When we enter the lifeworlds of everyday subjects, however, we find a more complex picture. Crossing into the domains of sociality, subjectivity, and the body, our line breaks up, diminishes, refracts, and scatters. For even in the shining subjectivities of born-again ethnics like Pemba, there is always more to the story. There are always other lines.

It is this breakdown of governmentality that concerns me in the phe-nomenological analysis that follows. That said, if we are to understand how recognition's ethno-logics do—and do not—make their way into the body and the body politic, we must first come to terms with the power gradients of their circulation. This requires starting at the top—i.e., with those propagating these (re)formations of the tribal subject.

ETHNOLOGY REPURPOSED

"There must be attraction. We have to create attraction. If the attraction is there . . ." The man breaks off, realizing that his associates are nodding in full agreement. On an otherwise quiet afternoon in the offices of AITBA, six men discuss the details of a proposed Tamang calendar demonstrating traditional Tamang dress, ritual schedules, and the like. Sitting in an office teeming with magazines, books, and stacks of mailers awaiting the week's round of dissemination, they are no strangers to documentation. But these ethnic elites face certain challenges in representing their community.[16]

The president raises the tricky issue of language. "If we put it in Tamang, who will have learned the Tamang to be able to read it?" With rare exceptions, the Tamangs have collectively lost their native tongue since migrating from Nepal. The leaders therefore decide the calendar will be printed in Tamang and Nepali, their lingua franca. More importantly, one of the men asserts, "the calendar must go in each and every home. For there it will bring knowledge."

This matter resolved, conversation turns to a more ambitious project, the making of an ethnographic film to properly document Tamang culture. The circumstances that spawned this idea are noteworthy. Earlier in 2006, the Darjeeling Gorkha Hill Council (operating at the behest of Subash Ghisingh) began making a documentary demonstrating the tribal traits of *all* Gorkhas—Tamangs, Sherpas, Gurungs, etc. The film was to show each constituent ethnic group wearing its respective dress and performing its unique tribal customs. Ghisingh's administration would then send the film to Delhi to bolster the bid for Sixth Schedule tribal autonomy. When Tamang leaders learned of the DGHC's film, they were furious that they had not been consulted and that Tamangs were subsequently shown singing and dancing while wearing *daurā suruwāl* and *chaubandi choli*, which are not AITBA-sanctioned attire. With their representational authority circumvented and their people misrepresented, AITBA leaders wanted to set the record straight. Further, they had little interest in contributing to the broader efforts to make Darjeeling tribal. Having won ST status in 2003, the Tamang had their own identity, their own recognition, their own relations to the state. These were to be guarded tightly.

And so, two weeks after these leaders hatched the film idea, they pitched the project to AITBA's Central Committee. The meeting consisted of fifteen elites (all men) from around the region.[17] The president began by contextualizing the need for the film:

> Because of all the political hooliganism [*gundāgari*] these days, it is difficult
> to make any statement at the moment. And there are other hurdles too. That

is why we ought to preserve and conserve our culture. And we should promote our culture. Some Tamangs have been forced from above to put *tikā* on their foreheads and celebrate Dasain [a Nepali Hindu holiday]. We, the Tamangs, will not even mention the "D" of Dasain, and this has to be enforced very strongly, and totally, and should be disseminated by all the different branches. . . . We must make a CD, a cassette, or a picture based on our complete dharma and traditional dress. We have our own dress. Our own festivals too.

"Yes," another man chimed in in mixed English and Nepali. "It should be fully technical. From the technical point of view, we should shoot it. From the time before our child's birth. According to our culture and tradition. What kind of practices, from the name-giving ceremony, marriage, and things like that."

"Yes," another opined. "It is a time to bring our own fellows into understanding, to instill communal feeling [*jātitwa*]. With the help of our culture, let us instill *jātitwa* among our fellows!"

For two hours, the CC members discussed the details of the documentary and its potential to awaken *jātitwa*. The film was not just for Tamang viewers; it was also to serve political purposes. As a representative from Sikkim suggested:

Over all of India and in the interest of all Tamangs, decisions have to be taken. We can create, whatever you may call it, a think tank, an intellectual [*buddhijibi*] group. It could be you all! Even now when I look at it, this high command body, why don't we meet the Chief Minister of West Bengal? . . . If we make this film, then why can't we meet this high body? We can go as a delegation. We can talk to the Government of West Bengal, the Chief Secretary, the Home Secretary, and *show them exactly what we are*. This is the big thing, the Government of India. To send it to the Government of India. It can convince the government. [emphasis added]

AITBA had been in the business of convincing for a long while. Over the twenty-two years it took to achieve ST status, the organization produced countless "convincing" representations: various forms of ethnic media; specially written essays on distinct Tamang customs, language, religions, and rituals; and vivid performances of Tamang identity, none more important than when the government anthropologists came to certify their tribal claims. These auto-ethnological endeavors aimed to show the government—and Tamangs—"exactly what they were." Notably, the commitment to self-representation did not wane with the achievement of ST status in 2003. As the pitch for this ethnographic film in 2006 made clear, maintaining a proper Tamang identity required constant upkeep, representation, and, above all, performance.[18]

EPISTEMOLOGY MATTERS

For Darjeeling's aspiring tribes, auto-ethnological representations like documentaries, magazines, and calendars were key instruments of cultural revitalization and the quest for ST recognition. In turning ethnology upon themselves, their endeavors shared a great deal with techniques of representation employed by indigenous movements and heritage projects around the world.[19] Whether in the Native museums of Canada or the courtrooms of Australia, the ability to represent identity and difference in ethnological ways has become vital to marginalized communities' pursuits of rights, justice, and economic prosperity. That these self-representations should entail their fair degree of strategic essentialism is understandable.[20] These essentialist tendencies have caught the attention of Heritage Studies and communities themselves. Scholars and communities today are consequently collaborating to represent collective difference in new ways that are, at once, rooted in cultural tradition, yet also internally heterogeneous and historically dynamic.[21]

Legal recognition may require something different, however. For a group to become a Scheduled Tribe of India, essentialism is not only strategic but compulsory. Through both its written and its unwritten criteria, the Indian government effectively demands that communities essentialize themselves. In response, the people of Darjeeling have proven perfectly capable and willing to perform the tribal slot—as we saw in previous chapters.[22] We must remember, though, that strategic essentialism is a justification of a political register. Gayatri Spivak framed the concept as a politically geared and politically justified tactic. This says little about the deployment of strategic essentialism in the realms of sociality and subjectivity, however. Darjeeling's tribal reforms raise the complicated question of what happens when auto-essentialism crosses into other domains of human experience. What happens, in other words, when strategic essentialism's aims morph from political representation to social and subjective transformation?

Weighing these dynamics, epistemology matters—as does the context in which these ambiguously descriptive/prescriptive knowledges are produced and applied.[23] Upon closer inspection, the renderings of the tribal self in Darjeeling prove peculiar. Recall AITBA's calendar and its video: the content for these portrayals was to be gleaned from Tamangs in Nepal, not those in Darjeeling. Because Darjeeling's Tamangs have "lost" many attributes of ethnic distinction (distinct language, religious practice, custom, dress, etc.), they have looked to their contemporaries in Nepal as the bearers of pure (*suddha*) and original (*maulik*) culture. In this reckoning of authenticity, Tamang culture in India is conversely deemed diluted and impure (*asuddha*). In the interest of recognition and revitalization, the Tamangs consequently made numerous ethnographic trips into Nepal's interior to gather information on the "true" forms of their culture. These endeavors, along with extensive reviews of the anthropological literature, produced precisely the data that became the content of the calendar, the documentary, and the impassioned narratives of the CC member and Pemba. These auto-ethnological practices had an empirical element. However, *and this is crucial*, when brought back to Darjeeling, these representations obtained a different referentiality.[24] They came to refer not to subjects in Nepal, but instead to subjects in Darjeeling itself. In this way, ethnic associations furnished the cultural stuff of tribal recognition and rebirth—at once filling politically normative ethnological forms with sociocultural content, while erecting the informational scaffolding to revitalize culture and reconstruct ethnic selves.

This referential slippage was politically expedient, but it posed phenomenological quandaries for those looking to "find themselves" in their ethnology. The media that these groups produced for the government and themselves often bore little resemblance to day-to-day realities. At best, such representations depicted a people as they wanted to be—and perhaps were becoming. The epistemic peculiarity translated into everyday life in equally odd ways. Recall AITBA's branch meeting at the tea estate schoolhouse. The CC member's pedantry walked a slippery slope between ethnology-as-worldview (the world as it is) and ethnology-as-ethos (the world as it should be): *The Tamangs are Buddhists; the Tamangs wear such and such dress, practice such and such rituals, etc. When, where and for whom this is not the case, it should and must eventually be.* The ethical imperative established, the issue of referentiality—that is, the question of which Tamangs he was actually speaking about when he spouted off fact after ethnographic fact—goes unchallenged.

What I found most remarkable as I accompanied Pemba on his relay of AITBA's message down through the estate was how certain elements remained *in* Pemba's narrative while others dropped *out*. *In* were AITBA's political achievements; *out* was the locals' concern with AITBA's political entanglements. *In* was the ad nauseam litany of ethnographic facts; *out* was the locals' dissatisfaction with AITBA's cultural mandates. And so on and so on, Pemba forwarded AITBA's "technical point of view" to his family and friends. These dynamics illustrate how AITBA's agents and media made *exactitude* a powerful tool for convincing their constituents if not who they are, then what they should be. But exactitude works, in this case, as a matter of detail, not the referential accuracy of the representation itself. The referentiality question was largely obfuscated by a fog of ethnographic facts. For some, like Pemba, these facts condensed into resplendent streams of ethnic consciousness. For others, they remained a cloud hanging over everyday life—at once confusing, disorienting, and alienating.

The tribal turn was marked by varying degrees of subjectification.[25] Ultimately, how individuals found relation to the ideational form of the tribe depended largely on their ability and willingness to identify with its ethnological prescriptions. These makeovers entailed not only recognizing the self in this particular paradigm of the ethnos, but also taking on its attending sociocultural practices.[26] Reformation, in short, hinged on transforming the conceptual into the experiential.[27] This proved a difficult dialectic to embody.

DIVIDED SUBJECTS

It is months after I first accompanied Pemba on his rounds through the tea estate, spreading AITBA's message of Tamang awakening. For days, villagers have made their way to Pemba's home. In each hand they carry a plastic bag—one a kilo of sugar, the other a kilo of flour—the standard donation upon the death of a neighbor in Bidhuwā Busti. Two weeks ago Pemba's ailing mother passed away. During her life, she considered herself a Hindu, yet since her death Pemba has ensured that every detail of her passing be attended to in the proper Tamang Buddhist way. It being the sixteenth day since her death, the *lamas* who had taken up residence for the past several days have finally completed their duties. As I approach, I note that the house seems to lack its usual cheer. Outside I do not see the goat hides drying in the sun, soon to become the heads of one of Pemba's illustrious Tamang *damphu* drums. I call into the house to find Pemba alone. With his wife in the tea fields plucking her daily quota and the kids off at school, there is a solemn stillness inside the home. I wonder if I am intruding on the quietude of his mourning.

He greets me with warmth, as I offer him my two plastic bags and my apologies for being unable to attend his mother's *ghewā* (funerary rite). Pemba lacks his usual zeal. His mannerisms are unmistakably demure. He speaks in hushed tones. Yet something else is different. There is something about his appearance that seems off. He seems somehow younger, frailer, and smaller than the boisterous Pemba of before. I wonder if the grief could have taken a toll so quickly on his countenance. Then I realize he has recently shaved his head. His once close-cropped hair is now but stubble. When I ask him about it, he explains that he has shaved his head to mark the mourning of his deceased mother. This practice upon death is commonplace in Hindu homes. So why has Pemba, a born-again Buddhist, done so?

Pemba needs little prompting to explain the apparent contradiction. He tells me that he was uncertain whether he should shave his head. Particular family members and neighbors believed he should do so. They pressured him, he tells me. His explanation then wanders into a long-winded history of the Tamang, and how upon the death of Nepal's king, all subjects would be required by law to shave their head. This practice was part and parcel of the religious mandate in the Hindu kingdom, Pemba explains:

> It did not exist in our Buddhist dharma. But what to do now? It has become tradition [*paramparā*]. That is why. If I don't shave off my hair, my friends in the village will say, "Your mother has died, at least shave off your hair." This is

all. More and more, the people debate. Somebody says one thing and somebody else says another. The most important thing: what I wish to state is that our heart must be pure. If this is pure, then the soul will pass away peacefully.

What is particularly interesting about Pemba's explanation is that the embodied history—or as he frames it, the tradition (*parampara*)—that he calls upon to justify the shaving of his head is the very history of Hindu oppression that he and his AITBA cadres have railed against with such conviction. Their cultural purification programs have been implemented precisely to rid Tamang culture of this oppressive Hindu influence. But here, Pemba elicits this very history to justify his action. This was one of the many contradictions of his explanation. At one point he alluded to the troubling history through which Tamangs were forced to take up this practice;[28] at another, he offered veiled references to the pressures of local tradition; at still others, he reverted to his familiar idiom of identity-speak, reeling off a litany of ethnographic facts about how true Tamangs care for their dead.

I found Pemba's narrative difficult to follow. Ricocheting from one point to another, he seemed unable to justify his decision in any coherent manner. Clearly, he was torn between two traditions—one, the lived hybrid tradition of his family, friends, and neighbors, for whom the shaving of one's head was a routine marker of grief (irrespective of its Hindu or Buddhist origins); the other, the reconstructed "tradition" of an ostensibly "pure," "original," and recognizable Tamang culture. In the end, he chose to shave his head—the route of lived tradition. Clearly, though, this was a choice that challenged his commitments to Tamang revitalization.

Pemba's dilemma was but one instance of the ways in which ethnological schemas do—and do not—translate into sociocultural practice. The inherent tensions of his decision epitomized how individuals and communities negotiate these prescriptions of the tribe. For Pemba and organizations like AITBA, it was one thing to expound upon the details of tribal revitalization. It was quite another to transform these schemas into practice. Everyday life, after all, bore its own schemas of how the subject should act. Torn between two contending schemas, Pemba here gives voice to the subjective tensions of becoming tribal. Whether it is a question of how one expresses grief, how one celebrates a given holiday, or with whom one associates, defining the self vis-à-vis ethnological paradigms has become increasingly compulsive. More so than the choices individuals make in any given instance, it is this *compulsion* to render difference in conspicuously ethnological ways that marked the tribal turn in Darjeeling—and the politics of the ethno-contemporary more generally.

As we saw with his proselytizing down in the tea estate, Pemba was certainly one to trumpet the logics of ethnic rebirth. Tamang Buddhism, as he was wont to tell, had completely revolutionized his being, transforming him from a deadbeat alcoholic into a respectable, employed father and leader of ethnic renaissance within his community. Yet despite it all, on the occasion of his mother's death, he betrayed his own story of ethnic rebirth—arguably when it mattered most. It would have been easy to discount the shaving of his head as an erratic by-product of his grief. We could have also simply chalked it up to the richly syncretic lifeways of the hills. But as Pemba's own searching explanation made clear, he himself was deeply unsettled by his decision—especially so in the presence of me, a friend but always also an anthropologist. Sitting through his painful attempt at an explanation, I sensed my friend's shame and confusion. I couldn't help but feel implicated. Regrettably, my presence only added to his despair. Perhaps both of us were too committed to an ethnologically coherent point of view. If I were somehow able to return to this conversation, I would wish to tell him that a perfect rationale was not necessary. Considering his grief, perhaps neither was it possible.

Pemba's angst underscores the difficulties that the people of Darjeeling encountered as they struggled to fit themselves into the ethnological straitjacket of a twenty-first-century tribe. Tribal recognition asked them to undo hybrid sociocultural practices that had defined them for generations—to effectively disembody history. The affective impossibilities of that task engendered only further unease for a people already beset by anxieties about their identity and belonging in India.

Difficulties notwithstanding, the quests for recognition and revitalization were also generative. They were committed—and at times very successful—in making new kinds of subjects and new kinds of solidarity, precisely by resurrecting "old" forms of cultural practice. Engendering fluctuating degrees of discovery, confusion, and awkwardness, the effects and affects consequently ran the gamut within communities and within individuals themselves (as we saw with Pemba). To demonstrate the sometimes ungainly ways in which tribal ethno-logics took hold of the body, it is worth shifting from the Tamangs of Bidhuwā Busti to their Gurung neighbors—a people still struggling to remake themselves in a way that is both recognizable and feels right.

EMBODYING KNOWLEDGE

"No, you're doing it wrong. Like this, like this!" a voice exclaims from the corner of the barren concrete gomba.

Having just meandered in to attend her relative's *ghewā*, Anju, a Gurung woman in her mid-thirties, freezes in her tracks, then looks left to see her uncle seated in the rippling light of 108 butter lamps.

"What?" she says to him.

"Like this," he says, bringing his hands to prayer position at his forehead and then lowering them to his chest, as he bends forward in his chair. Anju mimics his motions, and then stops. Everyone is watching.

"Like this?" She pauses to ask, her hands still held in prayer position.

"No. Now prostrate! Go down."

"What?"

"Down! Down!" he insists, gesturing toward the floor.

"Down?"

"Yes, go down!" Still seated, he guides her by again bending forward in his chair.

Anju has never been all that involved in the Gurungs' cultural renaissance. But now, standing there just a few steps across the *gomba*'s threshold, she is, much to her chagrin, the center of attention. Everyone struggles to hold back laughter. This is supposed to be a somber occasion. Anju hesitantly starts lowering her body toward the concrete floor, looking left for approval that she is doing it right. A nod of approval. She continues moving to the floor in hesitant, segmented motions. Finally her chest touches down and she stretches her body out toward the Buddha statue that presides over the new temple. Once fully prone, she hears approval from the five or six relatives in the room and quickly returns to her feet with a smile. Now confident with the sequence, she hurriedly proceeds through the final two of three prostrations. Having passed the test, she holds back an embarrassed grin and sneaks, relieved, to the side of the room, joining the relatives who have gathered for the forty-ninth-day funerary rites of their recently deceased ancestor. Slowly, other Gurungs begin to trickle into the half-finished *gomba* to attend the *ghewā*.

. . .

Ten years ago, the death of a Gurung in Bidhuwā Busti would have typically been marked by a Hindu rite, but today the family has chosen the Buddhist route. Since early morning, the local branch leaders of the Gurung ethnic association, the Tamu Choj Dhin (TCD),[29] have been preparing the temple, along with several Buddhist monks who have been hired for the day. Unfortunately, the monks are not Gurungs, but these Tamang *lamas* will have to do until the Gomba Management Committee can afford to sponsor a Gurung *lama* to live in the village and see after the temple.[30] The temple itself, which doubles as a Gurung cultural center, is the pride of the local Gurung community. Their grassroots initiative to build the Guru Pema Choeling Gomba (est. 2006) has earned the local TCD branch fame across the hills.[31] Even in its incomplete construction, it is an important symbol of Gurung revitalization.

Still, the entire setting is somewhat unfamiliar for the family who has gathered on this particular morning. The warmth of the butter lamps, the wafting smoke of juniper, the cadence of the *lamas* chanting in a foreign tongue are all part of a Buddhist religious tradition that until very recently had far less traction in the village. That Anju would be so unsure of the proper Buddhist practice upon entering the new temple thus occurred through no fault of her own. In fact, her uncle who coached her through the prostrations had perfected them himself just minutes earlier. Nevertheless, they were there as a family making a conscious decision to relinquish the Hindu tradition of their past and embrace the more "original" practice of Gurung Buddhism.[32]

Like others in Darjeeling, the Gurungs were working to rid themselves of the trace of Hinduism. This was deemed necessary for the attainment of ST status and for the restoration of a "pure" Gurung identity.

Yet unlike, say, their Tamang neighbors whose socioreligious practice was and remains predominantly Buddhist with Hindu traces, Gurung syncretism was of a strong Hindu persuasion. There have always been Buddhist Gurungs in Bidhuwā Busti. But the last decade has seen a sea change toward the Buddhist tradition. The ethnic association has encouraged this shift, especially since the Gurungs' initial application for ST status was denied on the grounds of too much Hindu assimilation. The rejection underscored the need to embrace the kind of Buddhist practices that Anju was learning as she laid her body on the concrete floor of the *gomba*.

For Buddhist adepts, prostrating when one enters the temple is fluid and automatic. It is part of what Bourdieu, following Mauss, might deem a religious *habitus*—an embodied disposition that meanders between conscious and unconscious action.[33] Yet we see something very different upon Anju's entry into the temple. She wanders in and is suddenly put on the spot. Never mind that many in the temple are equally as unfamiliar with the act of prostration. Her uncle directs her to prostrate before the Buddha. As she lowers her body to the floor, her actions are calculated, hesitant, uncertain—quite different from Bourdieu's notion of *habitus*. Once her chest touches the concrete and she hears the approval of her peers, she realizes the proper form. She is able to synthesize the elemental *actions* as a single *act*.[34] More importantly, she can do it herself—and quickly! And so she races through her final two prostrations and sheepishly scurries away from the attention.

Anju's prostration was one momentary instance, but it signaled the broader conditions through which these reforms became embodied practice. Anju's hesitation; the social pressures of her peers; the looming exigencies of the state and recognition: these were hallmarks of the tribal turn in Darjeeling. While Anju may have hesitantly taken on these practices, others embraced them with zeal. For a people long denied a secure sense of identity and belonging in India, these revitalizations instilled both new promise and an array of difficulties.

AMBIVALENT HABITATIONS

Pemba's and Anju's stories give pause to consider how late liberalism's ethno-logics map onto—and into—people's ways of being in the world.

Their individual stories were, of course, embedded in broader social contours. In villages like Bidhuwā Busti, the movements for tribal recognition and rebirth reconfigured inter-ethnic relations in significant ways. When Pemba's Tamangs achieved ST status in 2003, it set them apart from Anju's Gurungs. Given the introduced inequality at hand, Gurungs increasingly looked to Tamangs with resentment, jealousy, and feelings of injustice. Tamangs reciprocated with a more-authentic-than-thou attitude toward the unrecognized. Unbending definitions of culture sharpened what earlier were more-fluid distinctions between these groups. This is not to say that these reforms created difference out of thin air. The Tamangs and Gurungs of Darjeeling have retained awareness of their ethnic distinction through the generations. But the tribal turn assigned new stakes to these distinctions, thereby transforming how ethnic difference was known and lived in Bidhuwā Busti. Following the orders of ethnic associations like AITBA, neighbors who once celebrated popular holidays like Dasain/Durga Pujā together now refused to join one another, for fear that their mingling would erode the cultural distinctiveness of a proper tribe or, worse yet, evince the corrupting presence of Hinduism. To mitigate this possibility, AITBA and the Gurungs' ethnic association promoted their respective versions of the Buddhist new year (*Lochar*) as sanctioned alternatives. My experiences of these holidays showed them to be ethnically exclusive affairs. My friends in Bidhuwā Busti expressed mixed feelings about these developments. At times, they appreciated the value of these ethnically exclusive affairs. At others, they lamented the new separations with their neighbors. This was just one of the many ways that the tribal turn rewrote the rules and realities of inter-ethnic sociality and solidarity.

Rifts also opened up *within* communities. Associations like AITBA and their orthodoxies gained credence from the state's criteria of tribal recognition, but when these organizations pushed the ethnological prescriptions onto their constituents, they often encountered resistance. Lauding one version of culture as pure and authentic inevitably cast others as inauthentic and of lesser value. Within a community, this meant telling fellow members that their sociocultural practices were corrupt, impure, and diluted. Not surprisingly, when ethnic elites marched into a village and proclaimed long-celebrated holidays like Dasain to be inauthentic, people took offense. Even those who supported the movements for cultural revitalization and ST status sometimes resisted the austerity of these impositions. (Recall the local villagers' complaints to the Central Committee member about the tensions caused by AITBA's reforms). These orthodox tendencies drove many away from becoming members. Others joined alternative organizations like the Tamang Gedung, sending schisms through the community.

Negotiating these circumstances, individuals had to decide whether to abandon practices they had always known in favor of newly invented traditions.[35] These decisions came with difficult considerations of how the choices made would affect one's standing in the community. Moreover, how might such *personal* decisions affect their *collective* chances of obtaining much-needed rights and entitlements from the state? Sociocultural practices that had earlier been taken for granted suddenly had new ramifications. One's choices—be it the observation of certain holidays or one's dress—became signals of one's ascription to these movements and the political parties backing them. On Diwali, Tamang and Gurung homes that used to glow through the night went dark. Even families were torn apart by divergent ethnological persuasions. The tribal turn thus came to rework even the most personal dynamics of everyday life. With remarkable speed and power, it transformed the everyday terms of difference. As even its staunchest supporters admitted, not all these changes were expected.

How then to weigh these intended and unintended outcomes? How then to balance the positive and negative ends to which communities are renegotiating state-sanctioned ethno-logics? Standard appeals, it seems, are unable to handle the complexities of these emergent dynamics. An attention to late liberal governmentality and its attending "politics of the governed" helps to plot the present contexts within which communities must struggle for rights and historical redress.[36] These analytics enable us to see the repurposing of ethnology as an innovative and necessary response to contemporary systems of recognition and social justice. Yet they tell us little of the tensions that shape these movements at every turn. Strategic essentialism similarly explains the epistemic character and political expedience of these appropriations, but stops short of justifying the impositions of tribal normativity in daily life. In these ethnologically affected circumstances, questions remain: Who is doing the imposing? Through what relations of power and expertise? And what may be said of the experiences of those who wittingly and unwittingly find themselves the subjects and objects of these reforms? To broach these questions is to bring agency back into the equation, but in a way that keeps in view the capacity to both resist *and* perpetuate existing forms of knowledge and power.[37] AITBA's reforms and Pemba and Anju's hesitant embodiments demand nothing less.

At the end of the day, the tribal turn proved phenomenologically uneven and fraught. Even when we look to its exemplars—be they ethnic association members gathered for their monthly meetings or born-again ethnics, like Pemba, struggling to practice what he preached—we see tensions, confusions, and above all, ambivalence. That ambivalence, let me suggest, may well be the signature experience of late liberal becoming. As these cases from Darjeeling show, finding oneself amid today's grids of ethno-intelligibility can be a categorically vexed affair. For a people whose ways of being—whose kind of difference—have never quite fit the norms of the day, the ambivalences of these habitations were all too familiar. The categorical unease would, in short time, instigate yet more shifts in the forms—and feelings—of identity and its politics in the hills. What followed was the stuff of political legend. It is to these more recent chapters of the ethno-contemporary in Darjeeling that I now turn.

CHAPTER 7

PERPETUATED PARADIGMS
At the Limits of Ethno-Intelligibility

SOME THINGS CHANGE quickly in Darjeeling. Others do not. In 2006, becoming tribal was the order of the day. The years since, however, have shown the tribal turn to be what it was: a moment—or a chapter—in a longer struggle for recognition, autonomy, and belonging. In the pages that follow, I turn attention to a series of more recent movements to ask: What happens *after* the tribal turn? From the vantage point of today, what are we to make of its ethnological means and dubious ends? And what might Darjeeling's mercurial ethnopolitics teach us about the terms of difference in India—and the ethno-contemporary more broadly?

These questions refocus the ethnographic lens at multiple levels. Locally, they force a reckoning of the often severe contingencies of life and politics in places like Darjeeling. Nationally, they prompt a plotting of the unstable grounds—and changing faces—of late liberalism in India. Globally, they beg comparison of the conditions that define the ethno-contemporary now versus those that defined it before. Toward that end, this chapter moves from 2007 to the present (2015) to track the latest permutations of a categorically searching politics. Thinking beyond the tribal turn, I advocate for a deeper, more historical reading of the ethno-contemporary—one agile enough to track its fluctuating forms, while grounded enough to reveal the enduring exclusions and affects at hand.

187

To this point: near the end of my 2007 fieldwork, anxious belonging made a shocking return, sending Darjeeling into a state of unthinkable turmoil. The events served as a powerful reminder of the histories of anxiety and non-belonging that undergird identity and its politics in the hills. Amid the ensuing chaos, the lesson was clear: the anthropology of the ethno-contemporary can ill afford to confine its scope to the present. Rather, it needs history. Ethnographic and historical perspective together afford a crucial means to unpack the interplays of continuity and change—reproduction and emergence—that define the ethno-contemporary now and going forward.[1] In Darjeeling, this requires thinking beyond the ethnological trappings of the tribal turn. So as to set the stage for the transformations that followed, let me briefly recap those pivotal years of the mid-2000s when becoming tribal ruled the day.

In the fall of 2006, the Sixth Schedule seemed on its way to becoming a reality. The government had recently completed its Ethnographic Survey (discussed in Chapter 4), giving reason to believe that the remaining "left-out" communities would be granted ST status. This would establish the tribal majority thought necessary for tribal autonomy. By all counts, things were progressing toward a tribal future. Still, the local administration was leaving nothing to chance. Subash Ghisingh commanded his Department of Information and Cultural Affairs (DICA) to promulgate tribal identity without question. Heeding orders, Ram Bahadur Koli and his DICA colleagues (whom we met in Chapter 3) engineered stunning displays of primitiveness, animism, tribal culture, and all the rest. When necessary, they enforced compliance with a heavy hand. Ethnic delegations meanwhile shuttled between Darjeeling, Kolkata, and Delhi, lobbying their communities' cause for ST status. With the quests for autonomy and recognition driving each other, the synergy was palpable.

Support for the Sixth Schedule surged throughout 2006. But it proved ephemeral. Come 2007, Ghisingh had yet to finalize the deal. The ST cases that would tilt the balance toward autonomy mysteriously vanished into governmental limbo. No one knew why. The opposition seized the opportunity. Spearheaded by Madan Tamang of the All India Gorkha League, the opposition harped upon the glaring disconnects between these tribal claims and the realities of daily life. The Sixth Schedule, they further argued, paled in comparison to the separate state of Gorkhaland that Ghisingh originally promised in the 1980s. Tribal politics, they claimed, would never fulfill the people's longings for authentic recognition, autonomy, and belonging in India. As the opposition had it, Ghisingh and his GNLF party were not just misrepresenting the people; they were forsaking their deepest desires.

Challenging Ghisingh and the seemingly within-reach promises of affirmative action and tribal autonomy was risky. Initially, the opposition's critiques struggled to gain traction. But as Ghisingh foundered and the cases stalled, the public began to listen. Throughout 2007, local intellectuals convened forums to raise public awareness of the Sixth Schedule's shortcomings. Op-eds filled the papers, debating the Sixth Schedule's ability to satisfy the people's desires for national inclusion in either a juridical or an affective sense. And slowly but surely, people began murmuring about whether tribal autonomy was really what they wanted and deserved.

Ghisingh responded by redoubling his efforts to get the bill to Parliament before the critiques gained further ground. National politics repeatedly deferred his efforts. The coalition government in New Delhi had more-pressing—and more-central—issues to manage, among them a suddenly fragile India-U.S. nuclear deal and politically volatile land expropriations in West Bengal and elsewhere. Despite promises otherwise, the Monsoon Session of Parliament (2007) came and went without any results, making it clear that Ghisingh was finding little purchase at the Centre.

At the margins, a public grew restive. Attendance at tribal rituals suddenly dropped. No longer willing to defend Ghisingh's tribal musings, many of my informants questioned whether the Old Man had lost a step in his old age. Some even questioned whether he was losing his mind. As dissent crept through the ranks, one had to wonder: Had Ghisingh finally lost his magic? Had he played upon the people's anxieties over belonging one too many times? Had he pushed the envelope of identity too far with these tribal politics? Time would soon tell. Unbeknownst to any of us, Indian pop culture was about to present the people of Darjeeling with an altogether new saga of being-in and being-of the nation. The terms of difference would shift accordingly.

INDIAN IDOL

The party began just after six p.m. on September 23, 2007.[2] The much-anticipated night had arrived. People poured into the streets. Jeeps and motorbikes overflowing with youths paraded through town, honking, chanting, and singing in anticipation. Across the nation the votes had been cast. In just a few short hours, a Gorkha of Darjeeling stood to become an Indian Idol.

Minutes before the winner of *Indian Idol* (India's version of the popular television show *American Idol*) was to be announced, Darjeeling's Prashant Tamang was handed the microphone, and the opportunity to sing one last, impromptu number. A boyish twenty-four years old, Prashant launched into "Bir Gorkhali," an a cappella ode to Gurkha warriors. On air before millions, Prashant's off-the-cuff rendition was a bit awkward and not nearly as polished as his competitor's. But it appeared as heartfelt as it could be. One of Darjeeling's own, for a celebrated moment, could bask in the national limelight.

FIGURE 7.1 *Celebrating Prashant's Indian Idol Victory*

Then, just before ten p.m., Bollywood star John Abraham reached into his magic box and confirmed what many already knew in their hearts: Prashant Tamang was this year's Indian Idol. Firecrackers exploded across the hills of Darjeeling. The promenade became a thicket of joy. People danced in the streets as live images of Prashant warped across public Jumbotrons. The Prashant Fan Club launched all-night parties. Local schools, colleges, tea gardens, and most businesses were given holiday so the carnival could continue into the next day.

Hailed as an ambassador of the Gorkha people, Prashant Tamang had become much more than an instant pop icon. For the people of Darjeeling, indeed for Nepali-speakers the world over, his victory was seen as a coming-out party on India's national stage. A Gorkha was Indian Idol. The fairy tale was real.

Yet, by September 25, the euphoria of the 23rd had morphed into outrage. The day after Prashant's victory, Red FM disc jockey Ulta Pulta Nitin went on air and sarcastically warned Delhi that if all Nepali *chowkidars* (guardsmen) became Indian Idols, who would guard the private property of India?[3] Riffing on common Gorkha stereotypes, Nitin joked, "Prashant Tamang has become Indian Idol. Tonight we need to guard our houses, malls, and restaurants by ourselves as there will be no Nepali people to guard these places." And further, "All *momo* [dumpling] shops will remain closed as the Nepali guy has become Indian Idol."[4] By the 25th, the Prashant Fan Club, led by then-GNLF muscle man Bimal Gurung, had declared a *bandh* (general strike) shutting down all commerce and travel in the hills. Effigies of DJ Nitin were ablaze in the streets.

On the morning of September 28, five thousand Prashant supporters gathered in Siliguri (a city in the plains, three hours to the south of Darjeeling Town) to file an official complaint against DJ Nitin. For those of us in Darjeeling, the details of what happened next remain hazy. Reports suggested a minor skirmish broke out at the front of the procession in a crowded commercial strip. The row quickly spread along communal lines. Bengali shop owners emerged from their stalls with sticks and attacked the Gorkha protestors. About eight hundred Gorkhas, including fifty children, fled into the courthouse grounds, seeking shelter from the barrage of bricks and rocks raining down upon them.

FIGURE 7.2 *Deriding DJ Nitin, Defending Gorkhas*

FIGURE 7.3 *Outside the Courthouse.*
Source: Kundan Yolmo

The Bengali mob now owned the streets. Tear gas was ineffective. The police then vanished, leaving the Gorkhas on their own to weather the storm. For eight hours they remained trapped inside the courthouse. Finally, at seven forty-five p.m., the Indian Army and Border Security Forces were called in to free the trapped Gorkhas.

The news broke piecemeal in Darjeeling. On the national channels, looped videos of burning vehicles, projectile-wielding mobs, and police idling at a safe distance played incessantly, as reporters tried to make sense of what was happening. Simultaneously, Darjeeling's local channel aired live footage of the All Gorkha Student Union (AGSU) protests going on in Darjeeling Town. There hundreds of enraged youths chanted, "The police procession should give us justice! All those who slander the Gorkhas, watch out! Death to the Bengali Government!" The streets of Darjeeling went dead as people awaited more news. No one was sure whether another *bandh* (strike) had been called. It didn't matter. The fantasy had turned into a nightmare. Needing a break from the slow drip of information, Eklavya and I switched off the television to take a walk. We needed to process everything that was happening.

. . .

Bandhs in South Asia bring an eerie peace. Without the drone and the wobbling headlights of the jeeps that typically ply Hill Cart Road, the crossroads is pleasantly quiet, and strangely dark. We happen upon Eklavya's old friend, Puran, who emerges from his freshly painted store sporting a three-piece beige suit. A budding entrepreneur who dabbles on the side in jazz guitar, Puran, with his long ponytail and laid-back style, cuts quite the figure as he ambles over, hand outstretched to greet us. As we talk, he tells us that earlier in the day he and friends almost beat up a carload of Bengali men who made a comment to a local girl as they passed through the very stretch of road where we are standing. Narrating the event, Puran suddenly bows up his chest and strikes at the air, as though the Bengalis were right there, close enough to feel his rage. I am taken aback; this is not the easygoing Puran I have come to know.

"What did they say to her?" I ask.

He doesn't remember. "Normally I wouldn't do such a thing, but at this moment, in the wave of the moment . . ." He can explain no more.

We discuss Prashant's win, Nitin's comments, the riot. I share with Puran my sympathy, but gently suggest to him how things could have been different had the people of Darjeeling not reacted so strongly to the comments made over the airwaves of Delhi. . . . if they had only let it roll off their back.

Puran listens intently, then rejects the grounds of my perspective. "But you see, this Prashant Tamang thing is really about more than Prashant Tamang."

That much is painfully clear.

GORKHA RESURGENCE

Indian Idol tapped into the people's long-standing anxieties over belonging in India—what, in Chapter 1, I termed "anxious belongings." The saga, in turn, triggered shocking ethnopolitical transformations. Consider the immediate aftermath. Just five days after the riots, the All Gorkha Student Union (AGSU) announced: "The recent Siliguri riots have prompted us to speak out. The incident made us feel that the Gorkhas are not safe. We always have to prove our identity in this country. This is happening because we do not have our own land . . . The Gorkhas require their own land!"[5]

That same week, the leader of the Prashant Fan Club, Bimal Gurung, quit the GNLF to float his own party. On October 7, 2007, twenty thousand people thronged to see the former GNLF henchman launch the Gorkha Janmukti Morcha—the Gorkha People's Liberation Front (hereafter "the Morcha"). With the crowd extending as far back into the bazaar as one could see, I found a perch on the beams of an unfinished construction project to witness the largest public gathering in Darjeeling since the 1980s Gorkhaland Agitation.

It would come to be known as "Foundation Day," the day Gurung put identity back on track to its lauded destiny: Gorkhaland. "Jai Gorkha! Jai Gorkhaland!" reverberated through the crowd, as twenty thousand strong chanted a new Liberation Front into existence. In the crowded streets below, the masses chanted, danced, and swayed, as specially written

FIGURE 7.4 *The Birth of a New Liberation Front*

songs flooded the scene with pinings for a separate state. There and then, the hot-blooded youth of AGSU, many of them drunken and shirtless, pledged their allegiance to Gurung's new Liberation Front—infusing an old cause with a new generation of vitriol. Gorkhaland was once again a movement.

Suddenly there were two competing movements afoot for autonomy: one, the Ghisingh-GNLF-led quest for Sixth Schedule tribal auton-omy; the other, the Gurung-Morcha-led agitation for a separate state of Gorkhaland. No one knew which way the political winds were blowing. On October 19, the following banner (see next page) went up in town depicting the complexities.

This complicated situation was unexpected and deeply contentious. *Indian Idol*, in this regard, became a watershed moment. While the saga demonstrated pop culture's ability to (re)charge publics and their politics, it also showed GNLF leader Subash Ghisingh to be woefully out of touch with his people and the times. Importantly, Ghisingh never supported

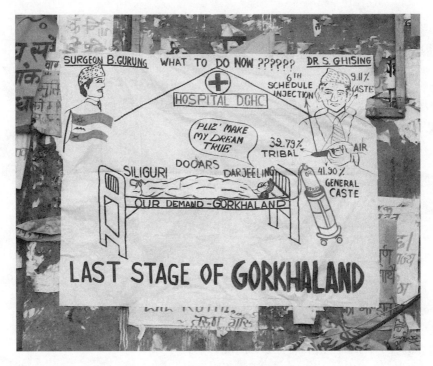

FIGURE 7.5 *The Political Scenario in the Fall of 2007*

Prashant's *Indian Idol* bid, seeing the hoopla as mere child's play. This hurt the people deeply—so much so that just days before the show's finale and with Ghisingh in Indonesia researching tribal tourism, posters went up in town warning that if Prashant didn't win, Ghisingh would not be allowed to return to Darjeeling. Betrayed by their paternal leader and strung out from the emotional roller coaster that followed Prashant's victory, the public was on edge. Meanwhile, having led the spirited campaign to *Indian Idol* victory, Bimal Gurung found his political capital surging. So with the masses once again beset with anxiety, the Morcha's muscular politics proved right for the time.

The Morcha went straight to work reinstating the primacy of Gorkha identity. Doing so, they championed an identity that they believed mapped closer to the sociocultural and affective realities of the people than did the tribal ploys of Ghisingh and the GNLF. Where the GNLF brought rocks, the Morcha told the people to celebrate as they always had. Where the GNLF struggled for Sixth Schedule tribal autonomy, the Morcha promised Gorkhaland. So sure was Bimal Gurung that *this* Gorkhaland Movement would be successful that he promised to commit suicide were a separate state not achieved by March 10, 2010. Galvanized by this firebrand rhetoric and with little to show for their tribal efforts of recent years, the public's support quickly shifted to the Morcha.

This Gorkha resurgence marked the latest in a long line of categorically searching politics. And like those movements that preceded it, the second Gorkhaland Movement was driven by deeper yearnings for belonging in India. No one could have foreseen the events that spawned the inception of Gorkhaland 2.0. Yet, when understood through the analytic of affect and anxious belonging, this seemingly unbelievable sequence through which a television show became the catalyst of political upheaval and subnationalist agitation proves more believable. How quickly the euphoria and cultural pride of Prashant's victory morphed into horror and anger. How quickly that horror and anger morphed into revived determination for Gorkhaland. Here we see anxious belonging shape-shifting into a range of political emotions—each of them pulsing with visceral energy and possibility. One moment joy, another hot-blooded rage, the next unbridled subnationalist desire: indeed, shape-shifting remains anxious belonging's signature mode of actualization—and therein its greatest potential to radically affect life and politics.

The events disrupted the delicate calculus of tribal becoming. While the bids for ST status went on, the rise of a second Gorkhaland Movement all but ended the bid for tribal autonomy. Just two months after *Indian Idol*, the Sixth Schedule bill finally made it to Parliament, in December of 2007. It was promptly shelved with requests for further inquiries (a clear nod to the opposition's headway in Delhi and the transformations unfolding in Darjeeling). With the bid for tribal autonomy effectively dead, the Morcha stormed to power in 2008. Promising Gorkhaland and relying heavily on political intimidation, the Morcha induced sweeping political conversions, taking over the municipality and triggering a volatile movement against Ghisingh and the GNLF. Interparty violence and protests turned the tide irrevocably against Ghisingh, and on February 29, 2008, the longtime savior of the Gorkhas was forced to resign—ending

FIGURE 7.6 *Banner Depicting Bimal Gurung and a Future Gorkhaland*

two decades of GNLF rule.[6] Taking his place was Bimal Gurung, a newly arisen demagogue to answer the people's longings.

Those who refused allegiance to the Morcha were labeled enemies of Gorkhaland and chased from the hills. Evoking Gandhi, the Morcha claimed their movement to be a nonviolent affair—a notable divergence from the violent agitations of the 1980s. But on the ground, interparty violence was rampant. Proponents of the tribal turn like Ram Bahadur Koli (DICA's executive director) were assaulted and their homes ransacked. Not wanting this to happen to them, people converted by the score. Though not elected, by March of 2008 the Morcha suddenly had a monopolistic grip on power and the public imagination. Whereas just a year earlier, becoming tribal had ruled the day, now only Gorkhaland would satisfy the people. With the terms shifted from "tribal" back to "Gorkha," Gorkhaland 2.0 proceeded accordingly.

The new agitation had devastating effects. Beginning in 2008, acerbic protests and indefinite strikes crippled the local economy. Interparty violence, assassinations, hunger strikes, and sporadic attacks on government offices became the hallmarks of the Morcha's ad hoc insurgency. Amid this day-to-day uncertainty, life necessarily proceeded in fits and starts. And so, much like in the 1980s, agitation made its uncanny return to the hills, becoming once again a political project and a socially embodied state.[7]

THE NEW REGIME

When the Morcha first emerged, many savvy commentators opined that the new party was just old wine in new bottles. The Morcha did look suspiciously like the GNLF of old, with its militant rhetoric; its green, yellow, and white flags; and, above all, its claims of Gorkha identity, its "crisis," and eventual resolution in Gorkhaland. The resemblance was not coincidental. Morcha founder Bimal Gurung had served as Ghisingh's henchman until just weeks before launching the Morcha. Likewise, most of the party's leadership and constituents had defected from the GNLF. But this was definitely *not* the Gorkhaland Movement of the 1980s. Even as the Morcha commenced with the well-worn tactics of subnationalist agitation, they advanced a discernibly new politics of difference—one articulated through the globally salient tropes of cultural difference, recognition, and self-determination. As anthropologist Sarah Besky has cogently noted, the movement similarly stressed the Gorkhas' primordial connection to the land.[8] The Gorkhas, the Morcha insisted, were "sons of the soil." Evoking these tropes of indigeneity, the Morcha borrowed liberally from the paradigms of their tribal predecessors. As they went about refashioning a singular Gorkha identity, the Morcha's ethnological tactics were, if anything, more severe.

This became increasingly clear as the Gorkhaland Movement unfolded. When the Morcha first appeared on the scene, the party promised a more tolerant and syncretic cultural politics. Throughout the holiday season of 2007, Morcha leaders invited people to celebrate Durga Pujā, Diwali, and other holidays as they always had: in their usual festival garb, with vermillion *sindur* streaking their hair in the familiar Hindu way, with *ṭikās* on their foreheads, and, of course, with Durga watching over them all. By honoring the syncretic lifeways of the Gorkhas writ large, the Morcha offered a compelling counter to the GNLF's mandates of tribal culture. With one party (the Morcha) pushing a syncretic vision

of the Gorkhas and the other (the GNLF) championing a vision of Darjeeling's tribes, the holiday season of 2007 turned into a cultural battle-
field. The competing movements leveraged their respective ethno-logics,
parades, and claims upon the subject. The everyday citizen thus found
herself caught in the crossfire of yet another cultural politics.

But that was the fall of 2007, when the GNLF was still in the picture.
Once the Morcha chased Ghisingh and the GNLF from the hills (taking
with them their tribal politics), the new regime asserted Gorkha identity
in increasingly non-negotiable terms. These stridently *cultural* politics
distinguished the twenty-first-century Gorkhaland Movement from the
1980s Gorkhaland Movement. At the same time, these ethnological tactics marked a telling continuity between these new Gorkha politics and
the tribal movements of the 1990s and 2000s. The Morcha's tightening
cultural grip coincided with the intensification of agitation. Throughout 2008, *bandhs* crippled the hills, as the masses took to the streets demanding a separate state. Darjeeling came to be glossed in the familiar
white, green, and yellow of Gorkhaland. Place-making became key to the
Morcha's program. The party mandated that businesses and homes fly
Morcha flags. They erected signage announcing the "state" of Gorkhaland and created corresponding license plates for Gorkha vehicles. To
patrol and ensure order, the Morcha created its own paramilitary force,
known as the Gorkhaland Personnel. Thousands of young men and
women swelled the ranks, donning their signature tracksuit uniforms.
Those who opposed the Morcha faced violent repercussions. The making
of Gorkhaland went hand in hand with an increasingly austere cultural
politics. Every state, after all, needs its nation.

Heading into the holiday season of 2008, the Morcha announced
a strict dress code to be in force from Durga Pujā through the end of
Diwali. Turning against the tribal imperatives of years past (and against
their own tolerant principles of just a year before), the party proclaimed
the official and only authentic dress of the Gorkhas to be *daurā suruwāl*
(traditional Nepali coat and cap) for men and *chowbandi choli* (Nepali
dress and blouse) for women.[9] The order sparked immediate protests
from groups like the Tamangs, Lepchas, and others, who noted that as
discrete ethnicities (and recognized Scheduled Tribes) they had their

own authentic ethnic attire and their own socioreligious practices, which did not allow for the celebration of Hindu holidays like Durga Pujā and Diwali. These identities, they claimed, prevented them from complying with the Morcha's prescriptions of a pan-ethnic Gorkha culture. Morcha president Bimal Gurung responded to the dissenting groups as follows:

> Lepchas, Sherpas, and Tamangs want to wear their respective dresses, but I insist that they wear *daurā suruwāl* because, being the inhabitants of this place, they are Gorkhas . . . I am not interfering in your faith or culture like Subash Ghisingh and neither asking you to shed blood for Gorkhaland. We have to prove that we share no cultural or linguistic affinity with West Bengal and hence are demanding a separate state . . . These communities should don the traditional Gorkha attire to show solidarity with the Gorkhaland Movement.[10]

After several days of controversy, exceptions were eventually granted to these communities.[11] The order was subsequently relaxed from a "compulsion" to a "request." Terminology notwithstanding, the Morcha worked to ensure compliance. The Morcha's Women's Wing, the Nari Morcha, organized a "Dress Code Road Show" to demonstrate authentic Gorkha dress.[12] Signaling their growing propensity for moral policing, the Morcha took the campaign door-to-door to impart firsthand lessons of proper Gorkha attire. Word began circulating that Morcha cadres found not wearing the prescribed attire would be suspended from the party for three months.

On the morning of October 14, 2008, in the thick of holiday festivities, a poster went up in Darjeeling warning the public that violation of the dress code would be equated with opposition to Gorkhaland. Importantly, the poster bore the signature of the Gorkha Janmukti Yuva Morcha, the Morcha's Youth Wing. Hours later, havoc broke out on the streets as a gang of Morcha cadres rushed about Darjeeling's main bazaar brandishing paintbrushes and buckets of paint, blackfacing violators of the dress code. Those not in compliance quickly fled public spaces to the safe haven of their private homes.[13]

As news of the incidents spread, outrage rippled through the community. By late afternoon, Morcha leaders condemned the blackfacing, taking to task the rogue doings of their party cadres. The party secretary issued a statement decrying the Youth Wing's actions, but not without reiterating the party's logic: "Those wearing traditional dresses," the statement claimed, "are helping a cultural revolution, which is aimed at establishing the difference between us and the rest of Bengal."[14]

A new poster was subsequently pasted directly over the Youth Wing's earlier warning, condemning the vulgar acts of blackfacing that had transpired earlier in the day. Faced with such sudden public backlash, Morcha leaders were clearly trying to distance themselves from the events. The facts proved not so easy to paste over. Pictures of the incident soon emerged, showing members of the administration among the dozen or so well-dressed older men applying the blackface, shaming unsuspecting citizens for their non-compliance, marking them in the darkest way—and just as the so-called Youth's poster warned—as opponents of Gorkhaland.

.   .   .

Ethnographers have long been concerned with identity and its politics. Of late, many of us have come to see communities' representations of culture and identity as integral to a new politics of difference, which continues to reconfigure the sociopolitical possibilities of indigenous and marginalized communities in promising ways.[15] Yet for all the attention to the external representations of culture, identity, tradition, and the like, less attention has been directed to the *internal* cultural politics of these movements.[16] Dynamics of cultural enforcement, moral policing, and imposed orthodoxies remain uncomfortable topics among those of us who support these movements but find their ethnological impositions troubling. The justification of strategic essentialism works far better when applied to communities' external representations of culture. But, concerning movements' internal mandates of homogeneity, it leaves difficult questions unanswered. What are the dynamics of these ethnological enforcements? To what degree are the logics of strategic essentialism serving budding fundamentalisms?[17] What might academics make of once-disciplinary paradigms put to alternative "disciplinary" uses? These are uncomfortable and under-asked questions in the anthropology of indigeneity. But if Darjeeling is any indication, such disciplinary endeavors may—for better and for worse—do much to shape the lived realities of otherwise well-intended movements.

Weighing these stakes, we might do well to record the other side of these ethnological imperatives—namely, the resistance that these paradigms face when forced upon communities. The blackfacing incident may have shown the Morcha's heavy cultural hand, but crucially, it also showed the public's limited tolerance of such mandates. As the public backlash made clear, it is one thing to represent a singular Gorkha subject; it is quite another to violently remake a people as such.

Upon closer scrutiny, then, the second Gorkhaland Movement exhibits both continuities and differences with its 1980s *Gorkha* and 1990s/2000s *tribal* antecedents. The movement recouped an old term (*Gorkha*) and an old cause (Gorkhaland), but it has articulated these in fundamentally new ways. In its ethnological predilections, the movement has, in fact, appeared to be far more similar to the tribal movements of the 1990s and 2000s than its leaders might care to acknowledge. The terms have shifted from *tribal* back to *Gorkha*, but the ethno-logics remain notably the same. Recombinant, shifting, and contingent, these are the interplays of old and new that define this Gorkhaland Agitation as a movement of the ethno-contemporary. As Paul Rabinow has similarly noted in his writings on the contemporary writ large, such are the dialectics of reproduction and emergence that constitute the present day.[18]

That said, for the people of Darjeeling, it is not just the means of these movements that have proven eerily familiar. So have the ends. And is here where *failure* must figure into our reckonings of the ethno-contemporary in this particular corner of India.

FAMILIAR ENDS

When the Morcha first appeared on the scene, the party seemed to have struck upon a perfect balance of old and new. With the public's hopes and anxieties roused by *Indian Idol* and the drama that followed, the Morcha channeled those energies into a new, but perfectly familiar cause: Gorkhaland. Through their aesthetic and affective technologies, Bimal Gurung and his party had seemingly mastered the politics of the uncanny. In its look and feel, Gorkhaland 2.0 was strangely familiar. But so too was the language of indigeneity through which this old cause was resurrected. Thanks to the tribal movements of the 1990s and 2000s, Darjeeling's public had grown accustomed to the idioms of cultural difference, rights, and self-determination now adopted by the Morcha. As the party rendered the old anew, the antinomy was precisely the point. Through new means, the Morcha promised a different, more successful end to *this* Gorkhaland Movement. That perfect balance of the familiar and unfamiliar—what Freud would call the uncanny[19]—proved difficult to maintain, however.

By 2010, three years of agitation had yielded little. The Morcha, West Bengal, and the Centre had gone through multiple rounds of tripartite talks to resolve the crisis. Yet as news of the negotiations leaked, the focus seemed to be not a separate state of Gorkhaland (as the Morcha had promised), but rather the creation of an "interim set-up" with dubious autonomy. This sounded suspiciously like the DGHC administration, which summarily failed to satisfy the people's desires following the 1980s Gorkhaland Agitation. With the second Gorkhaland Movement toiling on, the Morcha's double-speak became increasingly apparent. The public, meanwhile, was growing weary and wary. The violence, the tactics, the false promises—they had seen it all before. Coming as no surprise to anyone, March 10, 2010—the day Bimal Gurung was to deliver Gorkhaland or martyr himself—came and went with little ado.

Discussing identity and politics at this time was difficult. While people spoke to me privately about widespread dissension, few dared speak openly against the Morcha, for fear of violent repercussions. Sensing that they were losing their base, Morcha leaders tightened their grip on power. Since the Morcha had chased nearly all opposing parties out of the hills, opposition leaders like Madan Tamang of the All India Gorkha League had little choice but to work through the press from the plains below. This opposition in exile took the Morcha to task for their assault on democracy and their failed promises of Gorkhaland. As Madan Tamang told me himself from his home in the plains in March 2010, there was simply no space for democratic intervention in the hills. His point was tragically confirmed weeks later when he was brutally assassinated en route to a political rally that he had convened in Darjeeling in defiance of the Morcha.

Implicated in Tamang's murder and faltering on its promises of Gorkhaland, the Morcha was desperate to rekindle support.[20] The party subsequently began 2011 with what it called the Long March.[21] This event would see thousands of Gorkha protestors march to the future borders of Gorkhaland to stake a symbolic and physical claim upon the nation-state. Fittingly, West Bengal police stopped the Long March as it left the geopolitical confines of the hills.

Prevented from advancing into the plains of the Dooars, Bimal Gurung and his thousand-person entourage set up camp in protest. During the two-week standoff that ensued, Morcha agitators, state police, and para-military forces of the Central Government flocked to the scene. Tensions reached their breaking point on the morning of February 8, when police and paramilitary personnel resorted to *lathi*-charges and tear gas to

FIGURE 7.7 *West Bengal Police Block the Long March.*
Source: Vikash Pradhan

disperse the now three-thousand-strong camp-in. The protestors initially scattered, but then reassembled for a vengeful clash with the state. The ensuing violence left two dead and many more injured.

The events triggered a volley of aftereffects in the hills. Angry mobs took to the streets chanting "Gorkhaland," torching government offices, police outposts, and whatever other symbols of West Bengal's authority lay in their path. Exacerbating the alarm, the Morcha called an indefinite strike, crippling daily life until further notice. With the Central Reserve Police Force called in to preempt further unrest, Darjeeling entered into a state of emergency. Pregnant with symbolism from start to finish, the fate of the Long March was all too familiar. Yet again the Gorkhas had attempted to claim their place in India. Yet again they had been relegated to their corner of the nation.

. . .

By 2011, the optimism that marked the tribal movements of 2006–7 and the Gorkhaland Movement (2008–11) had given way to the sobering inefficacy of these identities. The Sixth Schedule was off the table. Most had accepted that Gorkhaland was also currently out of reach. Darjeeling's home state of West Bengal was undergoing major political transformations as well. Mamata Banerjee's Trinamool Congress Party had finally ended the CPI-Marxist's thirty-four-year hold over the state government. Initially, there was speculation that these changes might shift the fortunes of the Gorkhas, but the Trinamool's stance against Gorkhaland only extended the status quo: West Bengal would not be divided.

In July 2011, the Morcha, West Bengal, and the Centre agreed to the establishment of the Gorkhaland Territorial Administration (GTA), a local administrative setup with limited autonomy that remained within West Bengal. The Morcha tried to save face by lauding the inclusion of "Gorkhaland" in the title. Bimal Gurung went so far as to say the Gorkhas were "proud to have a new identity through the Gorkhaland Territorial Administration."[22] But the GTA was not the separate state the Morcha had promised. Instead, it looked like a slightly improved DGHC—the unsatisfactory administration that had followed the first Gorkhaland Agitation. Not surprisingly, the GTA met a lukewarm reception on the streets. By this point, much of the public had resigned itself to this unsatisfactory end. Strung out after years of agitation and having endured the identificational shifts from *Gorkha* to *tribal* and back again—fraught as they were with misidentification, division, and failure—what the masses wanted now was a return to normalcy, governance, and above all, peace.

Agitation had taken its toll on the body politic, leaving the people unsatisfied and exhausted. Evaluating these familiar ends, we might profitably recall Povinelli's framing of exhaustion as the antithesis of late liberal endurance.[23] This tiring out of communities and their politics has become a familiar story in Darjeeling. These movements—involving an array of alternating ethnopolitical forms—suggest that the ability to constantly redefine the self in the logics and language of late liberalism may be a key to enduring its turbulence. But there is only so much that communities can do—and only so much they can take—in the face of unrelenting marginalization. In such instances, exhaustion figures as an endgame of late liberal control: a wearing down, and perhaps wearing out, of minorities' claims upon the state.

UNVIABLE IDENTITIES

Like the bids for autonomy, the quests for Scheduled Tribe recognition took similarly disappointing turns. In 2011, for example, the Gurungs learned that their ST application had been rejected, despite earlier assurances of its success. Unlike their first rejection, where the government deemed them too Hindu, this time around the government provided no reasons for the denial. When I entered the Gurung ethnic association (the Tamu Choj Dhin, TCD) offices in the spring of 2011, the leaders shared with me their dismay over the government's decision and its deleterious effects on their community. They told me another Gurung ethnic association, the All India Gurung Buddhist Association (AIGBA), had emerged in the wake of the rejection, luring constituents with claims of a singular Gurung Buddhist identity. This Buddhist identity, the new faction promised, would bring the entitlements and recognition that the Gurungs' earlier "secular" identity had not. From the way the TCD leaders described it, this was an acrimonious split—one that inevitably asked everyday Gurungs to choose between the "secular" path of one organization (which embraced heterogeneity and hybridity) and the "communal" path of another (which claimed Buddhism to be the only pure and authentic Gurung tradition).

These were troubling developments. The Gurungs, who had carefully avoided the fundamentalist tendencies that divided other groups, now were falling sway to factionalism and internal division. Eager to get the other side of the story, I phoned the new faction's president to arrange a meeting—ideally, a one-on-one chat over tea. Days later, I arrived at a room teeming with ethnic leaders waiting to meet me. This was not a new scenario for me as an academic anthropologist. Groups often looked to me for input and endorsement of their tribal identities. These encounters, though fascinating in their own right, almost always entailed awkward moments. Thankfully, this time around, there were familiar faces in the room, as many of those present were former members of the Gurung (TCD) association that I had worked with for years. With tea poured, we moved straight into a discussion of the government's rejection of the Gurungs' ST bid. The president explained the problem as follows: "By birth Gurungs are Buddhist tribals. But due to Hinduism's influence, the Government of India decided not to include the Gurungs in the List of Scheduled Tribes. That's why there was the defect."

Elaborating on this syncretic, Hinduized history, an elderly gentleman in a tweed suit added, "The Gurungs were under the influence of the Hindus, but they were ignorant. They didn't have knowledge of that. They were not conscious of it. Now everyone has realized and now they don't want to be considered in this position. They want to be Buddhist, so this is our main ambition."

I nodded my head, trying to follow his logic. Yes, the Gurungs of Darjeeling had in recent years been reviving Buddhist practices. I had seen this firsthand through my experiences living in Bidhuwā Busti. But to suggest a wholesale abandonment of Hindu practices belied the syncretic realities of everyday practice. "We are trying to bring them into the mainstream," the president clarified. "But there are Gurungs who practice different religions. However, they have to understand that when the government recognizes someone as tribal, they will not recognize the Hindus as tribals. There are criteria for becoming tribals, so this Buddhist organization is demanding the status within those criteria. From the time of our forefathers in India, we have not been able to establish our Gurung identity. We need to have our identity. Right?"

The leaders had a compelling argument—supported, as it was, by the Indian state's rejection of the Gurungs' ST application. But their efforts to re-represent and reform the Gurungs promised to divide the Gurungs in new ways. To their credit, these leaders understood the stakes of their efforts. And it was here that they sought my "expert" opinion. The elder in tweed put it to me in the following terms: "Looking at us before and now, from a religious point of view, which side do you think we ought to be on? For advantage, which side should we lean to?"

I weighed my words carefully. "Well, it's difficult because modern governments tell you that if you want to go 'forward,' you should have one religion. But that is not really how culture works."

Unsatisfied with these offerings of twenty-first-century anthropology, he pushed me further. "What I mean to say is: Is it more advantageous for us to remain as we are now or should we be Buddhist? This is a direct question to you."

I searched for a suitable answer, but there seemed to be little escape from the imposed ethno-logics. I could only turn to the Gurungs' history of syncretism and suggest that they carry on as they had been for centuries—by continuing to "mix it up," as I awkwardly put it. Obviously, this was unsatisfactory advice. As an academic, I had the luxury of ducking out of these normative paradigms of recognition through a simple appeal to the realities of life and history in Darjeeling. As members of a minority seeking rights, recognition, and national inclusion, they did not. Therein lay the rub for them. If the Gurungs wanted official recognition, they would have to translate their heterogeneous cultural forms (and their emic understandings thereof) into the singularly etic terms of the state. Such were the exigencies of late liberal recognition.

. . .

The Buddhist faction pressed on. Citing the Gurungs' need for governmental attention, the organization promised a different political strategy. First, they would appeal to the Indian government to be notified as an official

Religious Minority, in this case Buddhist.[24] Then, they would re-initiate the bid for Scheduled Tribe status. With a new politics in the offing, everyday Gurungs began changing their allegiance in large numbers. By 2013, the Buddhist AIGBA had supplanted the secular Tamu Choj Dhin (TCD) as the dominant Gurung organization of the region—effectively birthing a newfangled communalism from the failures of an earlier secularism.

The rollover was not uniform. In villages like Bidhuwā Busti, the change from one organization to another went relatively smoothly. Most of my Gurung neighbors had already embraced Buddhism. And while they lamented abandoning the secular TCD (which had been so instrumental in making Bidhuwā Busti a model of Gurung revitalization), they were also eager for alternatives that could bring them the affirmative action they desired. For political expediency, the Gurungs of Bidhuwā Busti therefore changed over wholesale.

Elsewhere, the splits were more fractious. Leaders of the two organizations fired accusations of failure, misidentification, and communalism at one another. Not wanting to be mired in these intra-ethnic conflicts, some elites rescinded involvement, taking with them precious financial and social capital. The impacts reverberated across the sociological spectrum, as native intellectuals, activists, and everyday Gurungs argued over the best way forward. The rifts asked Gurungs of all kinds to make choices that, by definition, would affect their politics, sociality, and solidarity in meaningful ways. It bears remembering that all of this stemmed from the Indian government's rejection of the Gurungs' ST application— not once, but twice. Chronicling these developments, I could not help but ponder the divisive, paradoxical impacts of state multiculturalism on this marginalized minority. Here again, the Indian state was proving the consummate difference maker. Only this time, its ethno-logics were not drawing lines around and between ethnic communities, but rather straight through them.

REVAMPING COMMUNITIES

I caught up with the fast-growing Buddhist Gurung faction in June 2013 for one of their general meetings. Navigating our way through Darjeeling's central bazaar, my Gurung friends and I squeezed our rain-soaked umbrellas through the door to find the community hall packed with Gurungs. Chairs were arranged on the stage; ledgers were open and recording the names of those walking through the door; and boxes of newly printed calendars were stowed about, awaiting their debut. The meeting looked like many I had attended in my years of fieldwork. But as it got under way, it signaled the changing times. As usual, the meeting began with formal introductions, but then it took a notable turn. One speaker after another took the podium to inform the Gurungs of the socioeconomic opportunities open to them in a rapidly transforming India. They discussed the prospects of minority scholarships and distance-learning programs that would help the Gurungs overcome the confinement of the hills. They discussed the matriculation standards that Gurung students would need in order to enroll in universities—the degrees from which would propel them into jobs in thriving economic centers like Delhi, Hyderabad, and Bangalore. Government-sponsored self-help and micro-credit schemes appeared repeatedly in these presentations, as did the special provisions allotted to Scheduled Tribes and officially recognized Religious Minorities. The economically minded presentations charted a discernible geography of opportunity in post-liberalization India. The message was clear: The opportunities—and future—lay beyond the hills.[25] How then to gain entry into this rapidly evolving national "mainstream"?

Cultural recognition figured centrally in their strategies. The speakers reiterated that affirmative action was the key to economic inclusion. And if they wanted affirmative action, they would need to overhaul not only their organizational structure but also themselves. At this point, the leaders shifted attention to their ethnic association's organizational structure. With lists in hand, they began reading out the names of locales targeted for new branches, requesting any residents in attendance to step forth as branch "conveners." Some did so willingly. Others found themselves the lone representative of their village and had little choice but to volunteer. For twenty minutes, the community hall devolved into seeming chaos as AIGBA leaders scrambled to match conveners to locales. But by the end, the organization had its roll of new branches.[26]

The leaders restored order by announcing the conveners' names and graciously thanking them for their civic engagement. The leaders then began offering a litany of instructions about how to recruit and register members, how to spread the word about Gurung Buddhism, and how to market the ethnic association. With impeccable timing, AIGBA leaders then unveiled their freshly printed calendars, depicting Gurungs in various states of ethnic uplift and Buddhist repose. The meeting came to a cacophonous end, as people maneuvered to get their hands on the calendar. Right on cue, tea began circulating through the aisles, adding warmth as the audience pored over the calendar's contents, with hot, flimsy plastic cups in hand.

The scene was indicative of the times. This was a civil association in the making—and the start of a new foray into Indian political society. The Gurungs' cause would now be led by a new organization, with a more refined cultural and economic focus. These makeovers are sure to engender varying degrees of division, transformation, and hope as they unfold in the years to come. The organization's leaders are keenly aware of these potential effects. Yet, as they also note, such dynamics may be necessary given the present circumstances. The strategies of their secular predecessors failed, leaving the Gurungs little choice but to risk a more communal assertion of their identity. Their case, in this regard, portends a sometimes slippery slope from multicultural governance to ethnic fundamentalism.

More broadly, the developments evince the compounding impacts of recognition's failures on the marginalized. Throughout these cycles of identification and rejection, the Gurungs' need for governmental attention has only grown—especially as India continues its acceleration into the neoliberal world order. The initiative to be recognized as a Religious Minority has emerged as merely a stopgap. The scholarships, stipends, micro-credit schemas, and legal safeguards it provides pale in comparison to the affirmative action advantages accorded to Scheduled Tribes. The Gurungs' new leaders are the first to admit that this is not the recognition the Gurungs believe they deserve. This is not the recognition the Gurungs desire. Given their histories of rejection, one may reasonably wonder what other options are available for this community as it seeks a way out of this literal and figurative corner of the nation-state.

These developments reflect both the fluidity and strictures of the ethno-contemporary. On the one hand, the Gurungs' redefinition of their cause illustrates the innovation and resilience that defines minority politics across South Asia. On the other, these attempts to revamp themselves in a way that is legible to the state illustrate just how susceptible these communities are to modern forms of governmentality—ethnological and otherwise. How these factionalist and fundamentalist tendencies will rework Gurung sociality remains to be seen. Local precedents, where communities have divided at even the most intimate levels, do not bode well. Viewed as but the latest chapter of a people seeking, yet continually denied, their place in India, none of these dynamics—present or future—should come as a surprise. And it is for precisely these reasons that they have become an immediate concern for all parties involved.

CATEGORICAL UNCERTAINTIES

Darjeeling's trajectory since the tribal turn provides a case study of the possibilities and quandaries of the ethno-contemporary in India and elsewhere. We encounter here the lives and politics of those who live at—and beyond—the limits of late liberal ethno-intelligibility. Surveying these protean contours, we find there is more at play than just the paradigms through which communities and their differences are known. Deeper exclusions, deeper needs, deeper affects run through these fluctuating forms of identity and its politics in the hills. *Indian Idol* and the stunning inception of Gorkhaland 2.0 serve as timely notice of the reactivity of these politics at the margins. The saga further evidences the histories of anxious belonging that undergird these and other subnationalist struggles. Such conditions cannot be dissociated from the emergences—and emergencies—of our current moment. This is why the anthropology of the ethno-contemporary needs history. Building upon grounded historical perspective, we can get more out of our engagements with this ethnologically marked present. Seen in this light, Darjeeling's recent oscillations offer especially important lessons. The sudden shift from *tribal* back to *Gorkha* politics certainly caught many by surprise. Yet upon closer scrutiny, the underlying affects and operative ethno-logics of these tribal and post-tribal movements, tellingly, prove to be the same. Tragically, so too do the outcomes.

Since its capricious birth from the whims of Indian pop culture, the second Gorkhaland Agitation has limped into the second decade of the twenty-first-century unfulfilled. Contingencies at the national level have periodically rekindled the movement's original spark. In the summer of 2013, Darjeeling erupted at the news that the Centre was moving forward with plans to create a separate state of Telangana in southern India. The Morcha had long pegged the cause of Gorkhaland to that of Telangana, so when the news broke, violent protests and self-immolations ensued. The outbreak marked a spike in subnationalist desire. But the intensity has not held.

In the meantime, the quests for recognition and autonomy have become entangled in a complicated web of state- and national-level politics. Nationally, hope has come from an unlikely source, the Hindu nationalist Bharatiya Janata Party (BJP). Under the aegis of its controversial leader Narendra Modi, the BJP stormed to national power with a resounding defeat of the Indian National Congress Party in the Lok Sabha elections of 2014. Compared to the Congress, the BJP has been far more sympathetic to the idea of Gorkhaland. Not surprisingly, Darjeeling's Morcha pledged its allegiance to the BJP in the run-up to the election. The BJP's victory in May 2014 thus ushered in a new wave of optimism in the hills. But it remains to be seen whether intimations of Gorkhaland on the BJP's campaign trail will translate into the reality of a separate state. As has so often been the case, the promise remains outstanding.

If the 2014 election rekindled hope for Gorkhaland, it also played upon the question of tribal difference. This involved the complicated power-politics of West Bengal, Darjeeling's home state. In order to attract votes for her Trinamool Congress Party, West Bengal's chief minister, Mamata Bannerjee, promised to bring ST status to all of Darjeeling's "left-out" communities. The gesture was part of the Trinamool's ongoing strategy to infiltrate the hills. But there were counter-insurgency undertones. Recall that Bannerjee and her party steadfastly opposed Gorkhaland. By luring votes with the promise of ST status, the move promised to help break the Morcha's stranglehold on power in the hills—and with it, the demands for Gorkhaland.

Counter-insurgency tactics notwithstanding, the Gorkhaland-friendly BJP defeated the Trinamool's candidate in Darjeeling. The electoral defeat sent a clear message: the cause of Gorkhaland was not dead.

With the Trinamool's advance thwarted, it remains to be seen whether Bannerjee will—or even can—fulfill her promises of ST status. By policy, ST status is not hers to grant. But as we have seen, there are unwritten ways of becoming a Scheduled Tribe of India.

ST status was not the only card Mamata Bannerjee played in her tribal dealings with Darjeeling. In 2013 and 2014, Bannerjee's government announced the creation of separate Development and Cultural Boards for the Lepcha and Tamangs of Darjeeling. These semi-autonomous boards would allow these two tribal communities to safeguard their cultural, economic, and social welfare. Importantly, these tribal administrations would operate beyond the purview of the Morcha-led Gorkhaland Territorial Administration (GTA)—thus eroding the power of the Morcha and GTA. As with the promise of ST status, the conferral of tribal development boards would lure the Lepchas and Tamangs away from the Morcha and to the Trinamool. Per the logics of counter-insurgency, these tribal development boards would further divide the Gorkhas and undercut the movement for Gorkhaland. In short, while Bannerjee proved willing to dangle the carrots of tribal recognition and limited autonomy, under no circumstances would her West Bengal be divided.

If this all sounds complicated, that is precisely the point. These dynamics illustrate the complicated—often contending—forms of multicultural governance that minorities must navigate en route to rights and social justice. Around the world, state and non-state actors have developed a complicated array of institutions to protect and manage diversity. For marginalized peoples, these administrations of difference remain a field of operation and hope. But, as we have seen, they can also be a space of cross-purposed politics, where the aims of communities themselves are subordinated to bigger interests. In such instances where gestures to autonomy, rights, and cultural preservation are conveyed in disingenuous ways, multiculturalism can indeed "menace"—as Charles Hale has suggested.[27] Given the situation in Darjeeling, one has to wonder about the underlying motives and eventual impacts of these recent developments.

These are the complex political, moral, and ethnological configurations within which marginalized communities must struggle in late liberalism. I introduce these most recent dynamics in Darjeeling to highlight the realpolitik of these institutionalized grids of ethno-intelligibility. What is remarkable in this case is how one kind of difference (tribal) is played off—and pitted against—another (Gorkha). Undercutting local power and solidarity, these developments put a curiously late liberal twist on the age-old axiom of *divide and rule*. Indeed, the people of Darjeeling are quick to invoke this axiom when assessing their current situation. Amid the realpolitik of the Indian ethno-contemporary, none of this should be written off as coincidental. But it bears asking: With their difference becoming the stuff of a politics operating far beyond them, where does this leave the people of Darjeeling? What are they to make of these overlapping and contradictory schemas of multicultural governance? How are they to find their way—and themselves—amid these politically loaded grids of ethno-intelligibility?

These questions return us to this book's core concerns and the people of Darjeeling. In this particular corner of India, resilience, need, and categorical instability have been—and remain—the operative conditions of life and politics. Despite these communities' enduring struggles, despite the shifts from *Gorkha* to *tribal* and back again, despite the governmental systems in place to recognize and respect their difference, the outcomes remain troublingly similar. Here we find a populace beset with anxieties over who they are and who they must be in order to belong in India. We find communities increasingly torn by which terms of difference and which politics will serve them best. And we find a people *still* searching for the recognition, autonomy, and belonging they need and deserve. As I hope these chapters have shown, their circumstances raise questions for us all about how diversity is not only known and ruled, but also lived and negotiated.

To question these terms of difference is to interrogate the concepts, contexts, and conditions by which communities are recognized, affirmed, and denied at our current juncture. Surveying the protean contours of the present, the Indian ethno-contemporary looks patently unstable. With a Hindu-nationalist return to power, the question of minority rights and belonging has become an urgent concern. Prime Minister Narendra Modi has captured the national and global imagination with his promises of economic and governmental reform. But how these neoliberal commitments will translate into the lives of India's minorities remains unknown. Looking ahead, the quandaries of late liberalism promise to deepen. And as they do, the terms of twenty-first-century difference promise to morph. How communities like those from Darjeeling will navigate these shifting grounds of the ethno-contemporary remains to be seen. From the turbulence of the present, the future looks categorically uncertain.

NEGOTIATING THE ETHNO-CONTEMPORARY

THE ETHNO-CONTEMPORARY is a time-space of uneven implication and possibility. Pick up any piece of Gorkhaland propaganda, attend any political rally today, and you will hear cries of a people unrequited, of difference denied, of identity in "crisis." Experiences of loss, rejection, and crisis span the sociopolitical spectrum in Darjeeling. As the Gurung leaders put it to me back in 2011, "From the time of our forefathers in India, we have not been able to establish our Gurung identity. We need to have our identity. Right?" Whether in the agitations of the Gorkhas or the quests to become tribal, a sense of crisis and anxious belonging imbues these politics with unmistakable urgency. These anxieties emanate from unsettling histories. And, as the *Indian Idol* saga and subsequent Gorkhaland Agitation make clear, they frequent present-day life with alarming volatility.

These histories and their effects and affects must be respected. But with regard to an "identity crisis," I will offer a different reading. Communities like the Gurungs and the greater Gorkha conglomerate of which they are a part do not lack identity. Generations of shared history and ethno-genesis have imparted to these communities strong senses of membership, group solidarity, and culture. Their recurrent ethnopolitical mobilizations—some of them subnationalist, others more legal—confirm as much. Per these terms, these communities "have" an identity. What they lack is that sacred stuff of recognition to affirm their being-in-and-of

India—and, in more Hegelian terms, their being-in-and-of themselves.[1] The crisis, in short, is not one of identity, but rather one of difference and its recognition.[2]

With the terms shifted accordingly, we can begin to rethink the mercurial contours of identity and its politics in places like Darjeeling. The intermittently violent and ethnological politics featured throughout this book are as notable for their fluctuating *forms* as they are for their perpetual *failures* to achieve their intended aims. Crucially, though, failure figures here not as the shortcomings of a people and their sociocultural practices, but rather as the shortcomings of the system of recognition within which they have but little choice to operate. The failure, in other words, falls not to communities but to the paradigms through which the state does—and does not—recognize and "see" their difference.[3] As the people of Darjeeling by now know well, not all forms of identity are admitted into the imagined community of the nation. Not all forms of difference are legible in the eyes of the state.

For communities, policy makers, and academics, transferring the onus of failure *from* communities *to* the postcolonial state is of paramount importance. It raises timely questions about how late liberal recognition works, how it does not, and how its logics affect those who do and do not fit its molds. That the recent cycles of identification, mobilization, and denial have fed back into a shared sense of "crisis" in the hills confirms the stakes of these late liberal reckonings. Shifting so suddenly from *Gorkha* to *tribal* politics and back again, these communities' search for a secure sense of being-in-and-of India has only amplified their anxieties about who they are—and who they must be—if they are to attain the recognition, autonomy, and belonging they desire. Of all the paradoxes presented in this book, this is perhaps the most tragic and telling.

ANTHROPOLOGICAL FUTURES

My aim has been to shed some light on these conditions of the Indian ethno-contemporary—as they are lived and negotiated by the people of Darjeeling. Their struggles give pause to consider just what kinds of life and politics are possible amid late liberalism's systems of intelligibility. Questions of difference and its legibility have emerged as key concerns in the study of indigeneity, particularly in the Latin American context. For scholars like Arturo Escobar, Mario Blaser, and Marisol de la Cadena, finding ways of conveying alternative ways of being in the world has become vital to the constitution of a more inclusive and "pluriversal" global future.[4] The reassertion of indigenous communities' cultural and ontological difference has become a dignified way of offsetting the dominant Eurocentric episteme—and thereby "decolonizing" the present.[5]

These concerns bear heavily on the ethno-contemporary. The decolonial bent, however, becomes especially complicated in the South Asian context, where colonial paradigms have long since bled into postcolonial life. This is to say nothing of the dynamics by which communities are now putting old colonial paradigms (like "tribe") to new uses. As we have seen, these groups are not just turning governmental ethno-logics back upon the state; they are also turning them upon themselves to represent—and remake—themselves into recognizable tribes. The result is an ethnologically confounded present where ethnos and logos continue to bleed into each other in newly generative ways. This bleed between human reality (ethnos) and its representation (logos)—or what we may trace historically as ethnology's seep into the world it studies—remains a signature condition of the ethno-contemporary in India and beyond. As we have seen, these involutions continue to reconfigure communities, their politics, and their difference in unforeseen ways.

These dynamics open up new concerns about how the human sciences might negotiate the protean contours of the ethno-contemporary. They likewise put tough questions to the discipline that is perhaps most directly implicated in it: anthropology. It is important to remember that contemporary anthropology and ethnology are not one and the same. Their colonial collusions do raise problems, however. Because of these collusions, ethnology (and by association, anthropology) is built into the problem-space of the ethno-contemporary. This, for me, was an inescapable fact of fieldwork. Communities and government anthropologists alike looked to me with expectations seemingly born of ethnology's past. These encounters were awkward. But while their presumptions and requests may have seemed dated, they were timely and relevant for the groups I was working with. What then is the twenty-first-century anthropologist to make of this uncanny precession of the discipline in the world s/he studies? Where might s/he find herself among these confounding circumstances?

Given the discipline's past and present implications, one might argue that the last thing the world needs now is another anthropology. In *Against Race*, Paul Gilroy has charted designs for what he calls a "planetary humanism." Central to this utopian world order, Gilroy avers, will be a "*postanthropological* version of what it means to be human."[6] Historically speaking, Gilroy's idea is sound. From India to Africa and the Americas, colonial anthropology helped to naturalize classificatory divisions that have since spawned communal tensions and unimaginable violence. Modern conceptions of race, caste, tribe, etc.—insofar as they are hybrids of colonial and indigenous taxonomies—may accordingly be counted among the discipline's bastard progeny. Indeed, as we saw with the abandonment of the category "tribe" on the eve of India's independence, colonial anthropology was all too prone to cut and run once these categories had taken on a life of their own. Postcolonial anthropology can ill afford to do the same.

Gilroy's call for a "postanthropological" future is suggestive, but it warrants some additional consideration. What Gilroy appears to be calling for is not so much a postanthropological future (from a disciplinary standpoint), but a post*ethnological* future—one that transcends the divisive legacies of colonial taxonomies. To that end, we might ask, what role does the *discipline* of anthropology play in understanding, reworking, and moving beyond the lingering legacies of colonial ethnology?

A logical step, let me suggest, is to first come to terms with the various "lives" of ethnology out there in the world today. This requires a careful combination of historical and ethnographic engagement. If history helps us understand how various assemblages of the ethno-contemporary have come into being, ethnography provides a method for engaging its current dynamics, agents, and habitations. Through these techniques we can venture a deeper, more critical study of how particular ethno-logics are reshaping contemporary life. For the academic, it is uncanny that many of the categories our disciplines once helped to produce, and that we have since struggled so hard to unmake, have now reappeared with such force. But this is the reality we are charged with understanding. Sorting through our various implications in this eerily old, yet new circumstance is therefore a key task—and the uncanny, a key trope—for studying the ethno-contemporary.[7] As these chapters from Darjeeling have worked to show, ethnology's return to the lives and politics of modern India continues to generate an array of outcomes—some of them promising, some of them troubling, and all of them worthy of critical ethnographic concern.

Ethnographic critique, however, runs its share of risks—especially in the context of the ethno-contemporary. Even when encountering something as conspicuously colonial as tribal recognition, the Fanonian impulse to "analyze and destroy" may prove misguided and irresponsible.[8] Millions of lives are invested in—and dependent on—this system of recognition, no matter how problematic. Countless more remain in need of its benefits and care, including the people of Darjeeling. Any attempt to think our way out of these ethnologically occluded circumstances must be realistic. Across the board, the vested interests are formidable. Quandaries abound. It would be utopian and reckless to propose wholesale changes.

Which is not to say that we should shy away from critique. Given today's contending claims upon the ethnos, the anthropologist may find his/herself in a position to critique existing forms of knowledge and power that everyday subjects simply cannot. Darjeeling's tribal turn— and this book—offer working examples. While the ethnic leaders, politicians, and activists I worked with in Darjeeling were well versed in the language of tribal becoming, many of my friends and neighbors in Bidhuwā Busti harbored very different orientations to the tribal movements at hand. They found themselves ensnared in ethnological schemas often framed in foreign terms, yet bearing real social and political consequences. Wrought with varying degrees of hope, commitment, confusion, and ambivalence, their predicaments posed important challenges for me as an ethnographer. What was I to make of their often silenced experiences? Could my research and writing lend voice to those whom the tribal turn—with its imperious ethno-logics—had rendered subalterns? By bringing their experiences to light, how might I develop critiques of late liberal recognition that my neighbors—with so many ethnological expectations foisted upon them—could not?

Pondering these predicaments, we could evoke Liisa Malkki's point that the "objects" of ethnological knowledge—unlike the dumb matters of, say, plants, rocks, or bugs—are uniquely equipped with the power to "categorize back."[9] The reality, however, is that today's imposition of ethnological norms (like "tribe") operate through oftentimes insurmountable gradients of political power, class inequality, and expertise. Thanks to ethnology's institutionalization in India, particular distinctions like "tribe" now come loaded with sociopolitical, material, and affective promise—especially for marginalized communities. For the average person, "categorizing back" against this discursive juggernaut and its local agents may be neither possible nor desirable.

In such instances, the ethnographer may find his/herself in an uncomfortable but important position. On the one hand, s/he may be able to provide much-needed awareness of these dynamics and their often deleterious consequences. On the other, s/he may be called upon to perform the functions of the very colonial ethnology that s/he may be struggling to work past. This happened repeatedly to me in the field, as time and time again I was called upon to endorse precisely the categories and logics I was working to ethnographically critique. I have included some of these instances throughout the book in order to underscore the often uncomfortable place of the anthropologist in our contemporary moment. Negotiating our way out of these past and present implications, the work of critical ethnography is not to judge the relative success or authenticity of these ethnological paradigms and their subsequent embodiments. Rather, it is to expose their underlying structures, compulsions, and experiences.

This has been my aim in writing this book. My hope is that the historical and ethnographic perspectives it provides can prompt a timely rethinking of how difference—tribal an otherwise—is known, ruled, and lived in India and elsewhere. The *terms of difference* figure in these pages as something more than just the concepts and labels that we assign to communities and their lifeways—and something more than the conditions upon which minorities are deemed eligible for rights and social justice. As I hope this anthropology of the ethno-contemporary shows, the terms of difference and its recognition are a negotiated and decidedly human thing. So long as this is the case, they remain mutable and a source of collective concern.

This is the critical impulse that has driven my multi-sited, multi-sided engagements with the people of Darjeeling and their government an-thropologists. Moving between a *people* and the *state*, the *past* and the *present*, and the *conceptual* and *experiential*, this book has been a project build around interfaces from the start. Through these interfaces of the ethno-contemporary, I have endeavored to understand how a particu-lar system of recognition has come into being, and how its ethno-logics are structuring the lives and politics of those who do—and do not—fall under its ambit. This has meant delving into the human dimensions of this ethnologically affected circumstance and asking: Who holds the handle and who holds the blade of late liberal recognition? What are the stakes of its unevenly distributed compulsions? And more poignantly: What are the experiences of those who must find themselves within—or else outside—these grids of ethno-intelligibility?

These concerns are particularly acute amid Darjeeling's ongoing struggles. But at the end of the day, they implicate us all. Let me then end by offering a few open-ended thoughts on how we, collectively, might negotiate the ethno-contemporary now and in the years to come.

THINKING BEYOND RECOGNITION

The ethno-contemporary today is protean and contingent. Tomorrow's is yet to be determined. The road ahead will require a careful balance of critical and creative engagement. In both capacities, thinking beyond our current systems of recognition—and their terms of difference—promises to be vital.

To think beyond recognition in the critical spirit is to question how the ethno-logics of late liberalism impact life well beyond classificatory encounters like the Ethnographic Survey with which we began. At this in-terface of government anthropologists and twenty-first-century tribes, we can rightly expect to find ethnological paradigms at work. Such findings, however, tell us little of the actual lives and politics of those who found themselves the un/witting objects of the state's ethnographic gaze. Moving our analysis into the domains of sociality, subjectivity, and embodied affect we may venture deeper reading of how particular ethno-logics are (and are not) reconfiguring what it means and how it feels to be an ethnic subject. These effects and affects afford us the grounds for an ethnographic critique of both the power of late liberal recognition—and its ultimate failure—to shape the world in its own image.

Here we may find the ethnographic leverage to pry open the in/commensurabilities of ethnological governmentality and communities' actual ways of being in the world. As civil servant anthropologists are the first to admit, the "objects" of tribal recognition seldom fit the state's mold. That minorities in need are now turning governmental ethno-logics back upon the state—and themselves—marks but the latest example of humanity's strategic renegotiation of the schemes foisted upon it.[10] Repurposing paradigms in this way, these tactics profitably undercut the state's classificatory endeavor—frustrating civil servant anthropologists to no end. The generative paradox, of course, is that these strategies spawn ever-new configurations of difference and ever-new demands upon the postcolonial state. The Indian government consequently finds itself forever struggling to keep pace with the constantly evolving needs and forms of its people. So go the dialectics of difference and late liberal recognition. Operating adjacent to these dialectics,[11] critical ethnography offers a means of exposing their operative contradictions and often deleterious consequences. Thinking beyond recognition accordingly becomes a way of if not "destroying" these regimes of recognition (in the Fanonian sense), then at least unsettling their pretenses, so as to create some breathing room for alternative ways of knowing and living the ethnos.

This brings me to the second, more creative way of thinking beyond recognition, which concerns those forms of humanity that our current schemas of recognition have rendered us unable to see. To think beyond recognition in this way is to embrace the possibility that there are ways of being and forms of difference "out there" that hold important lessons for moving forward. The challenge concerns how all of us—native, governmental, and academic anthropologists, as well as the communities we serve—can work together to develop new forms of recognition that promise a better future for all parties. Taken up in this collaboratively creative spirit, we should remember that moving beyond established paradigms, should we wish to do so, will not be easy. The way forward will necessarily be slow, dialogic, and fraught. The academic/non-academic encounters to come will likewise be wrought with differences of all kinds (epistemological, ontological, and professional, to name a few). Yet precisely because of their mutually transformative potential, these encounters are worth pursuing. Entering into such conversations, we may find both hope and cause for concern among the ethnologies now loosed upon the world. Amid this widening gyre, these second comings serve as powerful reminders of anthropology's long-term—and potential—impacts upon the world.[12] In doing so, they underscore the stakes of the reckonings to come.

Engaged accordingly, the ethno-contemporary comes into view as an intellectual "problem" and opportunity—one that invites academics and non-academics alike to think critically, creatively, and, collaboratively about what kinds of recognition we can develop for the future. Thinking beyond recognition, in both senses, provides a vital tool for coming to terms with this ethnologically affected present *and* perhaps for constituting a different kind of anthropological future. The interfaces ahead will be challenging, but in them stirs the possibility that we—all of us—may find ways of knowing and being that will serve us well. Whatever these interfaces may bring, one thing by now seems certain: the anthropologies to come will be something more than just "academic."

NOTES

NOTES TO INTRODUCTION

1. Here and throughout this book, I follow local usages in referring to the three sub-divisions of Darjeeling, Kurseong, and Kalimpong collectively as the Darjeeling Hills.

2. Exemplary anthropologies of recognition and indigeneity include: Cadena and Starn 2007; Clifford 2013; French 2009; Ghosh 2006; Niezen 2003; Povinelli 2002, 2011; Shah 2010. For recent treatments of the postcolonial state in South Asia, see Gupta 2012; Gupta and Sivaramakrishnan 2012; Fuller and Bénéï 2000; Hansen and Stepputat 2001; Hull 2012.

3. On "late liberalism," see Povinelli 2011:ix; also Povinelli 2002.

4. See Cohn 1987, 1996; Dirks 2001, 2004; Dudley-Jenkins 2003; Haller 1971; Pels and Salemink 2000; Pinney 1991; Uberoi, Sunar, and Deshpande 2008; Young 1995.

5. I do not mean to suggest a uniform development of anthropology and ethnology across colonial contexts. As Asad (1973), Binsbergen (1985), Sanjek (1993), and Schumaker (2001) have shown, anthropology's development was variegated and regionally specific. On the native question, see Mamdani 1996: 16.

6. See, e.g., Clifford 1988; Hale 2006; Povinelli 2002.

7. Davidson and Henley 2007.

8. Cf. Clifford 2004, 2013; Eriksen 2002, 2004; Handler 1996; McAnany and Parks 2012; Phillips 2003.

9. On the haunting un/familiarity of the uncanny, see Freud (1919) 2003.

10. Yeats, "The Second Coming" (1920) 1994.

11. Population figures based on the 2011 censuses of India, the UK, and Canada. Because the government recognizes and administers STs on a state-by-state basis, I have followed suit to arrive at the 700+ tally. See *The Constitution (Scheduled Tribes) Order, 1950: c.o. 22* (as of 2014).

12. Available in *The National Commission for Scheduled Tribes Handbook 2005* (Government of India, 2005).

13. Helpful overviews include Davidson and Henley 2007: 7–12 and Niezen 2003.

14. *Adivasi* is a term used widely throughout India, meaning, loosely, "autochthonous or original inhabitant."

15. Indigenous leaders from India began participating in the UN Working Group of Indigenous Peoples in the mid-1980s. Participation has been steady ever since. See Ghosh 2006; Karlsson 2006: 52–59. See also Shneiderman's (2015, ch. 6) cogent discussion of communities' uneven access to this global arena.

16. See Ghosh 2006; Karlsson and Subba 2006; Shah 2010.

17. Gupta and Sivaramakrishnan 2012.

18. Rao 2009.

19. On the tensions of tribal recognition in the Northeast, see Baruah 2005, 2009, 2010; Karlsson 2000, 2006, 2011; McDuie-Ra 2009. More broadly, see Karlsson and Subba's edited volume, *Indigeneity in India* (2006).

20. Moodie 2013, 2015.

21. The literature on Nepal's People's Movement/s and *janājāti* politics is significant. Gellner (2007) provides a succinct overview. On the interplays of Nepal's *janājāti* politics and the tribal movements of Darjeeling, see Middleton and Shneiderman 2008; Shneiderman 2009.

22. Appadurai 1991; also Shneiderman 2015.

23. The Tamangs first requested ST status in the early 1980s, but abandoned their demands during the Gorkhaland Agitation. With the Limbus, they eventually achieved ST status in 2003. As of 2014, none of Darjeeling's other aspiring tribes had attained recognition.

24. Middleton 2011a and Middleton 2013c; Shneiderman 2009; Shneiderman and Turin 2006.

25. See Indian Constitution, Articles 244(2) and 275(1).

26. As Darjeeling's leaders studied—and networked with—these cases from the Northeast, the creation of the Bodoland Territorial Council in nearby Assam in 2003 was an often-invoked model. On the Sixth Schedule and "ethnic homelands" in the Northeast, see Baruah 2005, 2009, 2010; also Dasgupta 1997; Karlsson 2011; McDuie-Ra 2009.

27. "Nothing Short of a Separate State," *Frontline*, August 9–22, 1986, in Lama 1996: 54.

28. Material from Kuper 2003.

29. See Clifford 2004. These concerns also resonate with the recent discussions of paraethnographics and para-sites. See Boyer 2010; Holmes and Marcus 2005, 2006; Marcus 2000.

30. Snapshot from Hale 2006: 111.

31. Material for this snapshot cribbed from Comaroff and Comaroff 2009.

32. On Indian nationalists' historical turns, see, e.g., Chakrabarty 2000; Chatterjee 1986, 1992, 1993; Kaviraj 1995. On nationalism and historiography more broadly, Adas 2004; Burton 1997; Duara 1995.

33. These anthropological turns sparked heated debates over the relationship of academic and native anthropology, particularly in the North American context. See Biolsi and Zimmerman 1997; Deloria 1969; Dombrowski 2001; Ranco 2006; Simpson 2007; Smith 1999. On the sensitive relationships of anthropology and indigenous struggles, cf. Hale 2006; Hodgson 2002; Sylvain 2014; Warren and Jackson 2005: 66.

34. Wording borrowed from Jung 2008.

35. The genuineness of these gestures remains debatable. See Hale 2002.

36. Rabinow 2003: 30. My framings of the ethno-contemporary have been aided by the work of Paul Rabinow and others on the "anthropology of the contemporary." Though

Rabinow, Faubion, Rees, and Marcus (2008) ponder an anthropology of the contemporary through much different findings than I offer, we nevertheless share a critical concern with academic anthropology's place among other knowledge forms (including, in my case, other forms of anthropological knowledge). See Rabinow 2003, 2007; Rabinow et al. 2008; also, Westbrook 2008.

37. Archives consulted include: the West Bengal State Archives, the National Library of India, and the Asiatic Society in Kolkata; the National Archives of India in New Delhi; and the India Office Records at the British Library in London.

38. Cohn 1996.

39. Ann Stoler (2009) makes a similar point about epistemic anxiety and colonial circumstances in the Indonesian context.

40. I crib "tribal slot" from Li 2000; see Trouillot 1991 on the "savage slot."

41. Dirks 2001, 2004.

42. Foucault 1977, 1980, 1994.

43. Malkki 1995: 8. Also referenced in Karlsson 2000: 31–32.

NOTES TO CHAPTER 1

1. This was not my research assistant Eklavya, whom I have written about and with. See Middleton and Pradhan 2014.

2. This and other portions of this chapter have been adapted from previously published articles; see Middleton 2013a and Middleton 2013c.

3. Though not engaging the question of anxiety, recent papers by Thapa (2009) and Dhakal (2009) also note the long-standing desires among the people of Darjeeling for belonging in India.

4. Cf. Karlsson and Subba 2006.

5. Hutt 1997; Subha 2009; Subba and Sinha 2003.

6. Hutt 2003: 193–94.

7. *The Voice of Gorkhaland*, November 25, 1987.

8. Chatterjee 2004.

9. Classical theories of ethnicity would be quick to point out the political instrumentality of these movements (cf. A. Cohen 1974; R. Cohen 1978). Other classical readings—situationalist, primordialist, constructivist, etc.—also apply. The tribal movements aimed for sociopolitical gain (instrumentalist), yet they also advanced the re-discovery and re-construction of culture (constructivist) as a means to rekindle long-lost forms of ethnic solidarity (primordialist). As Brass (1985, 1991) would predict, this often involved ethnic elites manipulating cultural forms to achieve specific goals. But there were everyday dynamics to consider. Redefining the tribal self entailed redrawing the boundaries with the ethnic other—an anthropological concern typically associated with the seminal work of Fredrik Barth (1969). Viewed accordingly, the tribal turn confirms—yet transcends—many of the core attentions that shaped the ethnicity debates over the latter half of the twentieth century. The discussions have been long-winded. Some touchstone texts include the following: On situational and instrumental ethnicity, Barth 1969; A. Cohen 1974; R. Cohen 1978. On the primordialist view of ethnicity, Geertz 1973; Isaacs 1975; Shils 1957. On

constructed ethnicity, Anderson's work on imagined communities (1983) and seriality (1998), Hobsbawm and Ranger's edited volume on "invented tradition" (1983), and Fardon (1987) and Roosens's (1989) work on "ethnogenesis."

10. See Hegel's "Lordship and Bondage," popularly known as the master-slave dialectic. Hegel 1977: 111.

11. My thoughts on belonging owe much to the interdisciplinary work of Arjun Appadurai (1998), Lauren Berlant (2005, 2007), Jason Cons (2012, 2013), Elspeth Probyn (1996), and others (Bell 1999; Fortier 2000; Game 2001; Stoler 2004). On anxiety in the psychoanalytic tradition, see Freud 1959: 19, 1966; Green 1999; Lacan, in Harari 2001. On affect and its political possibilities, see Massumi 1995; Mazzarella 2009; Protevi 2009; Stewart 2007.

12. Here I join Teresa Brennan (2004: 3) and Joseph Masco (2008) in advocating a consideration of affect in its social context of production.

13. Letter 154, 29 October 1854, India, Foreign, 29 December 1854, 22–34 SC.

14. Letter 568, 9 November 1854, India, Foreign, 29 December 1854, 22–34 SC.

15. India, Foreign, 31 December 1858, 2522–6 FC.

16. India, Foreign, 30 December 1859, 1431–1446 FC/SUP.

17. Bengal, Political, Political, 27–28 November 1864.

18. India, Foreign, July 1864, 132–133, Political A; India, Foreign, November 1864, 152–154, Political A.

19. India, Foreign, 2 March 1860, 243–255 FC; India, Foreign, July 1864, 132–133, Political A.

20. India, Foreign, December 1864, 206–8, Political A.

21. The archive mentions Nepal, Bhutan, and Sikkim as the sources of the Nepali immigrants. The historical demographics of the region remain unclear for this period. And while not all of the "Nepali immigrants" came directly from Nepal (some came from Sikkim and Bhutan; others seem to have been already in Darjeeling [Subba 1992: 39–50]), Nepal nevertheless emerged as the principal labor pool for the British. India, Foreign, August 1837, 139–140; India, Foreign, 28 June 1841, 135–6 FC; India, Foreign, 27 April 1855, 63 FC.

22. Darjeeling in this sense had its own "market for aboriginality," a term coined by Kaushik Ghosh (1999) elsewhere in India.

23. India, General, Colonial Emigration B, 1–4, July 1888.

24. On these circumstances, see Holmberg and March 1999; Whelpton 2005: 50–55.

25. Chatterjee 2001: 65–80; Hutt 1997: 109–13; Subba 1989, 1992: 39–44; Subba and Sinha 2003: 14–17.

26. The Nepali government allowed Gurkha military recruitment elsewhere in Nepal, but it refused to sanction civilian emigration to Darjeeling. Quite to the contrary, the Nepali state demanded the immediate return of emigrants, promising amnesty to refugee slaves or else the denial of future entry and citizenship in Nepal. These demands, along with intermittent trade embargos, signal the Nepali government's concern with controlling the flow of both goods and people across its eastern border into British Darjeeling. India, Foreign, 31 December 1858, 2522–6 FC.

27. Besky (2014: 74–77) has also written on Darjeeling's *sardārs*.

28. Consolidated census data available in Samanta 2000.

29. Vocabulary borrowed from Van Gennep's (1965) and V. Turner's (1967) classic theorizations of liminality.

30. The British frequently evoked slavery in Nepal, Sikkim, and Bhutan to justify their tacit encouragement of immigration of labor to Darjeeling. India, Foreign, 28 June 1841, 135–6 FC.

31. This helps to explain the paucity of archival materials on Darjeeling's labor populations in the nineteenth century. This is in marked contrast to the archive's considerable attention to labor in the tea plantations of Assam, where the *sardār* recruitment system became increasingly formalized and regulated.

32. India, Foreign, August 1868, 219–220, Political A; India, Foreign, August 1868, 404–5, Political A; India, Foreign, February 1869, 9, Political A; India, Foreign, March 1878, 1–8, Political A; India, Foreign, January 1864, 222–223, Political A; India, Foreign July 1866, 63, Political A; Bengal, Judicial, 206–209, August 1868.

33. Singh 1996: 34–35, 68–77.

34. Sivaramakrishnan 1996, 1999.

35. Popular Gorkha histories claim that a memorandum was submitted in 1907 (ten years earlier) with a demand for self-governance. Having searched local holdings and archives in Kolkata, Delhi, and London where such a memorandum would be, I have found no evidence of a 1907 memorandum. Until and unless this memorandum surfaces, 1917 strikes me as a sounder starting date.

36. Bengal, Public, January 1921, 13/22.

37. Ibid.

38. Bengal, Appointment, December 1930, 12–19.

39. Bakhtin 1981: 359. On ethnicities as political interest groups, see Cohen 1974.

40. Cf. Weber 1998: 22.

41. The Gorkha League was first established in Dehradun in 1924. Darjeeling's branch was founded in 1943. Whelpton 2005: 80.

42. See also Besky 2014: 76; Des Chenes 1991: 123.

43. Intelligence Bureau Translation. India, Home, Political F, 14/9, 1931.

44. See Berlant 2007; Fortier 2009: 19; Mookherjee 2005. On "structures of feeling," see Williams 1961, 1977.

45. India, Home, Political F, 14/9, 1931.

46. Letter to Gorkha League leader Damber Singh Gurung (8 August 1938), cited in Roy 2012: 333–34.

47. The Gorkha League's message to its constituents was notably different, however. League leader Dambar Singh Gurung told local Gorkhas in 1943, "The Britishers have treated us like animals, but the Bengalis are worse than the Britishers!" Ibid.

48. Bagchi 2012: 72.

49. Sarkar 2010.

50. For more on the postcolonial history of tea and its politics, I refer the reader to Sarah Besky's *The Darjeeling Distinction* (2014). On tea's colonial history, Piya Chatterjee's *A Time for Tea* (2001) is particularly insightful.

51. On the Nepali Language Movement, see Booth 2010.

52. Dhakal 2009: 157; Samanta 2000: 101.

53. "The Years of Living Dangerously," *The Illustrated Weekly of India*, October 2, 1988. Available in Lama 1996: 260.

54. Ibid., 261.

55. Probyn 1996: 13, 8.

56. In "The Sorcerer and His Magic," Levi-Strauss (1963: 191) (borrowing from psychoanalysis) worked with the notion of "abreaction" to explain how sorcerers conjured and reenacted the ailments of their patients so as to cure them of their affliction.

57. For example, Nagaland (1963), Meghalaya (1972), Manipur (1972), and Mizoram (1987). The subsequent creation of other states like Jharkhand (2000), Uttarakhand (2000), and Telangana (2014)—all of them based on reasons exceeding the linguistic paradigms laid out by the States Reorganization Act of 1956—further stoked hope for Gorkhaland. On Khalistan, see Oberoi 1987. On insurgency in the Northeast, see Baruah 2005, 2009, 2010; Chasie and Hazarika 2009; Hazarika 1995, 2008; Karlsson 2011; McDuie-Ra 2009. On Jharkhand, see Shah 2010.

58. Ghisingh spoke, in particular, of being personally moved by the Nagaland struggle. Likewise, Khalistan figured into Ghisingh's claims and negotiations with the government. See, e.g., "Fire on the Mountain," *Illustrated Weekly of India*, February 22, 1987. Also available in Lama 1996: 122–34. Karlsson (2000: 222) notes Ghisingh's subsequent 1990s alliances with comparable movements in Jharkhand, Bodoland, and the Koch Rajbanshi of Assam/North Bengal.

59. Constitution of India, Section 2, Article 5.

60. Lama 1996: 22–27.

61. "Letter to Prime Minister of India, Sri Rajiv Gandhi," in Lama 1996: 40.

62. "Nothing Short of a Separate State," *India Today*, 66, October 31, 1986. Available in Lama 1996: 50.

63. The thirteen-day strike began on June 20, 1987, and was ultimately called off on the ninth day, citing progress in negotiations with the state. Lama 1996: 139.

64. Taussig 1992.

65. Figures from Samanta 2000: 54.

66. Lama 1996: 241–45.

67. This has become a common pattern for Northeastern peoples throughout India. See McDuie-Ra's *Northeast Migrants in Delhi*, 2012.

68. See Subba's "Indigenising the Limbus" (2006). Also, Karlsson 2011: 61–64; Karlsson and Subba 2006; Shneiderman 2015.

69. For comparative studies of the Sixth Schedule in the Northeast, see Dasgupta 1997; Karlsson 2011: 227–65; McDuie-Ra 2009.

70. Point 11 reads: "This in principle Memorandum of Settlement is the full and final settlement of the Darjeeling Hills Area issue and no further demands in this regard would be entertained."

71. Taylor 1992: 5.

72. Fanon 1967; Marx 1978: 52.

73. Memo BGJMS/DJ/12/06, *Bharatiya Gorkha Janajati Manyata Samity.*

74. I return to Koli (a pseudonym) in Chapter 3. On my working relationship with Eklavya, please see our co-written article "Dynamic Duos" in the *Fieldwork(ers)* special issue of *Ethnography*, which I co-edited with Jason Cons; Middleton and Pradhan 2014.

NOTES FOR CHAPTER 2

1. Stoler 2004, 2009.

2. On ethnology's implications in South Asia, see Cohn 1987, 1996; Dirks 2001, 2004; Dudley-Jenkins 2003; Haller 1971; Pels and Salemink 2000; Pinney 1991; Uberoi, Sundar, and Deshpande 2008; Young 1995. On anthropology's colonial legacy more generally, see Asad 1973; Binsbergen 1985; Foucault 1988; Schumaker 2001.

3. Foucault 1979, 1988, 1994.

4. Exemplary studies from Africa include: Binsbergen 1985; Fardon 1987; Malkki 1995; Ranger 1982; Werbner and Ranger 1996.

5. Kaviraj 1992; Mitchell 1988, 2002.

6. Dirks 2001.

7. On the colonial roots of ethnicity, Chakrabarty 2002. On caste, Bates 1995; Bayly 1995, 1999; Dirks 1987, 2001, 2004. On race, Epperson 1994; Ranger 1982; Robb 1995; Young 1995. On gender, Bannerji 2001; Burton 1994, 2003; Ghosh 2008; Mani 1998; Sangari and Vaid 1990; Sarkar 2001.

8. The work of Shail Mayaram (2004) is exemplary. Also, Radhakrishna 2001.

9. Cf. Rao 2009.

10. "Statistical Sketch of Kumaun," *Asiatic Researches* 16, no. 1 (Calcutta, 1828). *The Official Reports of the Province of Kumaun* (Agra: Secundra Orphan Press, 1851); see *Imperial Gazetteer* (volumes on northwestern provinces), August 31, 1877.

11. Hunter (1896) 1991: 234. On Hodgson, see Dhungel 2007; Gaenszle 2004; Pels 1999; Waterhouse 2004.

12. "Classification of Military Tribes of Nepal," Hodgson Collection, MSS6, vol. 6/1/1–12; "Letter dated July 8, 1833," Hodgson Collection, MSS7/20/119–22; See also the 1840s "Tribes of Hillmen" essays, Hodgson Collection, MSS7, vol. 5/1/1–78. Following the Rebellion of 1857, the British increased Gurkha regiments considerably. See Des Chenes 1991; Hunter (1896) 1991: 259–60.

13. See B. Hodgson, "Comparative Vocabulary of Languages of the Broken Tribes of Nepal," *Journal of the Asiatic Society of Bengal* 26 (1857): 317–522.

14. Early in the nineteenth century the EIC began seeking more systematic knowledge. Buchanan's general survey work in Mysore and Colin Mackenzie's work as the first surveyor general are examples; see Metcalf 1995: 25. Kim Wagner's work (2009) on the *thugees* demonstrates some early ethnographic practices of the EIC.

15. See Hunter's biography *The Life of Brian Hodgson* (1896), where Latham (289), Baron Von Humboldt, and Max Müller (286) all praise Hodgson. See also Risley's *The Tribes and Castes of Bengal*, 1891.

16. Dirks 2001.

17. Hunter's phrase, (1896) 1991: 284.

18. *Proceedings of the Asiatic Society*, August 1865.

19. Ibid.

20. Ibid., February 1866.

21. "Letter from Fayrer to J. Anderson," *Proceedings of the Asiatic Society*, April 1866. Kaushik Ghosh has briefly touched upon the Ethnological Congress in his important article "A Market for Aboriginality" (1999).

22. *Proceedings of the Asiatic Society*, April 1866.

23. "Letter 139, Anderson to Bayley," *Proceedings of the Asiatic Society*, April 1866. See also Bengal, General, Proc 40, 1866.

24. On non-events, Stoler 2009: 106–8.

25. Mehta 1999: 12.

26. Metcalf 1995: 46–47.

27. Foucault 1994: 73.

28. Bengal, General, 1–2, February 1869.

29. See, for instance, Bandyopadhaya 2004: 144; Bayly 1995; Dirks 2001: 200–25; Metcalf 1995: 11, 106; Pels 2000; Raheja 2000.

30. Dalton 1872: 123.

31. Young 1995: 25.

32. Beverley's Census Report of 1872, as cited by *Census Report of 1881* (1883: 20).

33. See Kaviraj 1992.

34. Cf. Stoler 2009: 36.

35. Risley 1891:vi. Also, Bengal, Financial, Misc 1–55, March 1887.

36. Bengal, Financial, Misc 1–55, March 1887, 43.

37. Dirks 2001: ch. 10.

38. Underlying concerns with race were emblematic and constitutive of Indian ethnology. See Bayly 1995.

39. Bengal, Financial, Misc 1–55, March 1887.

40. Ibid.

41. Demi-official letter from Risley to W. H. Flowers, June 9, 1885, ibid., 95.

42. Dirks 2001: 222.

43. Letter No. 51, from Risley to Secretary of the Government of Bengal, March 8, 1886, in Bengal, Financial, Misc, March 1887, 83–84.

44. *Census Report of 1881* (1883: 21).

45. Ibid., 158.

46. See *General Report on the Census of India, 1891* (1893): 121, 158, 190, 193.

47. Report on the Census of India, 1901: 312–13.

48. See "Ethnographic Survey in India in Connection with the Census of 1901," *Man* (1901) 1: 137–41. Also Bengal, Financial, Misc, File M-3C-18, Proc B1–2, December 1900. With regard to Darjeeling, a special "Note on the religion, castes and languages of the inhabitant of Nepal for Guidance of Census Officers" was sent to clarify enumerators' confusion. It read: "Religion.—It is the fashion in India to be a Hindu. Hence most Nepalese tribes in India will so describe themselves, including the Gurungs, who are Buddhists in Western Nepal. Some tribes are neither Hindu nor Buddhist. It is believed

that many Limbus belong to this class. In such cases the tribal name should be entered in the column for religion." Elsewhere, it broke "the more important tribes of Nepal" into four major designations: Religious Castes; Military and Dominant Tribes; Other Tribes; and Menial Tribes and Castes. See Bengal, Financial, Misc, File M-3c-26, Proc B 86, July 1900.

49. Resolution 3219–32, Bengal, General, Misc File 6E–1, Proc B 69, No. 1902.

50. Report on the Census of India 1911: 129.

51. Ibid., 370.

52. Ibid.: 382–84.

53. Report on the Census of India 1921: 112.

54. Ibid., 113.

55. Ibid.

56. On enframing, see Mitchell 2002: 289–301.

57. Ibid., 222.

58. Hacking (2006) develops this idea with regard to psychiatric classifications.

59. Report on the Census of India 1921: 112.

60. Mitchell 2002: 111, 118.

61. Report on the Census of India 1931: 379.

62. Ibid., 506.

63. Appendix II, 1931 Census.

64. Khilnani 1997.

65. Rao 2009: 18.

66. Originally, in 1916, the Indian Legislative Council included under this designation "criminal and wandering tribes," "aboriginals," and "untouchables." But the Southborough Committee of 1919 gave this distinction a decidedly Hindu inflection by basing it on the test of untouchability. Revankar 1971: 105.

67. On this history of Dalit becoming, see Rao 2007, 2009.

68. One exception was British-born ethnologist Verrier Elwin, who advocated the protection of India's tribals throughout the independence movement, eventually splitting with the Congress over the issue. I return to Elwin in Chapter 3.

69. Report on the Census of 1941: 18.

70. Ibid., 28.

71. Ibid., 20.

72. The philosophically minded may here consult Kant 1998 (1787).

73. Stoler 2008.

74. Rabinow 2007.

NOTES TO CHAPTER 3

1. On Eklavya as fixer, see our article Middleton and Pradhan 2014.

2. Cohn 1996.

3. Dirks 2001.

4. There are now more than 75 semi-autonomous Scheduled Areas and 9 semi-autonomous Tribal Areas designated by the Fifth and Sixth Schedules of the Indian

Constitution respectively. There are 194 Integrated Tribal Development Projects (ITDPs) and some 259 Modified Area Development Approaches (MADA) for regions with high densities of tribal populations. This is in addition to the more than 700 Scheduled Tribes entitled to affirmative action.

5.   See Gupta and Sivaramakrishnan 2012.

6.   Povinelli 2011.

7.   Gupta 2012; Hansen and Stepputat 2001; Hull 2012.

8.   Gramsci 1971: 243.

9.   These are broader questions, which Partha Chatterjee has taken up in his writings on the politics of the governed, 2004.

10.   Middleton 2011b. Materials in this section adapted from Middleton, T. 2011. "Ethno-logics: Paradigms of Modern Identity." In *Handbook of Modernity in South Asia: Modern Makeovers,* edited by Saurabh Dube, 200–213. New Delhi: Oxford University Press, (pp. 206–7). Reprinted by permission of Oxford University Press.

11.   Rao 2007, 2009.

12.   Ibid.

13.   Rodrigues 2002.

14.   Rao 2007, 2009.

15.   "Communal Deadlock and a Way to Solve It," in *Dr. Babasaheb Ambedkar: Writings and Speeches (BAWS).* Bombay: Government of Maharashtra, 1979.

16.   Chakrabarty 2000. Johannes Fabian's *Time and the Other* (1983) makes similar arguments, but focuses on how academic anthropology denies coevalness to its object communities.

17.   Mehta 1999: 48.

18.   On false liberalism, see Scott 1995.

19.   On savage slot, Trouillot 1991. On tribal slot, Li 2007.

20.   As Ambedkar once put it, "Humanity is not capable of assortment and classification. The statesman therefore, must follow some rough and ready rule, and that rough and ready rule is to treat all men alike not because they are alike but because classification and assortment are impossible"; Ambedkar, in Rodrigues 2002: 58.

21.   Gramsci 1971: 243.

22.   All passages quoted are from the Constituent Assembly Debates on September 5 and 6, 1949. India, Constituent Assembly Debates, Official Report, 1950.

23.   See, e.g., Chatterjee 1993; Khilnani 1997; Metcalf and Metcalf 2002; Sarkar 1997.

24.   Guha 1999; Nongbri 2006: 78–79; McDuie-Ra 2009: 51.

25.   Stoler 2008.

26.   See Chapter 2.

27.   Anthropological engagements with these processes are many, but see Jan French's excellent work in Brazil by the same name, *Legalizing Identities* (2009).

28.   Despite its notoriety, the ASI plays little administrative role in the scheduling of tribes. Also of note during this period was the Ayyangar Committee's 1949 recommendation to repeal the Criminal Tribes Act, which had been on the books in various forms since the nineteenth century. The listed Criminal Tribes were subsequently "denotified" by

the Criminal Tribes Act of 1952. See also "Ayyangar Report on Repeal of Criminal Tribes Act of 1924," Government of India, 1949.

29. Article 342 outlines ST provisions. See also Articles 15(4), 46, 330, 332, 335, 338, 339.

30. See Constitution (Scheduled Tribes) Order of 1950. Less-formalized precedents included the list of "primitive tribes" from the 1931 Census, as well as the list of "backward tribes" in the Government of India Act of 1935. See Chapter 2.

31. "Report of the Commissioner for SC and ST for 1952," India, Ministry of Home Affairs, 1953.

32. "Resolution of the Government of India," Department of Social Security, June 1, 1965.

33. B. N. Lokur (Chairman), 1965, "The Report of the Advisory Committee on the Revision of the Lists of Scheduled Castes and Tribes," India, Department of Social Security: 12.

34. Darjeeling's All India Nepali Scheduled Castes Association (AINSCA) (est. 1947) opposed Koli's organization on fears that the Dalits could lose all designation through such finagling. Op-ed debates between rival factions appeared in the papers, and divisions increasingly mapped to local party politics. At least one assault related to the controversy occurred (on March 17, 2007 in Chyanga, Panighatta) when a supporter of AINSCA was attacked by GNLF supporters in the course of trying to convene a local branch meeting. *Himal Darpan*, March 20, 2007.

35. Foucault 1977, 1980.

36. A nod here to the seminal work of the late Mary Douglas (1966). On the application of her thoughts on "purity and danger" to ethnicity, see Appadurai 1998 and Malkki 1995.

37. Durkheim (1912) 1995: 163.

38. Students of Indian historiography will see resonances here with the Cambridge School's attentions to colonialism's administrative history.

39. Subaltern historians Dipesh Chakrabarty (2002, 2000) and Partha Chatterjee (1993: 13) have advocated similar strategies, but for historiography.

NOTES TO CHAPTER 4

1. Middleton 2011a and Middleton 2011b. Materials in this chapter adapted from Middleton, T. 2011. "Across the Interface of State Ethnography: Rethinking Ethnology and Its Subjects in Multicultural India," *American Ethnologist* 38 (2): 249–66. Materials in this chapter also adapted from Middleton, T. 2011. "Ethno-logics: Paradigms of Modern Identity." In *Handbook of Modernity in South Asia: Modern Makeovers,* edited by Saurabh Dube, 200–213. New Delhi: Oxford University Press, (pp. 206–7). Reprinted by permission of Oxford University Press.

2. Since the cases are still pending, I use pseudo-ethnonyms and places throughout this chapter (Lekh, Molung, Laharā Gāū, etc.).

3. As a compliment to the courtrooms and indigenous rights cases that have rightly been a major site of study (cf. Clifford 1988; Hale 2002, 2006; Povinelli 2002), here I take a page from anthropology's recent fascinations with paraethnographic encounters (Boyer

2010; Holmes and Marcus 2005, 2006; Holmes, Marcus, and Westbrook 2006; Westbrook 2008) to examine the field of state ethnography itself. Claudio Lomnitz's *Deep Mexico, Silent Mexico* (2001) offers a comparison of anthropologists' governmental involvement, although he does not address the ethnographic practices of recognition.

4. Available in *The National Commission for Scheduled Tribes Handbook 2005* (Government of India, 2005).

5. For comparative perspective on different multicultural orders, see, e.g., Béteille 1998; French 2009; Gunew 2004; Hale 2002; Li 2000; Miller 2003; Povinelli 2002; Shah 2010; Taylor 1992.

6. Cf. Povinelli 2002: 226.

7. On the politics of mediation vs. immediation, see Mazzarella 2006.

8. On the particularity/generality of *the example*, see Agamben 1993: 10–11.

9. Spivak 1988a.

10. Dombrowski 2004: 23.

11. Cf. Li 2000; Shah 2010.

12. Baudrillard 1994.

13. Fabian 1983: 31–32.

14. On pure antecedent pasts, see Young 1995: 25.

15. Gadamer 1997: 277–307.

16. Corrigan and Sayer 1985: 4

17. This was not a final ruling. See Chapter 7.

18. Cf. Needham and Rajan 2007; Nigam 2006.

19. Cf. Povinelli 2002: 226.

20. Chatterjee 2004: 41.

21. Sayer 1994: 374.

22. Cf. Wedeen's work in Syria, 1999. Also Gramsci 1971; Povinelli 2002; Sayer 1994.

NOTES TO CHAPTER 5

1. Some of the materials in this chapter have been adapted from Middleton 2013b.

2. Dirks 2001.

3. On the anthropology of bureaucracy, see, e.g., Gupta and Sharma 2006; Herzfeld 1992; Hetherington 2012; Weber 1978. My inquiry is also indebted to recent treatments of postcolonial bureaucracy in South Asia, exemplified by the work of Akhil Gupta and James Ferguson 2002; Gupta 2012; Fuller and Bénéï 2000; Gupta and K. Sivaramakrishnan 2012; Hansen and Stepputat 2001; Hull 2012; Hull et al. 2013.

4. Clifford 1988; Hale 2006 Povinelli 2002;.

5. Gupta 2012; Hansen and Stepputat 2001; Hull 2012.

6. Gupta 2012: 76–77.

7. Recent studies of ST recognition have focused primarily on the communities involved. Less has been said of the government's side of things. Cf. Bisht 1994; Kapila 2008; Maaker and Schleiter 2010; Middleton 2011a, 2011b; Middleton and Shneiderman 2008; Moodie 2013, 2015; Shah and Shneiderman 2013; Shneiderman 2009, 2013, 2015; Shneiderman and Turin 2006; Xaxa 2008.

8. Abrams 1988; Fuller and Bénéï 2000; Gupta 2012; Gupta and Sharma 2006; Hansen and Stepputat 2001; Hull 2012.

9. A debt here to the Marxian sociology/anthropology of knowledge, in particular the foundational works of Marx 1978 and Mannheim 1952.

10. Hansen 2000: 43.

11. Hull 2012. See also Richland's symposium commentary, 2013.

12. Allochronism: the denial of coevalness between researcher and research subjects. Fabian 1983.

13. On waiting and its politics in India, see Jeffrey 2010.

14. Li 2000: 153.

15. Povinelli 2011: 31–32.

16. "Response to Queries on Inclusion of [. . .] Communities into the ST List of West Bengal," Cultural Research Institute, Backward Class Welfare Department, Government of West Bengal, 2006. (I have redacted the names of the groups in question.)

17. Abrams 1988: 79.

18. Hansen and Stepputat 2001: 29. Also relevant are Corrigan 1994; Corrigan and Sayer 1985; Gupta 2012; and Weber's (1978: 957–1002) foundational work on rational bureaucracy.

19. Hansen and Stepputat 2001: 16.

20. Weber 1978. On post/colonial technocracy, see Mitchell's *Rule of Experts* (2002).

21. Althusser 1971.

22. See Abrams, "Notes on the Difficulties of Studying the State" (1988).

23. More on this in Chapter 7.

24. On endurance and exhaustion, see Povinelli 2011: 31–32.

25. On these incidents, see Introduction.

26. See Jocelyn Chua's *In Pursuit of the Good Life*, 2014.

27. As Abrams (1988: 77) famously notes, "The state is, then, in every sense of the term a triumph of concealment . . . a mask of legitimating illusion . . . The real official secret, however, is the secret of the non-existence of the state."

28. Povinelli 2011: 31–32.

29. Cf. Baruah's work (2009, 2010) in India's Northeast.

30. The Chopra Commission Report, as cited in *Hindustani Times*, December 18, 2007.

NOTES TO CHAPTER 6

1. Ghisingh accusations preceded my fieldwork. See "Ghisingh Sees Hat Trick in Culture Shift," *Statesman*, February 24, 2006; "GNLF Talks Tribal Rule," *Statesman*, January 2, 2006; "Tamangs Defy Ghisingh Identity Whip," *Telegraph*, February 6, 2006; "Lochar Goes On despite Ghisingh," *Statesman*, February 6, 2006; "Chowrasta Chatter" and "Tamang Raise Ghisingh Hackles," *Statesman*, February 24, 2006; "Tamang Ire at Ghisingh," *Telegraph*, February 25, 2006; "Hill Tamangs Blink First," *Telegraph*, April 3, 2006.

2. The Tamang Buddhist Gedung (TBG) was founded in 1994 as an alternative to AITBA.

3. AITBA first demanded ST status on November 24, 1981. The bids went into re-mission during the 1980s Gorkhaland Agitations, but were re-initiated shortly after. The bill establishing the Tamangs' inclusion as STs passed Parliament on December 19, 2002. They were officially scheduled via Act 10 of 2003.

4. Headlines bespoke the surrounding controversy: "Durga Pujā Boycott Triggers Row," *Statesman*, October 4, 2003; "Tamangs Split over Dasain Celebrations," *Statesman*, October 7, 2003; "Diwali Splits Tamang Community," *Statesman*, October 24, 2003; "Tamangs Split over Lochar Celebrations," *Statesman*, December 12, 2003; "Tamangs Debate over Lochar," *Statesman*, November 29, 2005.

5. Italicized passage paraphrased from my notes.

6. Middleton 2011b. I have previously discussed this scene in Middleton, T. 2011. "Ethno-logics: Paradigms of Modern Identity." In *Modern Makeovers*, edited by Saurabh Dube, 200–213. New Delhi: Oxford University Press. (pp.209–10). Reprinted by permission of Oxford University Press.

7. See, e.g., Cadena and Starn 2007; Clifford 2013; Comaroff and Comaroff 2009; McAnany and Parks 2012; Povinelli 2002, 2011; Shneiderman 2009, 2015; Sylvain 2014.

8. See Clifford's *Returns: Becoming Indigenous in the Twenty-first Century* (2013).

9. On Darjeeling's tea industry, see Besky 2013.

10. The Buddhist Pema Tshoiling Monastery, est. 1951.

11. Chatterjee 2004: 57.

12. Shneiderman's work highlights ritual as a key domain of this production (2014, 2015).

13. In terms of gender and circulation, many of the ethnic associations I worked with had Women's Wings, which marked a strong feminine presence in these movements. While I interacted with the women leaders of these wings in the collective spaces of ethnic association offices, ethnic conventions, and a variety of cultural programs, my primary ethnographic relations with the associations were with men. Additional research would be needed to accurately depict the complicated gender dynamics through which these programs made claims upon male and female bodies.

14. Shah 2010: 9–35.

15. Foucault 1977, 1980, 1994.

16. On ethnic elites and representation, see Brass 1976, 1985.

17. Like other ethnic associations, AITBA's leadership was dominated by men.

18. On the performative nature of identity, see Butler 1990, 1993.

19. See Clifford 2004, 2013; Eriksen 2002, 2004; Handler 1996; McAnany and Parks 2012; Phillips 2003. Also Hale 2006. My discussions in this section also pertain to emerging literatures on indigenous media (see, e.g., Wilson and Stewart 2008) and its transformations of ethnic consciousness (Turner 1991). For regional comparison of codification of indigenous culture, see Karlsson 2011: 246–55.

20. Cf. Escarcega 2010; Nyamnjoh 2007: 305; Speed 2006: 73; Spivak 1988b; Sylvain 2014.

21. Clifford 2004, 2013.

22. Li 2000: 153.

23. A key point of the Marxian sociology of knowledge—and in particular the approach of Karl Mannheim, 1952, 1955, 1971. See also Gramsci 1971; Lukacs 1971; Marx 1978.

24. I use "referentiality" as Brentano (1874) 1995 and Husserl (1900) 1970 used "intentionality": the pointing to/aboutness of knowledge.

25. Translations of Foucault use both this term and "mode of subjection." For Foucault, *mode d'assujettisement* "is the way in which the individual establishes his relation to a rule and recognizes himself as obliged to put it into practice" (1986: 27).

26. George Mentore (2009) has written briefly (but beautifully) on recognizing the self in one's anthropology.

27. Philosophers from Kant (1998) to Heidegger (1962, 1982) and Schutz (1967) have weighed in on the debate about the distinction between epistemological (what I am calling *conceptual*) and embodied knowledge (what I am calling *experiential*). Charles Taylor offers a concise overview of these debates in "Overcoming Epistemology" (1995).

28. Anthropologist David Holmberg notes that Tamangs in Nepal still will shave their head upon the death of a family member. However, the meanings attributed to this act differ from those commonly held by Hindus. Nevertheless, these practices seem to emerge out of sustained histories of Hindu influence (Personal correspondence with Holmberg).

29. The TCD's registered English name is the Darjeeling Gurung (Tamu) Welfare Association.

30. Years later, the TCD succeeded in bringing a Gurung lama to the *gomba*. He and his handful of students now live at the *gomba*.

31. For the temple's inauguration in 2006, thousands descended on the village from Sikkim, Kalimpong, and Darjeeling.

32. This embrace of Buddhism has also occurred in Nepal (cf. McHugh 2006). And as in Darjeeling, significant rifts have opened up around the question of Hinduism and hybridity's place in Gurung sociocultural practice. These dynamics bespeak a growing historiographic consciousness among Nepal's *janājāti* communities that Hinduism was imposed upon them by the central powers of Nepal's Hindu monarchical state. Studies that have dealt with these histories and their contemporary effects include: Gellner, Pfaff-Czarnecka, and Whelpton 1997; Hangen 2005, 2007; Lecomte-Tilouine and Dolfuss 2003; Levine 1987; Onta 1996; Tamang 2008; Whelpton 2005.

33. Bourdieu 1977: 73, 1987: 77, 130–31; Mauss 1973: 97–104.

34. On *act* versus *action*, see the phenomenology of Alfred Schutz (1967: 39).

35. Hobsbawm and Ranger 1983.

36. Chatterjee 2004.

37. Cf. Mahmood 2001.

NOTES TO CHAPTER 7

1. Cf. Rabinow et al. 2008.

2. Middleton 2013a. Materials in this section and the next adapted from Middleton, T. 2013. "Anxious Belongings: Anxiety and the Politics of Belonging in Subnationalist Darjeeling." *American Anthropologist* 115 (4): 608–21.

3. See Chhetri 2008.

4. "The Hills Erupt Again—This Time in Protest," *Darjeeling Times*, September 26, 2007.

5. "Gorkhaland Demand Resurfaces," *Telegraph*, October 4, 2007.

6. See Lama 2008.

7. Cf. Taussig 1992.

8. See Besky's analysis of the movement's relationship to land and labor in Darjeeling's tea plantations (2013: 144–69).

9. Besky also discusses the Morcha's dress codes (2013: 122, 152–56).

10. "'Gorkhaland' to Have a Dress Code?" *Statesman*, September 11, 2008; "The Gorkha Dress Code of Discord," *Statesman*, September 12, 2008.

11. "Dress Code Row Goes On," *Telegraph*, September 23, 2008; "Dress Code Relaxation for Lepchas," *Statesman*, September 13, 2008.

12. "GJMM 'Road Show' to Enforce Dress Code," *Statesman*, October 13, 2008. On the Nari Morcha, women, and the movement, see Besky 2013: 164.

13. "Faces Blackened after Dress Code Defiance," *Telegraph*, October 15, 2008; "Dress Code Diktat Keeps People Indoors," *Statesman*, October 16, 2008.

14. "Faces Blackened after Dress Code Defiance," *Telegraph*, October 15, 2008.

15. The literatures here are numerous. See, e.g., Blaser 2010; Clifford 2004, 2013; Dennison 2012; Escobar 2008, 2011; Gellner 2010, 2011; Hale 2006; Richland 2007; Shah 2010; Shneiderman 2015.

16. Exceptions include Shah 2010; Dombrowski 2004; Escobar 2010: 43; Henley and Davidson 2007; Li 2007.

17. We are reminded here of how even hybridity—viz. the hybrid dress of *daurā suruwāl* and *chowbandi choli*—may be sucked into the same traps of auto-essentialism that structure fundamentalisms throughout the world. On hybridity as a progressive alternative to ethnic absolutism, see Gilroy 1990, 1993, 2000. On hybridity versus separation as cultural-political strategies, see Munasinghe 1997, 2001, 2002. Also, Brah and Coombes 2000; García Canclini 1995; Stewart and Shah 1994; Werbner and Modood 1997; Williams 1989; Young 2000.

18. Rabinow et al. 2008.

19. Freud (1919) 2003.

20. On the assassination and its fallout, also see Besky 2013: 140–43.

21. Middleton 2013c. I have previously written about the Long March. Materials in this section and the next are adapted from Middleton T. 2013c. "States of Difference: Refiguring Ethnicity and Its 'Crisis' at India's Borders." *Political Geography* 35: 14–24.

22. "All Fingers Are Crossed as They Sign Autonomy Pact." indianexpress.com, July 21, 2011 (accessed July 21, 2011).

23. Povinelli 2011: 99.

24. AIGBA appealed to the National Commission on Minorities (Government of India). However, it remained unclear how exactly Gurungs would attain Religious Minority status. See National Commission for Minorities Act, 1992.

25. Cf. McDuie-Ra 2012.

26. On standardization and indigenous mobilization, see Colloredo-Mansfeld 2009.

27. Hale 2002.

NOTES TO EPILOGUE

1. Hegel 1977.
2. Middleton 2013c.
3. On seeing and the failures of the state, Scott 1999.
4. Blaser 2010; Cadena and Starn 2007; Escobar 2008, 2010.
5. On decoloniality as an intellectual-political project, see Mignolo and Escobar 2009.
6. Gilroy 2000: 15.
7. On the uncanny, see Freud (1919) 2003.
8. Fanon 1967: 12.
9. Malkki 1995: 8.
10. Cf. Povinelli 2011: 73.
11. On ethnographic adjacency and its transformative potentials, see Rabinow 2007.
12. Imagery from Yeats's "The Second Coming" (1920) 1994.

BIBLIOGRAPHY

Abrams, Philip. 1988. "Notes on the Difficulties of Studying the State." *Journal of Historical Sociology* 1 (1): 58–89.

Adas, Michael. 2004. "Contested Hegemony: The Great War and the Afro-Asian Assault on the Civilizing Mission Ideology." In *Decolonization: Perspectives from Now and Then*, edited by Prasenjit Duara, 78–100. London: Routledge.

Agamben, Gorgio. 1993. *The Coming Community*. Minneapolis: University of Minnesota Press.

Althusser, Louis. 1971. "On Ideology and Ideological State Apparatuses: Notes toward an Investigation." In *Lenin and Philosophy and Other Essays*, 121–76. London: New Left Books.

Ambedkar, B. R. 1979. *Dr. Babasaheb Ambedkar: Writings and Speeches (BAWS)*, vol. 1, Bombay: Government of Maharashtra.

Anderson, Benedict. 1983. *Imagined Communities: Reflections on the Origin and Spread of Nationalism*. New York: Verso Books.

———. 1998. *The Spectre of Comparison: Nationalism, Southeast Asia, and the World*. London: Verso Books.

Appadurai, Arjun. 1991. "Global Ethnoscapes: Notes and Queries for a Transnational Anthropology." In *Recapturing Anthropology: Working in the Present*, edited by Richard G. Fox, 191–210. Santa Fe: School of American Research Press.

———. 1998. "Dead Certainty: Ethnic Violence in the Era of Globalization." *Public Culture* 10 (2): 225–47.

Asad, Talal, ed. 1973. *Anthropology and the Colonial Encounter*. London: Ithaca Press.

Bagchi, Romit. 2012. *Gorkhaland: Crisis of Statehood*. New Delhi: Sage.

Bakhtin, M. M. 1981. *The Dialogic Imagination: Four Essays*. Edited and translated by Michael Holquist. Austin: University of Texas Press.

Bandyopadhaya, Sekhara. 2004. *Caste, Culture, and Hegemony: Social Dominance in Colonial Bengal*. New Delhi: Sage.

Bannerji, Himani. 2001. *Inventing Subjects: Studies in Hegemony, Patriarchy, and Colonialism*. New Delhi: Tulika Publishers.

Barth, Fredrik, ed. 1969. *Ethnic Groups and Boundaries*. Boston: Little, Brown, and Co.

Baruah, Sanjib. 2005. *Durable Disorder: Understanding the Politics of Northeast India*. New Delhi: Oxford University Press.

———. 2009. "Introduction." In *Beyond Counter-Insurgency: Breaking the Impasse in Northeast India*, edited by Sanjib Baruah, 2–21. New Delhi: Oxford University Press.

————. 2010. "Introduction." In *Ethno-Nationalism in India: A Reader*, edited by Sanjib Baruah, 2–16. New Delhi: Oxford University Press.

Bates, Crispin. 1995. "Race, Caste, and Tribe in Central India: The Early Origins of Indian Anthropometry." In *The Concept of Race in South Asia*, edited by Peter Robb, 219–59. New Delhi: Oxford University Press.

Baudrillard, Jean. 1994. *Simulacra and Simulation*. Translated by Sheila Faria Glaser. Ann Arbor: University of Michigan Press.

Bayly, Susan. 1995. "'Caste' and 'Race' in the Colonial Ethnography of India." In *The Concept of Race in South Asia*, edited by Peter Robb, 165–218. New Delhi: Oxford University Press.

————. 1999. *Caste, Society, and Politics in India from the Eighteenth Century to the Modern Age*. Cambridge: Cambridge University Press.

Bell, Vikki. 1999. "Performativity and Belonging: An Introduction." In *Performativity and Belonging*, edited by Vikki Bell, 1–20. London: Sage Publications.

Berlant, Lauren. 2005. "The Epistemology of State Emotion." In *Dissent in Dangerous Times*, edited by Austin Sarat, 46–78. Ann Arbor: University of Michigan Press.

————. 2007. "Citizenship." In *Keywords for American Cultural Studies*, edited by Bruce Burgett and Glenn Hendler, 37–42. New York: New York University Press.

Besky, Sarah. 2013. *The Darjeeling Distinction: Labor and Justice on Fair-Trade Tea Plantations in India*. Berkeley: University of California Press.

Béteille, André. 1998. "The Idea of Indigenous People." *Current Anthropology* 39 (2): 187–91.

Biolsi, Thomas, and Larry Zimmerman. 1997. *Indians and Anthropologists: Vine Deloria, Jr., and the Critique of Anthropology*. Tucson: University of Arizona Press.

Binsbergen, Wim van. 1985. "From Tribe to Ethnicity in Western Zambia: The Unit of Study as an Ideological Problem." In *Old Modes of Production and Capitalist Encroachment: Anthropological Explorations in Africa*. Edited by W. van Binsbergen and P. Geschiere, 181–234. London: Routledge and Kegan Paul.

Bisht, B. S. 1994. *Tribes of India, Nepal, and Tibet Borderland: A Study of Cultural Transformation*. New Delhi: Gyan Publishing House.

Blaser, Mario. 2010. *Storytelling Globalization from the Chaco and Beyond*. Durham, NC: Duke University Press.

Booth, Chelsea. 2010. "'These People Deprived of This Country': Language and the Politics of Belonging among Indians of Nepali Descent." *Himalaya* 28 (1): Article 7. http://digitalcommons.macalester.edu/cgi/viewcontent.cgi?article=1752&context=himalaya (accessed 7/10/13).

Bourdieu, Pierre. 1977. *Outline of a Theory of Practice*. Cambridge: Cambridge University Press.

————. 1987. *In Other Words: Essays toward a Reflexive Sociology*. Translated by Mathew Adamson. Cambridge: Polity Press.

Boyer, Dominic. 2010. "On the Ethics and Practice of Contemporary Social Theory: From Crisis Talk to Multiattentional Method." *Dialectical Anthropology* 34 (3): 305–24.

Brah, Avtar, and Annie E. Coombes. 2000. "Introduction: The Conundrums of Mixing."

In *Hybridity and Its Discontents: Politics, Science, Culture*, edited by Avtar Brah and Annie E. Coombes, 1–16. New York: Routledge.

Brass, Paul. 1976. "Ethnicity and Nationality Formation." *Ethnicity* 3: 225–41.

———. ed. 1985. *Ethnic Groups and the State*. London: Croom Helm.

———. 1991. *Ethnicity and Nationalism: Theory and Comparison*. New Delhi: Sage.

Brennan, Teresa. 2004. *The Transmission of Affect*. Ithaca, NY: Cornell University Press.

Brentano. (1874) 1995. *Psychology from an Empirical Standpoint*. Translated by A. C. Rancurello, D. B. Terrell, and L. McAlister. London: Routledge and Kegan Paul.

Burton, Antoinette. 1994. *Burdens of History: British Feminists, Indian Women, and Imperial Culture, 1865–1915*. Chapel Hill: University of North Carolina Press.

———. 1997. "Who Needs the Nation? Interrogating 'British' History." *Journal of Historical Sociology* 10 (3): 227–48.

———. 2003. *Dwelling in the Archive: Women Writing House, Home, and History in Late Colonial India*. Oxford: Oxford University Press.

Butler, Judith. 1990. "Performative Acts and Gender Constitution: An Essay in Phenomenology and Feminist Theory." In *Performing Feminisms*, edited by Sue-Ellen Case, 279–82. Baltimore, MD: Johns Hopkins Press.

———. 1993. *Bodies That Matter: On the Discursive Limits of "Sex."* New York: Routledge.

Cadena, Marisol de la, and Orin Starn, eds. 2007. *Indigenous Experience Today*. London: Berg.

Chakrabarty, Dipesh. 2000. *Provincializing Europe: Postcolonial Thought and Historical Difference*. Princeton, NJ: Princeton University Press.

———. 2002. *Habitations of Modernity: Essays in the Wake of Subaltern Studies*. Chicago: University of Chicago Press.

Chasie, Charles, and Sanjoy Hazarika. 2009. *The State Strikes Back: India and the Naga Insurgency*. Washington, DC: East-West Center.

Chatterjee, Partha. 1986. *Nationalist Thought and the Colonial World: A Derivative Discourse*. Minneapolis: University of Minnesota Press.

———. 1992. "History and the Nationalization of Hinduism." *Social Research* 59 (1): 111–49.

———. 1993. *The Nation and Its Fragments: Colonial and Postcolonial Histories*. Princeton, NJ: Princeton University Press.

———. 2001. "On Civil and Political Society in Post-colonial Democracies." In *Civil Society: History and Possibilities*, edited by Sudipta Kaviraj and Sunil Kilnani, 165–78. Cambridge: Cambridge University Press.

———. 2004. *The Politics of the Governed: Reflections on Popular Politics in Most of the World*. New York: Columbia University Press.

Chatterjee, Piya. 2001. *A Time for Tea: Women, Labor, and Post/Colonial Politics on an Indian Plantation*. Durham, NC: Duke University Press.

Chhetri, Satyadeep. 2008. "No Chowkidar!" *Himal Southasian* 21 (1). http://old.himalmag .com/component/content/article/1072-no-chowkidar.html (accessed 11/16/14).

Chua, Jocelyn. 2014. *In Pursuit of the Good Life: Aspiration and Suicide in Globalizing South India*. Berkeley: University of California Press.

Clifford, James. 1988. "Identity at Mashpee." In *The Predicament of Culture: Twentieth-Century Ethnography, Literature, and Art*. Cambridge, MA: Harvard University Press.

———. 2004. "Looking Several Ways: Anthropology and Native Heritage in Alaska." *Current Anthropology* 45 (1): 5–30.

———. 2013. *Returns: Becoming Indigenous in the Twenty-First Century*. Cambridge, MA: Harvard University Press.

Cohen, Abner. 1974. "Lessons of Ethnicity." In *Urban Ethnicity*, edited by Abner Cohen, ix–xxiv. London: Tavistock Publications.

Cohen, R. 1978. "Ethnicity: Problem and Focus in Anthropology." *Annual Review of Anthropology* 7: 379–403.

Cohn, Bernard S. 1987. *An Anthropologist among the Historians and Other Essays*. London: Oxford University Press.

———. 1996. *Colonialism and Its Forms of Knowledge: The British in India*. Princeton, NJ: Princeton University Press.

Colloredo-Mansfeld, Rudi. 2009. *Fighting like a Community: Andean Civil Society in an Era of Indian Uprisings*. Chicago: University of Chicago Press.

Comaroff, John L., and Jean Comaroff. 2009. *Ethnicity, Inc.* Chicago: University of Chicago Press.

Cons, Jason. 2012. "Histories of Belonging(s): Narrating Territory, Possession, and Dispossession at the India- Bangladesh Border." *Modern Asian Studies* 46 (3): 527–58.

———. 2013. "Narrating Boundaries: Framing and Contesting Suffering, Community, and Belonging along the India-Bangladesh Border." *Political Geography* 35: 37–46.

Corrigan, Philip. 1994. "Preface: State Formation." In *Everyday Forms of State Formation: Revolution and the Negotiation of Rule in Modern Mexico*, edited by M. Joseph Gilbert and Daniel Nugent, xvii–xix. Durham, NC: Duke University Press.

Corrigan, Philip, and Derek Sayer. 1985. *The Great Arch: English State Formation as Cultural Revolution*. Oxford: Basil Blackwell.

Dalton, Edward Tuite. 1872. *Descriptive Ethnology of Bengal*. Calcutta: Government of India, under the Direction of Council of the Asiatic Society.

Dasgupta, Jyotirindra. 1997. "Community, Authenticity, and Autonomy: Insurgence and Institutional Development in India's Northeast." *Journal of Asian Studies* 56 (2): 345–70.

Davidson, Jamie S., and David Henley, eds. 2007. *The Revival of Tradition in Indonesian Politics: The Deployment of Adat from Colonialism to Indigenism*. New York: Routledge.

Deloria, Jr., Vine. 1969. *Custer Died for Your Sins: An Indian Manifesto*. New York: Macmillan.

Dennison, Jean. 2012. *Colonial Entanglement: Constituting a Twenty-First-Century Osage Nation*. Chapel Hill, NC: University of North Carolina Press.

Des Chenes, Mary Katherine. 1991. "Relics of Empire: A Cultural History of the Gurkhas, 1815–1987." Ph.D. diss., Stanford University.

Dhakal, Rajendra P. 2009. "The Urge to Belong: An Identity in Waiting." In *Indian Nepali: New Perspectives*, edited by D. R. Nepal, G. S. Nepal, A. C. Sinha, and T. B. Subba, 148–67. New Delhi: Concept Publishing House.

Dhungel, Ramesh K. 2007. "Opening the Chest of Nepal's History: The Survey of B. H. Hodgson's Manuscripts in the British Library and Royal Asiatic Society." *South Asia Library Group Newsletter* 3: 42–47.

Dirks, Nicholas B. 1987. *The Hollow Crown: Ethnohistory of an Indian Kingdom*. Cambridge: Cambridge University Press.

———. 2001. *Castes of Mind: Colonialism and the Making of Modern India*. Princeton, NJ: Princeton University Press.

———. 2004. "The Ethnographic State." In *Postcolonial Passages: Contemporary History-writing on India*, edited by Saurabh Dube and Shahid Amin, 70–88. New Delhi: Oxford University Press.

Dombrowski, Kirk. 2001. *Against Culture: Development, Politics, and Religion in Indian Alaska*. Lincoln: University of Nebraska Press.

———. 2004. "Reply to Clifford in 'Looking Several Ways.'" *Current Anthropology* 45 (1): 23–24.

Douglas, Mary. 1966. *Purity and Danger: An Analysis of Concepts of Pollution and Taboo*. New York: Routledge.

Duara, Prasenjit. 1995. *Rescuing History from the Nation: Questioning Narratives of Modern China*. Chicago: University of Chicago Press.

Dudley-Jenkins, Laura. 2003. *Identity and Identification in India: Defining the Disadvantaged*. New York: Routledge.

Durkheim, Emile. (1912) 1995. *The Elementary Forms of Religious Life*. Translated by Karen E. Fields. New York: Free Press.

Epperson, Terrence W. 1994. "The Politics of Empiricism and the Construction of Race as an Analytic Category." *Transforming Anthropology* 5 (1–2): 15–19.

Eriksen, Patricia Pierce. 2004. "Defining Ourselves through Baskets: Museum Autoethnography and the Makah Cultural and Research Center." In *Coming to Shore: Northwest Coast Ethnology, Traditions, and Visions*, edited by Marie Mauze, Michael Eugene Harkin, and Sergei Kan, 339–61. Lincoln: University of Nebraska Press.

Eriksen, Patricia Pierce, Helma Ward, Janine Bowechop, and Kirk Wachendorf. 2002. *Voices of a Thousand People*. Lincoln: University of Nebraska Press.

Escarcega, Sylvia. 2010. "Authenticating Strategic Essentialisms: The Politics of Indigenousness at the United Nations." *Cultural Dynamics* 22 (1): 3–28.

Escobar, Arturo. 2008. *Territories of Difference: Place, Movements, Life, Redes*. Durham, NC: Duke University Press.

———. 2010. "Latin America at a Crossroads." *Cultural Studies* 24 (1): 1–65.

Fabian, Johannes. 1983. *Time and the Other: How Anthropology Makes Its Object*. New York: Columbia University Press.

Fanon, Frantz. 1967. *Black Skin, White Masks*. Translated by Charles Lam Markman. New York: Grove Press.

Fardon, Richard. 1987. "'African Ethnogenesis': Limits to the Comparability of Ethnic Phenomena." In *Comparative Anthropology*, edited by Holy Ladislov, 168–88. Oxford: Basil Blackwell.

Fortier, Anne-Marie. 2000. *Migrant Belongings: Memory, Space, Identity*. Oxford: Berg.

———. 2009. "Proximity by Design: Affective Citizenship and the Management of Unease." *Citizenship Studies* 14 (1): 17–30.

Foucault, Michel. 1977. *Discipline and Punish: The Birth of the Prison*. Translated by Alan Sheridan. London: Penguin Books.

———. 1978. *The Birth of Biopolitics: Lectures at the College de France, 1978–79*. Edited by Michel Senellart. New York: Palgrave.

———. 1979. "Governmentality." *Ideology and Consciousness* 6: 5–21.

———. 1980. *Power/Knowledge: Selected Interviews and Other Writings, 1972–1977*. Edited by Colin Gordon. New York: Pantheon Books.

———. 1986. *The History of Sexuality Vol II: The Use of Pleasure*. Translated by Robert Hurley. New York: Vintage Books.

———. 1988. "The Political Technology of Individuals." In *Technologies of the Self*, edited by Luther H. Martin, Huck Gutman, and Patrick H. Hutton, 16–49. Amherst: University of Massachusetts Press.

———. 1994. *Ethics: Subjectivity and Truth*. Edited by Paul Rabinow. New York: New Press.

French, Jan Hoffman. 2009. *Legalizing Identities: Becoming Black or Indian in Brazil's Northeast*. Chapel Hill: University of North Carolina Press.

Freud, Sigmund. 1959. *Inhibitions, Symptoms, and Anxiety*. Translated by James Strachey. New York: W. W. Norton.

———. 1966. *Introductory Lectures on Psycho-Analysis*. Translated by James Strachey. New York: W. W. Norton.

———. (1919) 2003. *The Uncanny*. Translated by David McLintock. New York: Penguin Books.

Fuller, C. J., and Veronique Bénéï, eds. 2000. *The Everyday State and Society in Modern India*. New Delhi: Social Science Press.

Gadamer, Hans-Georg. 1997. *Truth and Method*. Translated by Donald G. Marshall and Joel Weinsheimer. New York: Continuum.

Gaenszle, Martin. 2004. "Brian Hodgson as Ethnographer and Ethnologist." In *The Origins of Himalayan Studies: Brian Houghton Hodgson in Nepal and Darjeeling, 1820–1858*, edited by David M. Waterhouse, 206–26. London: RoutledgeCurzon.

Game, Ann. 2001. "Belonging: Experience in Sacred Time and Space." In *Timespace: Geographies of Temporality*, edited by John May and Nigel Thrift, 226–38. New York: Routledge.

García Canclini, Néstor. 1995. *Hybrid Cultures: Strategies for Entering and Leaving Modernity*. Translated by Christopher L. Chippari and Silvia L. Lopez. Minneapolis: University of Minnesota Press.

Geertz, Clifford. 1973. "The Integrative Revolution: Primordialism and Civil Politics in the New States." In *The Interpretation of Cultures*, 255–310. New York: Basic Books.

Gellner, David N., ed. 2002. *Resistance and the State: Nepalese Experiences*. New Delhi: Social Science Press.

———. 2007. "Caste, Ethnicity, and Inequality in Nepal." *Economic and Political Weekly* 42 (20): 1823–28.

Gellner, David N., Joanna Pfaff-Czarnecka, and John Whelpton, eds. 1997. *Nationalism and Ethnicity in a Hindu Kingdom: The Politics of Culture in Contemporary Nepal.* Amsterdam: Harwood Academic Publishers.

Ghosh, Durba. 2008. *Sex and the Family in Colonial India: The Making of Empire.* Cambridge: Cambridge University Press.

Ghosh, Kaushik. 1999. "A Market for Aboriginality: Primitivism and Race Classification in the Indentured Labour Market of Colonial India." In *Subaltern Studies X: Writings on South Asian History and Society,* edited by Gautam Bhadra, Gyan Prakash, and Susie Tharu, 8–48. New Delhi: Oxford University Press.

———. 2006. "Between Global Flows and Local Dams: Indigenousness, Locality, and the Transnational Sphere in Jharkhand, India." *Cultural Anthropology* 21 (4): 501–34.

Gilroy, Paul. 1990. "Nationalism, History, and Ethnic Absolutism." *History Workshop Journal* 30: 114–20.

———. 1993. *Black Atlantic: Modernity and Double Consciousness.* Cambridge, MA: Harvard University Press.

———. 2000. *Against Race: Imagining Political Culture beyond the Color Line.* Cambridge, MA: Belknap Press of Harvard University Press.

Gramsci, Antonio. 1971. *Selections from the Prison Notebooks.* Edited and translated by Quentin Hoare and Geoffrey Nowell Smith. New York: International Publishers.

Green, Andre. 1999. *The Fabric of Affect in Psychoanalytic Discourse.* New York: Routledge.

Guha, Ramachandra. 1999. *Savaging the Civilized: Verrier Elwin, His Tribals, and India.* Chicago: University of Chicago Press.

Guha, Ranajit. 1989. "Dominance without Hegemony and Its Historiography." In *Subaltern Studies VI: Writings on South Asian History and Society,* edited by Ranajit Guha, 210–309. New Delhi: Oxford University Press.

Gunew, Sneja. 2004. *Haunted Nations: The Colonial Dimensions of Multiculturalisms.* New York: Routledge.

Gupta, Akhil. 2012. *Red Tape: Bureaucracy, Structural Violence, and Poverty in India.* Durham, NC: Duke University Press.

Gupta, Akhil, and James Ferguson. 2002. "Spatializing States: Toward an Ethnography of Neoliberal Governmentality." *American Ethnologist* 29 (4): 981–1002.

Gupta, Akhil, and Aradhana Sharma, eds. 2006. *The Anthropology of the State: A Reader.* Malden, MA: Blackwell.

Gupta, Akhil, and K. Sivaramakrishnan, eds. 2012. *The State in India after Liberalization: Interdisciplinary Perspectives.* New York: Routledge.

Hacking, Ian. 2006. "Making Up People." *London Review of Books* 28 (16): 23–26.

Hale, Charles. 2002. "Does Multiculturalism Menace? Governance, Cultural Rights, and the Politics of Identity in Guatemala." *Journal of Latin American Studies* 34 (3): 485–524.

———. 2006. "Activist Research v. Cultural Critique: Indigenous Land Rights and the Contradictions of Politically Engaged Anthropology." *Cultural Anthropology* 21 (1): 99–126.

Haller, John S., Jr. 1971. "Race and the Concept of Progress in Nineteenth Century American Ethnology." *American Anthropologist* 73 (3): 710–24.

Handler, Richard. 1996. "On Having a Culture." In *Objects and Others: Essays on Museums and Material Culture*, edited by George Stocking, 192–217. Madison: University of Wisconsin Press.

Hangen, Susan. 2005. "Boycotting Dasain: History, Memory, and Ethnic Politics in Nepal." *Studies in Nepali History and Society* 10 (1): 105–33.

———. 2007. *Creating a "New Nepal": The Ethnic Dimension.* Washington, DC: East-West Center.

Hansen, Thomas Blom. 2000. "Governance and Myths of State in Mumbai." In *The Everyday State and Society in Modern India*, edited by C. J. Fuller and Veronique Bénéï, 31–67. New Delhi: Social Science Press.

Hansen, Thomas Blom, and Finn Stepputat. 2001. *States of Imagination: Ethnographic Explorations of the Postcolonial State.* Durham, NC: Duke University Press.

Harari, Roberto. 2001. *Lacan's Seminar on "Anxiety".* Translated by Jane C. Lamb-Ruiz. New York: Other Press.

Hazarika, Sanjoy. 1995. *Strangers in the Midst: Tales of War and Peace from India's Northeast.* New Delhi: Penguin Books.

———. 2008. *Writing on the Wall: Reflections on India's North-East.* Gurgaon: Penguin Books.

Hegel, Georg W. F. 1977. *Phenomenology of Spirit.* Translated by A. V. Miller. Oxford: Oxford University Press.

Heidegger, Martin. 1962. *Being and Time.* Translated by John Macquarrie and Edward Robinson. New York: Harper.

———. 1982. *The Basic Problems of Phenomenology.* Translated by Albert Hofstadter. Bloomington: Indiana University Press.

Henley, David, and Jamie S. Davidson. 2007. "Introduction: Radical Conservatism—The Protean Politics of Adat." In *The Revival of Tradition in Indonesian Politics: The Deployment of Adat from Colonialism to Indigenism*, edited by David Henley and Jamie S. Davidson, 1–49. New York: Routledge.

Herzfeld, Michael. 1992. *The Social Production of Indifference: Exploring the Symbolic Roots of Western Bureaucracy.* Chicago: University of Chicago Press.

Hetherington, Keith. 2012. *Guerrilla Auditors: The Politics of Transparency in Neoliberal Paraguay.* Durham, NC: Duke University Press.

Hobsbawm, Eric, and Terrence Ranger, eds. 1983. *The Invention of Tradition.* Cambridge: Cambridge University Press.

Hodgson, Dorothy. 2002. "Introduction: Comparative Perspectives on the Indigenous Rights Movement in Africa and the Americas." *American Anthropologist* 104 (4): 1037–59.

Holmberg, David H., and Kathryn S. March. 1999. "Local Production/Local Knowledge: Forced Labour from Below." *Studies in Nepali History and Society* 4 (1): 5–64.

Holmes, Douglas, and George E. Marcus. 2005. "Cultures of Expertise and the Management of Globalization: Toward the Refunctioning of Ethnography." In *Global Assemblages: Technology, Politics, and Ethics as Anthropological Problems*, edited by Aiwha Ong and Stephen J. Collier, 235–52. Oxford: Blackwell Publishing Ltd.

————. 2006. "Fast Capitalism: Paraethnography and the Rise of the Symbolic Analyst." In *Frontiers of Capital: Ethnographic Perspectives on the New Economy*, edited by Melissa Fisher and Greg Downey, 33–57. Durham, NC: Duke University Press.

Holmes, Douglas, George E. Marcus, and David Westbrook. 2006. "Intellectual Vocations in the City of Gold." *PoLAR: Political and Legal Anthropology Review* 29 (1): 154–79.

Hull, Mathew. 2012. *Government of Paper: The Materiality of Bureaucracy in Urban Pakistan*. Berkeley: University of California Press.

Hull, Mathew, Constantine V. Nakassis, Katherine Verdery, Naveeda Khan, Justin Richland, Stephen M. Lyon, David Henig, Michael Gilsenan, Beatrice Fraenkel, and Akhil Gupta. 2013. "Symposium on *Government of Paper*." *Hau* 3 (3): 399–447.

Hunter, Sir William Wilson. (1896) 1991. *The Life of Brian Houghton Hodgson*. New Delhi: Asian Educational Services.

Husserl, Edmund. (1900) 1970. *Logical Investigations*. Translated by J. N. Findlay. London: Routledge and Kegan Paul.

Hutt, Michael. 1997. "Being Nepali without Nepal: Reflection on a South Asian Diaspora." In *Nationalism and Ethnicity in a Hindu Kingdom*, edited by Joanna Pfaff-Czarnecka, David N. Gellner, and John Whelpton, 101–44. Amsterdam: Harwood Academic Publishers.

————. 1998. "Going to Mugalan: Nepali Literary Representations of Migration to India and Bhutan." *South Asia Research* 18 (2): 195–214.

————. 2003. *Unbecoming Citizens: Culture, Nationhood, and the Flight of Refugees from Bhutan*. Oxford: Oxford University Press.

Isaacs, Harold R. 1975. *Idols of the Tribe: Group Identity and Political Change*. New York: Harper and Row.

Jeffrey, Craig. 2010. *Timepass: Youth, Class, and the Politics of Waiting in India*. Stanford: Stanford University Press.

Jung, Courtney. 2008. *The Moral Force of Indigenous Politics: Critical Liberalism and the Zapatistas*. Cambridge: Cambridge University Press.

Kant, Immanuel. 1998. *Critique of Pure Reason*. Translated by Paul Guyer and Allen W. Wood. Cambridge: Cambridge University Press.

Kapila, Kriti. 2008. "The Measure of a Tribe: The Cultural Politics of Constitutional Reclassification." *Journal of the Royal Anthropological Institute* 14: 117–34.

Karlsson, Bengt G. 2000. *Contested Belonging: An Indigenous People's Struggle for Forest and Identity in Sub-Himalayan Bengal*. New York: RoutledgeCurzon.

————. 2006. "Anthropology and the Indigenous Slot: Claims to and Debates about Indigenous Peoples' Status in India." In *Indigeneity in India*, edited by Bengt G. Karlsson and T. B. Subba, 51–73. New York: Kegan Paul.

————. 2011. *Unruly Hills: A Political Ecology of India's Northeast*. New York: Berghahn Books.

Karlsson, Bengt G., and T. B. Subba, eds. 2006. *Indigeneity in India*. New York: Kegan Paul.

Kaviraj, Sudipta. 1992. "The Imaginary Institution of India." In *Subaltern Studies VII: Writings on South Asian History and Society*, edited by Partha Chatterjee and G. Pandey, 1–39. New Delhi: Oxford University Press.

———. 1995. *The Unhappy Consciousness: Bankimchandra Chattopadhyay and the Formation of Nationalist Discourse in India*. New Delhi: Oxford University Press.

Khilnani, Sunil. 1997. *The Idea of India*. New York: Farrar, Straus, and Giroux.

Kuper, Adam. 2003. "The Return of the Native." *Current Anthropology* 44 (3): 389–402.

Lama, Mahendra P., ed. 1996. *Gorkhaland Movement: Quest for an Identity*. Darjeeling: Department of Information and Cultural Affairs, Darjeeling Gorkha Hill Council.

Lama, Niraj. 2008. "A 'Dictator' Deposed." *Himal Southasian* 21 (4). http://old.himalmag.com/himal-feed/48/4130-a-dictator-deposed.html (accessed 5/22/14).

Lecomte-Tilouine, Marie, and Pascale Dolfuss, eds. 2003. *Ethnic Revival and Religious Turmoil: Identities and Representations in the Himalayas*. New Delhi: Oxford University Press.

Levi-Strauss, Claude. 1963. "The Sorcerer and His Magic." In *Structural Anthropology*, 1: 167–85. New York: Basic Books.

Levine, N. E. 1987. "Caste, State, and Ethnic Boundaries in Nepal." *Journal of Asian Studies* 46: 76–88.

Li, Tania. 2000. "Articulating Indigenous Identity in Indonesia: Resource Politics and the Tribal Slot." *Comparative Studies in Society and History* 42 (1): 149–79.

———. 2007. *The Will to Improve: Governmentality, Development, and the Practice of Politics*. Durham, NC: Duke University Press.

Lomnitz, Claudio. 2001. *Deep Mexico, Silent Mexico: An Anthropology of Nationalism*. Minneapolis: University of Minnesota Press.

Lukacs, Georg. 1971. *History and Class Consciousness: Studies in Marxist Dialectics*. Translated by Rodney Livingston. Cambridge, MA: MIT Press.

Maaker, Erik de, and Markus Schleiter. 2010. "Indigeneity as a Cultural Practice: 'Tribe' and the State in India." *IIAS Newsletter: The Focus, Indigenous India* 53: 16–17.

Mahmood, Saba. 2001. "Feminist Theory, Embodiment, and the Docile Agent: Some Reflections on the Egyptian Islamic Revival." *Cultural Anthropology* 16 (2): 202–36.

Malkki, Liisa. 1995. *Purity and Exile: Violence, Memory, and National Cosmology among Hutu Refugees in Tanzania*. Chicago: University of Chicago Press.

Mamdani, Mahmood. 1996. *Citizen and Subject: Contemporary Africa and the Legacy of Late Colonialism*. Princeton, NJ: Princeton University Press.

Mani, Lata. 1998. *Contentious Traditions: The Debate on Sati in Colonial India*. Berkeley: University of California Press.

Mannheim, Karl. 1952. *Essays on a Sociology of Knowledge*. Edited by Paul Kecskemeti. New York: Oxford University Press.

———. 1955. *Ideology and Utopia: An Introduction to the Sociology of Knowledge*. Translated by L. Wirth and E. Shils. New York: Harcourt Brace.

———. 1971. *From Karl Mannheim*. Edited by Kurt H. Wolff. New York: Oxford University Press.

Marcus, George, ed. 2000. *Para-Sites: A Casebook against Cynical Reason*. Chicago: University of Chicago Press.

Marx, Karl. 1978. "The German Ideology, Part I." In *The Marx-Engels Reader*, edited by Robert C. Tucker, 146–200. New York: W. W. Norton.

———. 1978. "On the Jewish Question." In *The Marx-Engels Reader*, edited by Robert C. Tucker, 26–52. New York: W. W. Norton.

Masco, Joseph. 2008. "Survival Is Your Business: Engineering Ruins and Affect in Nuclear America." *Cultural Anthropology* 23 (2): 361–98.

Massumi, Brian. 1995. "The Autonomy of Affect." *Cultural Critique* 31: 83–109.

Mauss, Marcel. 1973. "Techniques of the Body." *Economy and Society* 2 (1): 70–85.

Mayaram, Shail. 2004. *Against History, Against State: Counterperspectives from the Margins.* New York: Columbia University Press.

Mazzarella, William. 2006. "Internet X-ray: E-Governance, Transparency, and the Politics of Immediation in India." *Public Culture* 18 (3): 473–505.

———. 2009. "Affect: What Is It Good For?" In *Enchantments of Modernity: Empire, Nation, Globalization*, edited by Saurabh Dube, 291–309. New York: Routledge.

McAnany, Patricia, and Shoshaunna Parks. 2012. "Casualties of Heritage Distancing: Children, Ch'orti' Indigeneity, and the Copán Archaeoscape." *Current Anthropology* 53 (1): 801–7.

McDuie-Ra. Duncan. 2009. *Civil Society, Democratization, and the Search for Human Security: The Politics of the Environment, Gender, and Identity in Northeast India.* New York: Nova Science Publishers.

———. 2012. *Northeast Migrants in Delhi: Race, Refuge, and Retail.* Amsterdam: Amsterdam University Press.

McHugh, Ernestine. 2006. "From Margin to Center: 'Tibet' as a Feature of Gurung Identity." In *Tibetan Borderlands: Proceedings of the 10th Seminar of the International Association for Tibetan Studies*, edited by P. C. Kleiger, 115–26. Leiden: Brill Publishers.

Mehta, Uday Singh. 1999. *Liberalism and Empire: A Study in Nineteenth-Century British Liberal Thought.* Chicago: University of Chicago Press.

Mentore, George. 2009. *Of Passionate Curves and Desirable Cadences: Themes on Wai-Wai Social Being.* Lincoln: University of Nebraska Press.

Metcalf, Barbara, and Thomas Metcalf. 2002. *A Concise History of India.* Cambridge: Cambridge University Press.

Metcalf, Thomas R. 1995. *Ideologies of the Raj.* Cambridge: Cambridge University Press.

Middleton, Townsend. 2011a. "Across the Interface of State Ethnography: Rethinking Ethnology and its Subjects in Multicultural India." *American Ethnologist* 38 (2): 249–66.

———. 2011b. "Ethno-logics: Paradigms of Modern Identity." In *Handbook of Modernity in South Asia: Modern Makeovers*, edited by Saurabh Dube, 200–213. New Delhi: Oxford University Press.

———. 2013a. "Anxious Belongings: Anxiety and the Politics of Belonging in Subnationalist Darjeeling." *American Anthropologist* 115 (4): 608–21.

———. 2013b. "Scheduling Tribes: A View from inside India's 'Ethnographic State.'" *Focaal: Journal of Global and Historical Anthropology* 65: 13–22.

———. 2013c. "States of Difference: Refiguring Ethnicity and Its 'Crisis' at India's Borders." *Political Geography* 35: 14–24.

Middleton, Townsend, and Jason Cons, eds. 2014. "Fieldworkers: Research Assistants,

Researchers, and the Production of Ethnographic Knowledge." Special issue, *Ethnography* 15 (3).

Middleton, Townsend, and Eklavya Pradhan. 2014. "Dynamic Duos: On Partnership and the Possibilities of Postcolonial Ethnography." Special issue, *Ethnography* 15 (3): 355–74.

Middleton, Townsend, and Sara Shneiderman. 2008. "Reservations, Federalism, and the Politics of Recognition in Nepal." *Economic and Political Weekly*, 43 (19): 39–45.

Mignolo, Walter, and Arturo Escobar. 2009. *Globalization and the Decolonial Option*. New York: Routledge.

Miller, Bruce G. 2003. *Invisible Indigenes: The Politics of Non-Recognition*. Lincoln: University of Nebraska Press.

Mitchell, Timothy. 1988. *Colonising Egypt*. Berkeley: University of California Press.

———. 2002. *Rule of Experts: Egypt, Techno-Politics, Modernity*. Berkeley: University of California Press.

Moodie, Megan. 2013. "Upward Mobility in a Forgotten Tribe: Notes on the 'Creamy Layer' Problem." *Focaal: Journal of Global and Historical Anthropology* 65: 23–32.

———. 2015. *We Were Adivasis: Aspiration in an India Scheduled Tribe*. Chicago: University of Chicago Press.

Mookherjee, Monica. 2005. "Affective Citizenship: Feminism, Postcolonialism, and the Politics of Recognition." *Critical Review of International Social and Political Philosophy* 8 (1): 31–50.

Munasinghe, Viranjini. 1997. "Culture Creators and Culture Bearers: The Interface between Race and Ethnicity in Trinidad". *Transforming Anthropology* 6 (1–2): 72–86.

———. 2001. *Callaloo or Tossed Salad? East Indians and the Cultural Politics of Identity in Trinidad*. Ithaca, NY: Cornell University Press.

———. 2002. "Nationalism in Hybrid Spaces: The Production of Impurity Out of Purity." *American Ethnologist* 29 (3): 663–92.

Needham, A. D., and R. S Rajan, eds. 2007. *The Crisis of Secularism in India*. Durham, NC: Duke University Press.

Niezen, Ronald. 2003. *The Origins of Indigenism: Human Rights and the Politics of Identity*. Berkeley: University of California Press.

Nigam, Aditya. 2006. *The Insurrection of the Little Selves: The Crisis of Secular-Nationalism in India*. New Delhi: Oxford University Press.

Nongbri, Tiplut. 2006. "Tribe, Caste, and the Indigenous Challenge in India." In *Indigeneity in India*, edited by Bengt G. Karlsson and T. B. Subba, 75–95. New York: Kegan Paul.

Nyamnjoh, Francis B. 2007. "Ever-Diminishing Circles: The Paradoxes of Belonging in Botswana." In *Indigenous Experience Today*, edited by Marisol de la Cadena and Orin Starn, 305–32. Oxford: Berg.

Oberoi, Harjat. 1987. "From Punjab to 'Khalistan': Territoriality and Meta-commentary." *Pacific Affairs* 60 (1): 26–41.

Onta, Pratyoush R. 1996. "The Politics of Bravery: A History of Nepali Nationalism." PhD diss., University of Pennsylvania.

Pels, Peter. 1999. "From Texts to Bodies: Brian Houghton Hodgson and the Emergence of Ethnology in India." In *Anthropology and Colonialism in Asia and Oceania*, edited by J. Breman and A. Shimizu, 65–92. Surrey: Curzon Press.

———. 2000. "The Rise and Fall of Indian Aborigines: Orientalism, Anglicism, and the Emergence of Ethnology of India." In *Colonial Subjects: Essays on the Practical History of Anthropology*, edited by Peter Pels and Oscar Salemink, 82–116. Ann Arbor: University of Michigan Press.

Pels, Peter, and Oscar Salemink, eds. 2000. *Colonial Subjects: Essays on the Practical History of Anthropology*. Ann Arbor: University of Michigan Press.

Phillips, Ruth B. 2003. "Introduction to Part III." In *Museums and Source Communities*, edited by Alison Brown and Laura Peers, 155–70. New York: Routledge.

Pinney, Christopher. 1991. "Colonial Anthropology in the 'Laboratory of Mankind.'" In *The Raj: India and the British, 1600–1947*, edited by Christopher Bayly, 252–63. London: National Portrait Gallery.

Povinelli, Elizabeth. 2002. *The Cunning of Recognition: Indigenous Alterities and the Making of Australian Multiculturalism*. Durham, NC: Duke University Press.

———. 2011. *Economies of Abandonment: Social Belonging and Endurance in Late Liberalism*. Durham, NC: Duke University Press.

Probyn, Elspeth. 1996. *Outside Belongings*. New York: Routledge.

Protevi, John. 2009. *Political Affect: Connecting the Social and the Somatic*. Minneapolis: University of Minnesota Press.

Rabinow, Paul. 2003. *Anthropos Today: Reflections on Modern Equipment*. Princeton, NJ: Princeton University Press.

———. 2007. *Marking Time: On the Anthropology of the Contemporary*. Princeton, NJ: Princeton University Press.

Rabinow, Paul, George E. Marcus, James Faubion, and Tobias Rees. 2008. *Designs for an Anthropology of the Contemporary*. Durham, NC: Duke University Press.

Radhakrishna, Meena. 2001. *Dishonoured by History: "Criminal Tribes" and British Colonial Policy*. Hyderabad: Orient Longman.

Raheja, Gloria. 2000. "The Illusion of Consent: Language, Caste, and Colonial Rule in India." In *Colonial Subjects: Essays on the Practical History of Anthropology*, edited by Peter Pels and Oscar Salemink, 117–52. Ann Arbor: University of Michigan Press.

Ranco, D. J. 2006. "Toward a Native Anthropology: Hermeneutics, Hunting Stories, and Theorizing from Within." *Wicazo Sa Review* 21 (2): 61–78.

Ranger, Terence. 1982. "Race and Tribe in Southern Africa: European Ideas and African Acceptance." In *Racism and Colonialism*, edited by R. Ross, 121–42. Leiden: Nijhoff.

Rao, Anupama. 2007. "Ambedkar and the Politics of Minority: A Reading." In *From the Colonial to the Postcolonial: India and Pakistan in Transition*, edited by Dipesh Chakrabarty, R. Majumdar, and A. Sartori, 137–58. Oxford: Oxford University Press.

———. 2009. *The Caste Question: Dalits and the Politics of Modern India*. Berkeley: University of California Press.

Revankar, Ratna G. 1971. *The Indian Constitution: A Case Study of Backward Classes*. Cranberry, NJ: Associated University Presses.

Richland, Justin. 2007. "Pragmatic Paradoxes and Ironies of Indigeneity at the 'Edge' of Hopi Sovereignty." *American Ethnologist* 34 (3): 540–57.

———. 2013. "Travels Among the Records: Some Thoughts Provoked by *Government of Paper*." *Hau: Journal of Ethnographic Theory* 3 (3): 417–20.

Risley, H. H. 1891. *The Tribes and Castes of Bengal*. Calcutta: Bengal Secretariat Press.

———. 1908. *The People of India*. London: W. Thacker.

Robb, Peter. 1995. *The Concept of Race in South Asia*. Oxford: Oxford University Press.

Rodrigues, Valerian. 2002. "Introduction." In *The Essential Writings of B. R. Ambedkar*, edited by Valerian Rodrigues. New Delhi: Oxford University Press.

Roosens, E. G. 1989. *Creating Ethnicity: The Process of Ethnogenesis*. London: Sage.

Roy, Barun. 2012. *Gorkhas and Gorkhaland: A Socio-Political Study of the Gorkha People and the Gorkhaland Movement*. Darjeeling: Parbati Roy Foundation.

Samanta, Amiya K. 2000. *Gorkhaland Movement: A Study in Ethnic Separatism*. New Delhi: APH Publishers.

Sangari, Kumkum, and Sudesh Vaid, eds. 1990. *Recasting Women: Essays in Colonial History*. New Brunswick, NJ: Rutgers University Press.

Sanjek, Roger. 1993. "Anthropology's Hidden Colonialism: Assistants and Their Ethnographers." *Anthropology Today* 9 (2): 13–18.

Sarkar, Sumit. 1997. *Writing Social History*. New Delhi: Oxford University Press.

Sarkar, Swatahsiddha. 2010. "The Land Question and Ethnicity in the Darjeeling Hills." *Journal of Rural Social Sciences* 25 (2): 81–121.

Sarkar, Tanika. 2001. *Hindu Wife, Hindu Nation: Community, Religion, and Cultural Nationalism*. Bloomington: Indiana University Press.

Sayer, Derek. 1994. "Everyday Forms of State Formation: Some Dissident Remarks on 'Hegemony.'" In *Everyday Forms of State Formation: Revolution and the Negotiation of Rule in Modern Mexico*, edited by Daniel Nugent and M. Joseph Gilbert, 367–77. Durham, NC: Duke University Press.

Schumaker, Lyn. 2001. *Africanizing Anthropology: Fieldwork, Networks, and the Making of Cultural Knowledge in Central Africa*. Durham, NC: Duke University Press.

Schutz, Alfred. 1967. *The Phenomenology of the Social World*. Translated by George Walsh and Frederick Lehnert. Evanston, IL: Northwestern University Press.

Scott, David. 1995. "Colonial Governmentality." *Social Text* 43: 191–220.

Scott, James C. 1999. *Seeing like a State: How Certain Schemes to Improve the Human Condition Have Failed*. New Haven, CT: Yale University Press.

Shah, Alpa. 2010. *In the Shadows of the State: Indigenous Politics, Environmentalism, and Insurgency in Jharkhand, India*. Durham, NC: Duke University Press.

Shah, Alpa, and Sara Shneiderman. 2013. "The Practices, Policies, and Politics of Transforming Inequality in South Asia: Ethnographies of Affirmative Action." *Focaal: Journal of Global and Historical Anthropology* 65: 3–12.

Shah, Alpa, and Sara Shneiderman, eds. 2013. *Toward an Anthropology of Affirmative Action*. Themes Section. *Focaal: Journal of Global and Historical Anthropology* 65.

Shils, Edward. 1957. "Primordial, Personal, Sacred, and Civil Ties." *British Journal of Sociology* 8: 130–45.

Shneiderman, Sara. 2009. "Ethnic (P)reservations: Comparing Thangmi Ethnic Activism in Nepal and India." In *Ethnic Activism and Civil Society in South Asia*, edited by David Gellner, 115–44. New Delhi: Sage.

———. 2013. "Developing a Culture of Marginality: Nepal's Current Classificatory Moment." *Focaal: Journal of Global and Historical Anthropology* 65: 42–55.

———. 2014. "Reframing Ethnicity: Academic Tropes, Recognition beyond Politics, and Ritualized Action between Nepal and India." *American Anthropologist* 116 (2): 279–95.

———. 2015. *Rituals of Ethnicity: Thangmi Identities between Nepal and India.* Philadelphia: University of Pennsylvania Press.

Shneiderman, Sara, and Mark Turin. 2006. "Seeking the Tribe: Ethno-Politics in Darjeeling and Sikkim." *Himal Southasian* 19 (2): 54–58.

Simpson, Audra. 2007. "On Ethnographic Refusal: Indigeneity, 'Voice,' and Colonial Citizenship." *Junctures* 9: 67–80.

Singh, Nagendra Kumar. 1996. *Nepal and British India.* New Delhi: Anmol Publications.

Sivaramakrishnan, K. 1996. "British Imperium and Forested Zones of Anomaly in Bengal, 1767–1833." *Indian Economic and Social History Review* 33: 242–82.

———. 1999. *Modern Forests: Statemaking and Environmental Change in Colonial Eastern India.* Stanford: Stanford University Press.

Smith, Linda Tuhiwai. 1999. *Decolonizing Methodologies: Research and Indigenous Peoples.* London: Zed Books.

Speed, Shannon. 2006. "At the Crossroads of Human Rights and Anthropology: Toward a Critically Engaged Activist Research." *American Anthropologist* no. 108 (1): 66–76.

Spivak, Gayatri Chakravorty. 1988a. "Can the Subaltern Speak?" In *Marxism and the Interpretation of Culture*, edited by Cary Nelson and Lawrence Grossberg, 271–316. Urbana, IL: University of Illinois Press.

———. 1988b. "Subaltern Studies: Deconstructing Historiography" in *Selected Subaltern Studies*, edited by R. Guha and G. Spivak. 3-32, New Delhi: Oxford University Press.

Stewart, Charles, and Rosalind Shah, eds. 1994. *Syncretism/Anti-Syncretism: The Politics of Religious Synthesis.* New York: Routledge.

Stewart, Kathleen. 2007. *Ordinary Affects.* Durham, NC: Duke University Press.

Stoler, Ann Laura. 2004. "Affective States." In *A Companion to the Anthropology of Politics*, edited by David Nugent and Joan Vincent, 4–20. Malden, MA: Wiley-Blackwell.

———. 2008. "Imperial Debris: Reflections on Ruin and Ruination." *Cultural Anthropology* no. 23 (2): 191–219.

———. 2009. *Along the Archival Grain: Epistemic Anxieties and Colonial Common Sense.* Princeton, NJ: Princeton University Press.

Subba, Tanka. 1989. *Dynamics of a Hill Society: The Nepalis in Darjeeling and Sikkim Himalayas.* Delhi: Mittal Publishers.

———. 1992. *Ethnicity, State, and Development: A Case Study of the Gorkhaland Movement in Darjeeling.* New Delhi: Vikas.

———. 2006. "Indigenising the Limbus: Trajectory of a Nation Divided into Two

Nation-States." In *Indigeneity in India*, edited by Bengt G. Karlsson and T. B. Subba, 152–69. New York: Kegan Paul.

———. 2009. "The Last Word So Far . . ." In *Indian Nepalis: Issues and Perspectives*, edited by D. R. Nepal, G. S. Nepal, A. C. Sinha, and T. B. Subba, 283–93. New Delhi: Concept Publishing.

Subba, Tanka, and A. C. Sinha, eds. 2003. *The Nepalis in Northeast India*. New Delhi: Indus.

Sylvain, Renee. 2014. "Essentialism and the Indigenous Politics of Recognition in Southern Africa." *American Anthropologist* no. 116 (2): 251–64.

Tamang, Mukta S. 2008. *Himalayan Indigeneity: Histories, Memory, and Identity among Tamang in Nepal*. PhD diss., Cornell University.

Taussig, Michael. 1992. *The Nervous System*. New York: Routledge.

Taylor, Charles. 1992. *Multiculturalism and the Politics of Recognition*. Princeton, NJ: Princeton University Press.

———. 1995. *Philosophical Arguments*. Cambridge, MA: Harvard University Press.

Thapa, Tapasya. 2009. "Being and Belonging: A Study of Indian Nepalis." In *Indian Nepalis: New Perspectives*, edited by D. R. Nepal, G. S. Nepal, A. C. Sinha, and T. B. Subba. New Delhi: Concept Publishing.

Thomas, Nicholas. 1994. *Colonialism's Culture*. Cambridge: Polity Press.

Trouillot, Michel-Rolph. 1991. "Anthropology and the Savage Slot: The Poetics and Politics of Otherness." In *Recapturing Anthropology: Working in the Present*, edited by Richard Fox, 17–44. Santa Fe: School of American Research Press.

Turner, Terrence. 1991. "Representing, Resisting, Rethinking: Historical Transformations of Kayapo Culture and Anthropological Consciousness." In *Colonial Situations: Essays on the Contextualization of Knowledge*, edited by George Stocking, 285–313. Madison: University of Wisconsin Press.

Turner, Victor. 1967. *The Forest of Symbols: Aspects of Ndembu Ritual*. Ithaca, NY: Cornell University Press.

Uberoi, Patricia, Nandini Sundar, and Satish Deshpande, eds. 2008. *Anthropology in the East: Founders of Indian Sociology and Anthropology*. Oxford: Seagull Books.

Van Gennep, A. 1965 [1908]. *The Rites of Passage*. London: Routledge and Kegan Paul.

Wagner, Kim. 2009. *Stranglers and Bandits: A Historical Anthology of Thuggee*. New Delhi: Oxford University Pres.

Warren, Kay B., and Jean E Jackson. 2005. "Introduction: Studying Indigenous Activism in Latin America." In *Indigenous Movements, Self-Representation, and the State in Latin America*, edited by Kay B. Warren and Jean E. Jackson, 1–46. Austin: University of Texas Press.

Waterhouse, David M., ed. 2004. *The Origins of Himalayan Studies: Brian Houghton Hodgson in Nepal and Darjeeling, 1820–1858*. London: RoutledgeCurzon.

Weber, Max. 1978. *Economy and Society: An Outline of Interpretive Sociology*. Edited by Guenther Roth and Claus Wittich. Berkeley: University of California Press.

———. 1998. "Ethnic Groups." In *New Tribalisms: The Resurgence of Race and Ethnicity*, edited by Michael W. Hughey, 17–30. New York: New York University Press.

Wedeen, Lisa. 1999. *Ambiguities of Domination: Politics, Rhetoric, and Symbols in Contemporary Syria.* Chicago: University of Chicago Press.

Werbner, Pnina, and Tariq Modood, eds. 1997. *Debating Cultural Hybridity: Multi-Cultural Identities and the Politics of Anti-Racism.* London: Zed Books.

Werbner, Richard, and Terence Ranger, eds. 1996. *Postcolonial Identities in Africa.* London: Zed Books.

Westbrook, David. 2008. *Navigators of the Contemporary: Why Ethnography Matters.* Chicago: University of Chicago Press.

Whelpton, John. 2005. *A History of Nepal.* Cambridge: Cambridge University Press.

Williams, Brackette F. 1989. "A Class Act: Anthropology and the Race to Nation across Ethnic Terrain." *Annual Review of Anthropology* 18: 401–44.

Williams, Raymond. 1961. *The Long Revolution.* New York: Columbia University Press.

———. 1977. *Marxism and Literature.* Oxford: Oxford University Press.

Wilson, Pamela, and Michelle Stewart, eds. 2008. *Global Indigenous Media.* Durham, NC: Duke University Press.

Xaxa, Virginius. 2008. *State, Society, and Tribes.* Delhi: Pearson Education.

Yeats, William Butler. (1920) 1994. "The Second Coming." In *Michael Robartes and the Dancer*, 19. Ithaca, NY: Cornell University Press.

Young, Lola. 2000. "Hybridity's Discontents: Rereading Science and 'Race.'" In *Hybridity and Its Discontents: Politics, Science, Culture*, edited by Avtar Brah and Annie E. Coombes, 154–70. New York: Routledge.

Young, Robert J. C. 1995. *Colonial Desire: Hybridity in Theory, Culture, and Race.* New York: Routledge.

INDEX

Page references followed by "*f*" refer to figures and photographs.